TAPE, I-C-E, & SOUND ADVICE

TAPE, I-C-E, & SOUND ADVICE

Life Lessons from a
Hall of Fame Athletic Trainer

ROD WALTERS

Rick Horrow
The Sports Professor

an imprint of Morgan James Publishing
NEW YORK

TAPE, I-C-E, & SOUND ADVICE

Life Lessons from a Hall of Fame Athletic Trainer

ISBN 978-1-61448-012-9 paperback
ISBN 978-1-61448-013-6 eBook
Library of Congress Control Number: 2012941101

an imprint of Morgan James Publishing
The Entrepreneurial Publisher
5 Penn Plaza, 23rd Floor,
New York City, New York 10001
(212) 655-5470 office • (516) 908-4496 fax
www.MorganJamesPublishing.com

Cover Photo Credit:
Keith E. McGraw, Jr.
Director of Photography
University Technology Services
Sub-Level 1 Law Center
Columbia, SC 29208

Cover Design by:
Rachel Lopez
www.r2cdesign.com

Interior Design by:
Bonnie Bushman
bonnie@caboodlegraphics.com

DEDICATION

THIS BOOK IS DEDICATED to three most important groups of people in my life. First and foremost, to my parents for your never ending love and support. You gave me a strong foundation for life in a Christian home, and from that I was able to grow and enjoy a most successful career.

Second, to the love of my life, my best friend, Susan. Thank you for your support and believing in me.

Finally, to my children. David and Ryan have been such a source of pride, and have made me see one's value. David and Rebecca's (Seibert) marriage brings things full-circle, especially with the birth of our first granddaughter Grace Christine. To Allison and Bradley, for allowing me to be an active part of your lives, and for being the best of the best.

TABLE OF CONTENTS

(List of)
ABBREVIATIONS:

AMSSM	American Medical Society for Sports Medicine
AOSSM	American Orthopaedic Society for Sports Medicine
BCS	Bowl Championship Subdivision
CFL	Canadian Football League
ESPN	Entertainment and Sports Programming Network
FCS	Football Championship Subdivision
MAATA	Mid-Atlantic Athletic Trainers Association
NATA	National Athletic Trainers' Association
NCAA	National Collegiate Athletic Association
SEC	Southeastern Conference

FOREWORD
By Lou Holtz

ABILITY IS WHAT YOU'RE capable of doing. Motivation determines what you do. Attitude determines how well you do it. Dr. Rod Walters succeeds on all three fronts.

There is a fine line between training and conditioning a team and working a group of athletes too hard. While at some points during my long football coaching career I didn't see that line as I blew past it, I always made a point of surrounding myself with smart, capable, caring people who were there to put the teams' best interests in front of me in those instances where I was too focused on on-field success to notice the trials of the individual athlete in front of me.

Dr. Rod Walters was one such gifted individual. In 1999, when I took the head football coaching job at the University of South Carolina, I inherited Rod and his capable staff of athletic trainers and physicians. Rod had been hired by my friend Dr. Mike McGee, who in turn had lured me away from my job at CBS and two-year "retirement" from coaching to try to turn around a Gamecocks team that had gone 1-10 in the previous season. Mike assured me that, despite the team's performance on the field, his department had plenty of positives on which to build, including the athletic training staff. I knew of the tradition and lure of the Southeastern Conference, and felt, with the proper plan, we could turn the program around.

The trust I soon built with Rod and his team was one of the many factors that soon helped me turn South Carolina into a winning football team. His ability to work with the University and community was tremendous, and I enjoyed reading his account of his time there and elsewhere. As an advocate for Rod's work, I want to do the same type of job for him that he did for us as our trainer.

Just like life itself, a sports-related injury is ten percent what happens to you and ninety percent how you respond to it. Often, as an athletic coach, the tendency to respond to a player's injury is some toxic combination of anger and denial, since most injuries kept the player off the field—the last thing a coach ever wants. Through his patience, conviction, and the quality of the care he provided, Rod was able to turn my frustrations with injuries and setbacks into committing to a long term plan and accepting the notion that truly, nothing but time heals all wounds. Rod understood the difference between pain and injury, and helped educate our players on this.

Rehabilitation of the athlete is fundamentally no different than rehabilitation of the non-athlete. What distinguishes athletic rehabilitation is the expectations and fears of the athlete, physician, athletic trainer, and coach—and the respect, trust, care, and commitment to common goals and objectives between them. While this trust and commitment is essential for sports teams, it also remains critical to success in business, and without a doubt, in the business of sports medicine. It is always important to remember that the principles that structure good teams are applicable to our personal life and business.

Just like in football, writing a book is a team effort where success requires a one hundred and ten percent effort from everyone involved. The excellent book by Rod Walters in your hands, and the lessons from the athletic training room it imparts, should help shape your thoughts about what it means to care for your body and mind, trusting a higher power, treating others as you want to be treated, and about what it means to be a team player.

Lou Holtz
2012

Lou Holtz retired from coaching in 2004 after six seasons at the University of South Carolina and 33 years as a head coach of five other institutions of higher learning. Over his coaching career, Holtz won one national championship (Notre Dame), received three national Coach of the Year honors, and is the only coach in NCAA football history to lead four different schools to postseason bowl games.

In 2005, Holtz joined ESPN as a college football analyst and commentator. He remains one of America's most sought-after motivational speakers.

PREFACE

WRITING A BOOK HAS BEEN a goal of mine for some time. I wanted to reflect on my career and share some experiences I dealt with in my work. These stories exemplify business and life principles. It is my goal to take you into all the behind-the-scenes locations, the locker room; the athletic training room; the staff rooms; and team charter flights, to see some of the lessons I have learned. You see, these stories exemplify what I see as the basic foundations of life. What produces success in life, works in business and vice-versa.

My experiences have been significant watermarks of some basic tenets of life. Readers are quickly introduced to the importance of priorities and how they apply to our personal and business lives. I truly believe if people are not happy at home, they are not going to be productive and happy at work. The same is true for the hostile work environment and its impact on one's family life.

Second, we must communicate. Failure to communicate is the beginning of the end. It tells you more about a relationship than anything. Information is so important, and the communication of the information is likewise.

Third, money can be the root of evil. Well, not money, but the lust for money. This is one of the biggest challenges families face. I tell my kids that money can have an impact on relationships more than anything else I have seen. Readers will see how money has changed so much in college athletics, and how it has had a great impact on decisions and logic of administrators and institutions. I have seen too many coaches and administrators let money dictate their life and the paths they follow. Money, or the lack of it, puts more stress on a family and marriage than one can ever imagine.

My parents, my wife, Susan, and our children have been the most influential people in my life. There will be some special stories about these people, as they are so important to me. Susan and I have laughed so many times as we review parenting. It is the toughest thing we do, with no instruction manual. Each of our children is different, and all are so special. I am so appreciative to David and Ryan, as well as Bradley and Allison—I am sure I have not always been the easiest person to invite into their lives during their challenging teenage years.

I have enjoyed a wonderful career in sports. As a freshman at Alexander Graham Junior High School in Fayetteville, North Carolina, I knew I wanted to be in the healthcare industry. During the summer of my ninth grade year, my parents arranged for me to attend the North Carolina Coaches Association's All-Star Student Trainer Clinic in Greensboro, North Carolina. Little did I know at this clinic I would meet some professionals who would mold my professional career while exposing me to my professional calling.

The world of athletic training and sports medicine involves so many facets of healthcare for participants. Regardless of the level of work, whether in the professional football arena, big-time college athletics, the highly competitive mid-levels of the NCAA, high school football under the Friday night lights, or the outreach role from a physical therapy clinic, athletic trainers all strive to provide patients the prevention, care, and rehabilitation of sports injuries.

Sports Medicine is good medical care applied to physically active populations. Many times, our team of specialists, including orthopedic surgeons and family practice physicians with specialization in sports medicine, may expedite diagnosis and treatment of this special group of individuals. The guiding factor is we do not speed up healing, we merely allow the patient to progress as their body allows. Regardless, the criteria for return to activity are the same for all: range of motion, strength, function, and a basal level of conditioning.

Rehabilitation of the student-athlete is fundamentally no different than rehabilitation of the non-athlete. What distinguish athletic rehabilitation are the expectations and fears of the student-athlete, coach, physician, and athletic trainer. The student-athlete expects the doctor and athletic trainer to have knowledge of the sport and demonstrate personal commitment, show concern, and be decisive. The student-athlete fears doctors forcing activity, benign neglect, and restrictions. The coach expects the doctor and athletic trainer to be available, give exact diagnosis, accurate prognosis and be concerned for the total student-athlete and team. Coaches fear long waiting periods, student-athlete apathy, and surgery. The physician and athletic trainer expect the student-athlete and coach to relinquish control, cooperate, be honest, and to have complete confidence. Physicians fear being called a scapegoat. They fear participation pressure will make them send student-athletes back too quickly and therefore fear early return and the loss of confidence of the student-athlete and coach.

Out of this quagmire, the fears and expectations in the medical field of sports medicine has mushroomed. Sports medicine has grown more rapidly than any other subspecialty in medicine. My aim is to take you into these areas and expose you to all these scenarios. Further, the reader will see why sports are so important, and how we can apply so much of life to the lessons learned in and around sports.

When an athletic trainer and team physician evaluate an injury during a game in a filled-to-capacity stadium on Saturday, they are the topic of discussion for all in the talk radio and blogosphere. Sports are a high-profile business—one receiving great amounts of attention daily. This exposure explodes with the boom of the Internet and ever-growing media exposure.

I walked the sideline of the University of South Carolina for seventeen years, dealing with the medical and ethical issues of three athletics directors and four head football coaches, plus a myriad of other head coaches from various sports and schools. Issues that must be dealt with range from patient care, to drug testing, to the financial provisions of healthcare, to NCAA Division I student-athletes. The athletic training job is a special challenge with so few of the people understanding just what we as a profession do!

The public does not understand the economics of college athletics and especially what healthcare provisions can be provided. It would shock many relative to the costs associated with the financing of healthcare for collegiate student-athletes. The mission statement and beliefs of the athletic department must reflect the practices and abilities of the department in relation to reimbursement of expenses.

It is so important to surround yourself with good people in sports medicine. We need specialists of all disciplines—orthopedists, family medicine practitioners, neurosurgeons, dentists—with the athletic trainer at the center of the team to facilitate the communication between the medical team and the patient, coaches, parents, etc. All members of the healthcare team must be willing to put themselves second, while making the care of the patient and the success of the team the primary goal. This is true in so many areas of work.

When Lou Holtz was the head football coach at South Carolina from 1999-2004, he was a very popular speaker. The colorful coach preached to his staff and team—and often to big businesses across the country—the importance of the team. He stressed the tenants of trust, commitment, and care. While this is true for teams, it also remains critical to success in business, and without a doubt in the business of sports medicine. It is critical to remember that principles which structure good teams are applicable to our personal life and business. This was one of the many tenants I learned from Coach Holtz. I share this valuable learning today, and I sincerely appreciate Coach Holtz agreeing to write this foreword. I have always appreciated his support. He was the most demanding and difficult person I ever worked with; yet I respected him so much. He was a proven winner.

I certainly enjoyed a wonderful career in athletics. The world of athletic training and sports medicine involves so many facets of healthcare today to provide participants a high standard of care. Regardless of one's level of participation, athletic trainers have a concerted mission to provide patients with care through prevention of injuries and rehabilitation of athletic injuries.

My philosophy of sports medicine always has focused on sound medical care applied to physically active populations. Being an educator by trade, I long have believed there is a direct relationship between good clinical care and good educational practice. Further, if I am successful in teaching a procedure or technique, this correlates to best-case practices. This term—best medical practice or best-case practices—is a common concept as we look at those programs with exemplary levels of care.

As state previously, the criteria for returning to activity are the same for all: range of motion, strength, function, and sport specific conditioning.

Case in point: During a game on a college football Saturday, we have an injury to a high profile student-athlete and immediately his care is the topic of discussion in the physician's dressing room, the local therapy clinics, sports talk radio shows and sometimes even national television. Sports have become a high-profile business—one generating great amounts of attention daily.

When I first entered the profession of athletic training it was a big event when a college football team appeared on television. Usually, there was a "Game of the Week" televised nationally, and that was it. Over the past twenty years, sporting events have exploded in popularity. All games are televised for teams in the bigger conferences. Games appear on television about every night of the week, and no longer are games on the West coast a rare occurrence to those in the East. The increased coverage of all college sports has meant a boom for athletic programs across the country. The Southeastern Conference has been the leader in generating revenue for its programs. In 2002, the SEC netted $28 million from football television coverage and bowl revenues. About $2 million was distributed to each member school at the end of the school year. Eight years later, the league was bringing in $210 million with nearly $18 million going to each school.

My hope is that *Tape, I-C-E, and Sound Advice* will take you to the sideline, to the athletic training room and see many of my experiences over my professional career. This book will feature key principles that form good business and family practice, and how they were molded and forged from the experiences.

Rod Walters
April 16, 2012

CHAPTER ONE

PLAN YOUR WORK AND WORK YOUR PLAN

Another group of eight Southeastern Conference football officials lined up for its mile and one-half run as part of the preseason physical screening program at Samford University. Already at 6 a.m. this day was unbearably humid as most are in July in Birmingham. The group of athletic trainers and physicians had drops of sweat to wipe from their brows just by standing and watching the session.

About the time we believed all had gone swimmingly well throughout the morning session, I turned to the cries of a woman standing in the lower rows of the football grandstand on one side of Seibert Stadium.

"Help! Help!" the woman shouted. "We need help! Somebody is down!"

At first glance, it appeared that one of our officials was engaged in a seizure. Ron Courson, an athletic trainer from the University of Georgia, and I were the first to arrive as John Gaston lay motionless on the third row of bleachers. The two of us conducted our primary assessment for an unconscious victim and found the official was not breathing. We checked the pulse. There was none. Courson administered mouth-to-mouth rescue breathing and I did cardiac compressions. We did this until on-site paramedics reached us. Gaston had an irregular heartbeat and would not recover without defibrillation.

The first time I compressed Gaston's chest, you could hear the counts I was taking through the eerie silence around the stadium. After about one minute of CPR, the ambulance originally stationed in the south end zone arrived and paramedics added advanced cardiac life support by use of an external defibrillator. The reading on the monitor clearly showed that Gaston's heart was in ventricular fibrillation. Before the first shock to the patient, I noticed Chris Patrick, an athletic trainer from the University of Florida, was holding Gaston's feet to keep him from rolling off the bleachers. Hastily, I pushed Chris' hand away to make certain he did not absorb any of the shock.

This was a cardiac anomaly, which was an electrical short-circuitry. If Gaston had not received an electrical shock, he would not have made it. This requires cardiac conversion, which an automated external defibrillator does. If we had just done cardiopulmonary resuscitation, there is a despairingly low—less than ten percent—chance there would have been a spontaneous conversion to a normal rhythm. In other words, this would have been a negative outcome.

The first shock was administered. No response. Still no pulse. The silence was deafening. The only sounds were from the two Northport paramedics, Steve Gamble and his partner, Edgar Calloway. Bill McDonald had arranged for them to be on site as part of our Emergency Action Plan.

A second shock was administered and I could hear that blood curdling cry when the air came out of Gaston's chest. Again, no response. Still no pulse. Paramedics continued their work.

A third shock was administered. Rhythm came back to Gaston's heart.

Six or seven minutes into the treatment, knowing Gaston's heart was back to full beat and was going to survive, I turned to Bill McDonald, the head athletic trainer at the University of Alabama, to inquire about why we were not transporting the patient to a hospital. McDonald smiled and pointed overhead where a helicopter was descending for a landing on the field. Within minutes, the official was transported to Birmingham's Carraway Methodist Medical Center, where we soon learned he was resting comfortably and would have a full recovery.

As the physicians and athletic trainers stood afterward I sensed all eyes were on me for the next decision. Should we continue the day's activities? I did not consider any other option and the fourth group of officials reported to the starting lineup. I have long since believed it was the correct decision. Had we not completed the screening, there is a chance the program would have been discontinued. The SEC would not be screening and testing officials today.

Testing was not the most popular event with the officials. For years prior, they had used preseason scrimmages as a way to get in shape. This way, we were using medical screenings in March and subsequent physical testing in July to make sure they were able to perform on athletic fields in a healthy manner and as a way of decreasing risk of injury.

I coordinated this project for the Southeastern Conference. This was a concept I brought from the Southern Conference during my tenure at Appalachian State University. The SEC protocol was on a much grander scale.

After the testing was completed that morning, I completed all paperwork regarding officials who were cleared, per our protocol. I passed the information along to Bobby Gaston, the supervisor of officials for the SEC who was no relation to John Gaston. Then I headed to Carraway Methodist Medical Center to check on John Gaston. He continued to be classified as "in stable condition."

John Gaston lived in Gainesville, Florida. Once he was assessed and stabilized in Birmingham, he was released to his hometown physician in Gainesville and he followed up with his primary care physician and cardiologist. I then followed with weekly phone calls to check on his progress. I soon learned that Gaston would be unable to officiate games that season. Instead, he was assigned to games as an officials' liaison to TV crews.

Our goal with the medical and functional screening was not to replace the relationship with the official's personal physician. Any finding the SEC medical screening team found was referred back to the personal physician for care and treatment decisions. It was up to the SEC medical screening team of physicians and athletic trainers to make final clearance decisions. This was initiated so physician friends of the SEC officials could not sign-off on treatments and make medical clearance as had been the case historically. There was a new day in standard of care for SEC football officials.

Our first game at the University of South Carolina that season was at home in Columbia and Gaston was assigned to work the game. When he strolled into the training room beneath the Williams-Brice Stadium grandstands that Saturday afternoon, I could not contain my emotions. I broke down in tears. They were tears of joy that Gaston was alive and with us. The administration and leadership within the SEC adopted many of my suggestions. One recommendation that I was most proud of was no official could be given an assignment as an official without clearing both our medical and functional screening. John was there as a television liaison and thus would not be subject to on-field work. Today, all clock operators must complete the testing in the event they are called into the game for an injured official.

In reflection over the years, it has become more and more apparent to me that careful planning is the hallmark to success in any profession, and athletic training is no exception. Without careful planning on that hot and humid day in Birmingham we likely would have lost a life.

There also is something to be said for making quick and accurate decisions. All of us that day were responsible for many spur-of-the-moment decisions and through our planning and knowledge they proved to be accurate ones.

The morning of that day's testing, Leroy Mullins and I rode in his truck from the Sheraton Hotel in downtown Birmingham to the Samford University campus. Mullins was the head athletic trainer at the University of Mississippi for twenty-nine years and he was one of the more well-respected athletic trainers in the business. Leroy was a jovial guy, but the one serious thing we discussed was good planning. He bragged about the great plan for assessing SEC officials. The last thing Leroy said as we got out of his truck was, "as a team, we plan our work and we work our plan."

Truer words were never spoken.

When I picked up the telephone in my University of South Carolina office in the spring of 1991, I thought I was the butt of another joke. I figured one of my assistants, or a fellow athletic trainer was setting me up. The voice on the other end of the line identified himself as Bobby Gaston, the assistant commissioner of the Southeastern Conference.

I was fortunate enough to be a member of the South Carolina athletic staff when the school accepted an invitation to join the SEC on September 25, 1990, joining Arkansas as the eleventh and twelfth members of the league. Arkansas and South Carolina departed conferences that had collapsed, the Southwestern and Metro Conferences, respectively. Actually, South Carolina had played football as an independent program since leaving the Atlantic Coast Conference in 1971.

As a newcomer to the league, I could not imagine a reason for Gaston to call me that spring day, so I immediately spoiled any prank attempt and hung up the phone. Before cutting the call short, "Gaston" identified himself as the supervisor of Southeastern Conference football officials. He inquired about a meeting to discuss the institution of a plan to better evaluate conference officials in a medical and functional program.

A few minutes after I rudely hung up on Gaston, he returned the call. He apologized for the bad connection, and I insisted our line must have been short-circuited.

Gaston again extended an invitation to meet with him in Atlanta, Georgia. This officials' testing was not new to me. During my tenure at Appalachian State University, I had coordinated and implemented an evaluation process for Southern Conference officials. The program was highly successful in bringing awareness of the need for better fitness training and nutritional habits.

I met with Gaston on July 26, 1991 in Atlanta, a red-letter day for me in my career and for the Southeastern Conference, which was on its way to establishing one of college football's most rigid and successful programs for officials. Gaston wanted the same type of program for SEC officials that we had implemented in the Southern Conference.

The mandatory screening would provide quantitative evidence of the ability to perform physically on the field. Bobby Gaston and the SEC were interested in including medical and functional assessment for screening of officials. This was a much more comprehensive program than I had put together a few years earlier in the Southern Conference. The budget of the

SEC was a little different than the limitations we had been given in Boone, North Carolina. The support from the Birmingham, Alabama offices of the SEC was unmatched in college athletics. They were leaders in so many aspects of college athletics.

To establish this program I believed it important to include athletic trainers from many SEC schools. The first group to get the preseason assessment of SEC football officials off the ground included me, Chris Patrick of Florida, Leroy Mullins of Mississippi, the late Tim Kerin of Tennessee, Bill McDonald of Alabama, Mike Roberts of Auburn and Al Green of Kentucky. All were supportive of a similar program we had established in the Southern Conference. Administratively, we had not only the support of Bobby Gaston, the Supervision of Football Officials, but also Associate Commissioner Jim McCullough. However, the program was effective due to the support of Roy Kramer. There was no one in college athletics with more power and influence that Commissioner Kramer. He is the one who crafted the SEC's Football Championship game and influenced so much of today's Bowl Championship Series. He was a big-time power player.

When a group of doctors and college athletic trainers work closely together from school year to school year, sophomoric pranks often become part of what makes everyone get along. One of my favorites occurred when Lou Holtz was the head football coach at South Carolina and his team was preparing to play the University of Arkansas in Little Rock. I received a telephone call from a Little Rock radio station, which was unusual for them to call me direct. I should have suspected something awry. Interviews were coordinated by the office and staff of Kerry Tharp, the sports information director.

The radio show host informed me that the University of Alabama had played in Little Rock the previous week and complained about numerous burns suffered by their players from the lime that was on the field. Again, I should have recognized something was amiss because lime had not been used to mark fields in years. The radio host asked what South Carolina had planned to prevent more burns.

I said we would protect the players, treat any wounds and make certain our doctors were aware of the problem. The interview went on for some five or six minutes with me avoiding any commitment to what we had planned. Finally, the host blurted out that I had been duped. This radio interview was a prank on me to the pleasure of the Little Rock, Arkansas radio audience.

The only ones not thrilled with the prospect of this new medical screening program were the game officials. They would now be required to pass an annual medical examination, which possibly included graded exercise testing. Then there was the mile and one-half run that required completion of the distance in accordance to Cooper's 1½-mile standards. The Cooper test is a physical fitness test designed by Kenneth H. Cooper in 1968, during his Air Force career. He devised a test (originally the distance run in 12 minutes) which correlated well with studies of oxygen uptake, a measure of aerobic fitness. The goal was to run as far as possible in the allotted twelve minutes. The test correlated with maximum oxygen uptake (VO_{2max}) a laboratory measure of aerobic conditioning or the ability of the heart and lung system to deliver oxygen throughout the body in an efficient manner. The test was meant to measure the condition of the person taking it and therefore it is supposed to be run at a steady pace instead of sprints and fast running. The outcome is based on the distance the test person ran, their age and gender. The test was later calibrated to a set distance of one and one-half miles, and standards established by age and gender. The results were classified as excellent, good, fair, or poor; and were specific to one's age.

For the SEC football officials, it was a difficult initiation process, but one that validated the assessment process. From the outset I realized just how much ground we needed to cover in our early years of making officials more fit for competition. One question that came out of our first meeting with SEC officials in 1991 came from Jimmy Harper, the legendary baritone-voiced official from Athens, Georgia.

"What, specifically, should we be eating for pre-game meals?" Harper asked.

It donned on me that most of our game officials played football during an era when the idea of a sound nutritional meal before a sporting event included steak, eggs and maybe potatoes. They generally were not afforded education on nutrition and the value of higher carbohydrate content, lower fats and hydration. We had a long way to go in the education of SEC officials, but it was a worthy endeavor that would prove to be beneficial to all parties concerned.

Annually, we completed medical screenings of the game officials in the spring. Anyone with concerns from our physicians was referred to the game official's personal physician to address the findings and provide documentation that the concerns had been resolved. All those cleared medically were assessed functionally with agility drills and the mile and one-half run. These functional tests were conducted in Birmingham in late July. The officials were broken into groups of ten, sorted by age with the older men running early in the morning to beat the excessive heat and humidity, which reached into the nineties with eighty-plus percent humidity.

We were prepared the day Gaston went down. As soon as the helicopter lifted off I knew we had a good program despite receiving a significant test. I knew that ninety percent of the game officials supported the testing. It was important that we immediately resume the testing or the entire program could be grounded for eternity. Forty minutes behind schedule, we resumed and no one ever looked back.

The lesson learned from the entire experience was failing to plan is planning to fail. This episode was one of many where my training in first aid and general athletic injuries prepared me to make educated, calculated decisions. Obviously, more experience helps one make better decisions.

Technically, I already had been offered the job as the head athletic trainer at the University of South Carolina in March of 1990 when I met with King Dixon, its athletic director. I was on campus to look over the facilities and my meeting with Dixon was a formal introduction.

While I was in Dixon's office in the Roundhouse building on the edge of the athletic campus, the athletic department's sports information director, Kerry Tharp, entered the office. Kerry delivered a proposed press release to Emily White, Dixon's administrative assistant. The release concerned the status of Joe Rhett, a men's basketball player who had some cardiac issues that resulted in the recent implantation of a cardiac pacemaker.

Rhett was an outstanding basketball player, a six-foot-eight forward who stayed at home to attend South Carolina. He would finish his four-year career with eleven-hundred-forty-two points. He also would be remembered forever by South Carolina fans because of his battle to overcome an irregular heart. Rhett and USC first became aware of the problem in January of 1990 when he blacked out in his Louisville, Kentucky hotel room. One month later, following a battery of tests and second opinions, doctors inserted the pacemaker.

Less than two weeks after the pacemaker was inserted near Rhett's left collarbone, Hank Gathers of Loyola-Marymount also gained national attention when he collapsed in cardiac arrest while playing basketball and died. I remember watching Gathers collapse on TV.

Naturally, we had physicians and all necessary equipment on the sideline for all of Rhett's games at South Carolina. That was standard procedure and part of our Emergency Action Plan. When we played road games, opposing teams' athletic trainers wanted to know what kind of special care was needed for Rhett. Our doctors' stance was that Rhett was cleared to play and nothing special was needed to care for him, just a functional Emergency Action Plan.

"I never think about it when I'm playing, but sometimes when I'm sitting alone in my room, I wonder what will happen if I get an elbow there or something," Rhett later told *Sports Illustrated*. "But three doctors have told me I'm fine, and I feel fine."

Then, on January 26, 1992, Rhett had a second syncopal episode. South Carolina was playing Mississippi State that Saturday evening at Carolina Coliseum in Columbia. Rhett fainted on the court during the game's second half in what was an extremely frightening episode. The local emergency medical staff of paramedics, athletic trainer Brainard Cooper and team physician Bill McKenzie stabilized the situation and managed Rhett's care. The following week Rhett was sent to Dr. Paul Walter and his staff at Emory University. It was determined that Rhett's bout the previous week had to do with fatigue and dehydration, nothing related to his heart issues and he later returned to complete his senior season.

At the time of the incident, we had twelve-thousand second opinions sitting in the stands, and one of them happened to be a Columbia physician who was very vocal about what had happened and how we had not handled the situation well. I always welcomed input and valued others' opinions. I would try to take the input and digest it and share with our healthcare providers.

The point is that the public often does not realize what has been done or what is being done behind the scenes to care for student-athletes. Nor does the public know how and why situations are handled in certain ways. Our team of physicians and athletic trainers were prepared for Rhett's situation, handled it in a professional manner and took extreme care in treating him. Athletic trainers must be on point and always prepared for any kind of situation, no matter how daunting.

I knew from that day forward there were some pretty exciting things happening at South Carolina.

When I first arrived in Columbia, South Carolina in March of 1990, Brainard Cooper was South Carolina's assistant athletic trainer for football, and Jim Price, the athletic trainer for men's basketball, and Malissa Martin worked with many of the women's sports and directed South Carolina Athletic Training educational program. There were several students assisting the full-time staff.

Jim Price was set to retire at the end of the spring. He was on the interview team that screened athletic training candidates for my position, and they made a recommendation to athletic director King Dixon. The plan was to move Cooper to men's basketball and he would handle baseball as well. Cooper was a couple of years younger than me and had worked previously at the University of Tennessee-Chattanooga where he was an athletic training student under Terry Lewis. Terry had now vacated my new position at South Carolina.

Cooper proved to be one of the best athletic trainers I have worked with over the years. Few people other than Ray Tanner, South Carolina's head baseball coach, know what an impact Brainard Cooper has had on Gamecock baseball success, which now includes national championships in 2010 and 2011. Brainard Cooper may have been one of the most under-appreciated people with the University of South Carolina athletic department. I realized his value more than ever after I departed the university.

I've been in athletics a long time and I certainly have seen a lot of situations develop with coaches. Every coach has strong rules when they first get hired: "We're going to make sure kids go to class. We're going to discipline kids who don't work out." Too often, though, coaches begin to take short cuts when their won-loss record begins to slip or they draw closer to the end of their contract. The problem is that coaches' priorities sometimes get skewed by the reality of the situation.

My good friend Sparky Woods, who coached football at South Carolina from 1989 to 1993, once said: "If I graduate ninety percent of my kids and win ten percent of my ball games, I'm going to get fired in three years. If I win ninety percent of my games and graduate ten percent of my kids, I'll be the coach of the year and play in a great bowl game and have all kinds of accolades." Woods embraced education as much as anyone at South Carolina and he made that point to his student-athletes. But Woods also understood the reality of coaching college football. If you do not win, you do not stick around long.

Coach Woods had good, sound principles just like any successful businessman. I remember one from an early staff meeting during his Appalachian State University tenure: "as a staff, we have two goals that we must remember and adhere to annually. First, we cannot afford to lose players. Recruiting mistakes will not be tolerated, and we must make sophomores out of freshmen. Second, in respect to game preparation, we cannot lose to teams we are better than. I would rather beat the teams we are supposed to, than upset a better team and lose to inferior opponents." Coach Woods was a motivator. My former athletic training students and graduate assistants remind me of their favorite Coach Woods pre-game talk annually at our meetings. Sparky Woods was a favorite.

The bottom line, coaches are constantly seeking any edge they can find to win games. Brad Scott succeeded Woods as USC's football coach for the 1994 season. Through his five seasons as head coach, Scott would call a meeting with the athletic trainers and strength coaches at the conclusion of every year. It generally was a review of where we were relative to our goals. In January of 1998, Scott met with me and Dennis Tripp, our strength coach at the time.

"What the heck is wrong with our kids?" Scott inquired. "Why are we so tired late in games, late in the season?"

As we were sitting there I could not help but recall the lectures from my undergraduate professor at Appalachian State University, Dr. Vaughn Christian. I admired him immensely. Dr. Christian was well-versed in the biological sciences as related to exercise science. One of his key lectures was the application of Hans Selye's stress adaptation model to the concepts of training he referred to as "periodization." That dated to the general adaptation syndrome and biological responses to stress. Selye's work has been used by the athletic community since the 1950s (Fleck, 1999).

General adaptation syndrome was described by Selye as three basic stages of response to stress:

a. The alarm stage, involving the initial shock of the stimulus on the system;
b. Resistance stage, involving the adaptation to the stimulus by the system; and
c. The exhaustion stage, when repairs are inadequate and a decrease in system functioning results.

The foundation of "periodization" training is that it keeps a body in the resistant stage without ever going into the exhaustion stage. By adhering to cyclic training, the body is given adequate time to recover from significant stress before additional training is undertaken. The response to a new stress is to first respond poorly, and the response or resistance is minimized. As the body is exposed to the sun, sunburn might develop. During the resistance stage, adaptation improves the response to a higher level than the previous level, and a suntan develops. The exhaustion stage is a continuation of the stimulus at too high a level and the increase gained from adaptation is now offset and all gains are lost. The resultant would be wrinkles, spots, or even skin cancer after the suntan.

The goal in sports "periodization" is to reduce the stress at the point where the resistance stage ends so the body has time to recover. In this way, the exhaustion stage does not reduce the gains achieved, the body can recover and remain above the original equilibrium point. The next cycle of increased stimulus now improves the response further and the equilibrium point continues to rise after each cycle.

Obviously, Scott realized his players were not being trained to cope with stress. Rather, they were peaking too early in the season and were not prepared for the rigors of our late-season schedule, when South Carolina traditionally plays its stiffest competition—what many fans called the "Orange Crush" of the schedule versus Tennessee, Florida and rival Clemson. Today, this seems to be the rule more than the exception, and far too few strength coaches understand this phenomenon.

Strength coaches have enjoyed significant pay increases in the 1990s and 2000s, reaching annual salaries in six figures in many cases, and I am ecstatic about that. Head football coaches have made certain strength coaches handsomely rewarded because NCAA rules have extended the amount of contact strength coaches have with players throughout the year. A person's value to a company is in direct proportion to the amount of money in his paycheck. As the value of strength coaches has increased, so have their salaries. Still, the fact remains they must understand the basic tenants of stress as related to strength and conditioning, and prudently apply conditioning principles.

South Carolina's Achilles heel during my tenure was its lack of depth in the offensive line. One thing that really affected college football during that period was the NCAA trimming football scholarships from ninety-five to eighty-five in the 1990s. All of the sudden, programs could no longer make poor decisions on recruits. Programs were allowed to bring in a maximum of twenty-five student-athletes per year. You could no longer over-sign student-athletes in a single class.

The official colors of the Southeastern Conference are blue and yellow, but I always have said they should be black and blue because it is such a tough conference and so darned competitive, particularly in football. It is not by luck that seven of the last nine national champions are from the SEC (2003 and 2006-2011) with Auburn, Alabama, Florida and Louisiana State all winning titles. There might be teams here and there that win with finesse, but for the most part, teams win in the SEC with a bruising style of football. The hallmark has been big and fast student-athletes with tremendous physicality. With that said, it always has been critical and imperative that a team maintain depth in its offensive and defensive lines.

When Woods arrived at South Carolina from Appalachian State for the 1989 season, he believed the quality of the South Carolina offensive linemen was inferior to those he had at Appalachian State. That was an eye-opening statement because Appalachian State competed at the NCAA Division I-AA level at the time, one step below South Carolina's NCAA Division I-A standing. Woods was speaking primarily about the quality of depth, or lack thereof, at South Carolina.

Woods and his coaching staff recruited the heck out of offensive linemen. So, did Brad Scott when he arrived at South Carolina. Scott hired Dennis Tripp as his strength and conditioning coordinator and the primary objective was to get our offensive linemen in top shape. Scott was an offensive line coach at Florida State previously and always had great linemen there, really athletic players. Florida State of the Atlantic Coast Conference was no different than Florida, Tennessee and Georgia of the SEC in having athletic lineman. It was something South Carolina sorely lacked. Part of developing that kind of necessary depth on the offensive line was by beginning to redshirt entire classes of recruits, giving them an extra year to develop in size, strength and ability.

I always believed I had a good understanding of student-athletes. I could read them well and could communicate effectively with them. I used humor at the appropriate time to keep the temperament of the athletic training room light, but the student-athletes knew I was confidant as well as an advocate. They also knew if they got between me and the head coach or an administrator, I would be loyal to the institution.

One Monday morning, following a home game during the 1997 season, I received a telephone call from the mother of an offensive lineman we were redshirting. The mother was concerned about her son, Todd Davis.

"Please don't let him know I called," she said.

These kinds of calls happened occasionally, and I always appreciated hearing from parents.

"Every time he hits, he complains about blacking out," the mother said of her son.

Our athletic trainers watched Todd before the next game. Since he was being redshirted, he could dress for games but was not allowed to play. In practice, he rarely was involved in contact because he was on a scout team. He was involved in dummy drills, but nothing full speed and none with contact. So, pre-game warm-ups were the best time to keep an eye on him.

At the conclusion of warm-ups, the team engaged in a drill called "Bull in the Ring." In this drill, a lineman stands in the middle of a circle, surrounded by another twelve or thirteen linemen. The bull in the ring then takes on one player after another in shoulder-to-shoulder contact. The drill is designed to make certain a player's pads are ready and to get the player into game mode. You do not want the player's first hit to be on the field during the game.

Sure enough, on this particular day, we noticed whenever Todd made a hit of any kind, he almost went to his knees. Rather than break confidentiality with Todd's mother, I went to him on Monday after practice.

"I was watching you warm up Saturday, I noticed you were almost dizzy after a hit," I recall saying. "It's almost like you went out. Is everything OK? Is there something you need to tell me about?"

He replied: "Dr. Rod, I don't know what's wrong, but whenever I hit, it feels like I just black out."

I immediately referred Todd to our team physician, Dr. Bob Peele, who examined him and took X-Rays. Dr. Peele did not find anything significant on his examination, but was not comfortable with the findings. So, he visited with Todd for about thirty minutes and said, "You know, something just doesn't seem right here, let's get an MRI." Three days later, Dr. Peele called and said, "Rod, we need to talk."

I said, "What's wrong?"

He said, "Todd has Arnold-Chiari malformation."

This malformation of the brain occurs when the brain stem, where it attaches to the spinal cord, attempts to pull down through the opening at the base of the skull. Basically, the stem is too large for the opening at the base of the skull (foramen magnum). Symptoms can include nausea, headaches, fatigue and dizziness. There are four or five classes of Arnold-Chiari malformation. His was the next to bottom class, but obviously there was some strangulation taking place upon contact. In Todd's case, this was congenital.

If Todd had absorbed extreme contact, it could have caused a very serious condition. He was disqualified from competition, and we sought a second opinion to validate the findings. The second opinion agreed with ours and recommended he avoid unnecessary contact. Todd would not be able to play football, but he would live a normal life. He is doing well today. He and his wife, Amy, live in Union, South Carolina, where he is employed by the Union County Schools and is a children's minister at New Life Baptist Church. Todd is like so many student-athletes: Todd Ellis, Steve Tanneyhill and Ryan Brewer, who settled in Columbia following their athletic careers at South Carolina.

Five or six years later, another student-athlete came to South Carolina having suffered "stingers" during his high school career. During his physical examination, we worked up his stingers and found the same Arnold-Chiari malformation. Interestingly, I had never heard of this malformation, and now dealt with two cases within a six-year span.

It was another great example of how an athletic trainer is not necessarily looking for things to find, but has to deal with findings and make certain these student-athletes are adequately treated.

I recall someone telling me early in my educational years at Appalachian that, "the top three reasons to teach in public schools or enter a career in education were June, July and August." I also heard that reasoning applied to athletics, and summers were supposed to be down time for those of us involved in an athletic endeavor. Obviously, folks who thought that way never worked in athletics. In my career in athletics, summers were always congested with workouts. The month of August was slammed with the genesis of the upcoming school year and preseason practices for football, soccer, volleyball, and cross country.

Although NCAA rules say otherwise, by the twenty-first century, summer workouts were really starting to be non-voluntary in basis. When I first started at South Carolina, we would have five to six student-athletes on campus for the summer to workout. Those student-athletes who remained on campus during the summer usually did so for academic reasons. Most were taking classes to regain their NCAA eligibility. There also were those we wanted to keep around for rehabilitation. By the time I left South Carolina in 2007, there may have been only five or six student-athletes who did not remain on campus. They remained during the summer to take classes and participate in off-season conditioning.

My first administrator and supervisor at South Carolina was Sterling Brown, a former football coach of twenty-nine years including one stint as the head football coach at Drexel University. He later served in athletic administration at Wyoming, Marshall, Virginia Tech and Georgia Tech. "Brownie" was a great administrator and advocate for me. He knew of the relationship between Sparky Woods and me. He supported me to do my job under the constraints of NCAA Division I athletics. As a former coach, he understood what I did and respected my work. "Brownie" was a meticulous rules guy. I heard him tell coaches in heated conversations, "just follow the rule" or "don't screw with kids," when coaches attempted to take shortcuts against the standards expected at South Carolina. "Brownie" was a great advocate for student-athletes.

"Brownie" was an old-school coach and administrator, and he believed student-athletes needed to get away from campus for the summer to get their batteries recharged. They needed the chance to be a person, according to Brown, and be out from under the watchful eye of their coaches. Brown was very supportive of healthcare, and always reminded me to take care of student-athletes. Likewise, he understood it was more efficient from a healthcare standpoint to rehabilitate a student-athlete on campus, and he supported that when he needed. If the student-athlete was vital to the program—one who we could not gamble that he or she might not do their work without a watchful and stern eye—Brown was supportive of keeping student-athletes in town for the summer.

I knew I was responsible to Sterling Brown, and ultimately to King Dixon, the athletic director. As the head athletic trainer, I knew I also was responsive to the head football coach. Though I coordinated the prevention, care and rehabilitation of injuries to our student-athletes as well as their daily healthcare needs, I knew if I did not meet the needs and expectations of the head football coach, my days would be numbered. This was true with coaches Sparky Woods, Brad Scott, Lou Holtz and Steve Spurrier. I was sensitive to this and also understood the necessity to do what was right.

I always believed "get rid of me because I failed to do my job, not because you have someone else you want to hire." Hey, I survived three athletic directors and four football coaches over a seventeen-year tenure at South Carolina.

There were times when we wished a student-athlete was on campus for the summer and not engaged in extra-curricular activities while on break. One such instance of that occurred in the summer of 2000. On July 15, I received a call from John Gutekunst, one of our assistant coaches to inform me that a signee from Myrtle Beach, South Carolina, had been involved in a four-wheel, off-road buggy accident. Daniel Weaver, who was recruited as a place-kicker by Lou Holtz's coaching staff, had dislocated his hip. This was a potentially catastrophic injury for the young man as well as for the team because he was slated to be involved in the team's plans for the season. Granted, Daniel's injury occurred prior to his initial University of South Carolina enrollment.

I immediately called Weaver's family to inquire about his health and overall condition. His mother was cordial and cooperative, and asked if our team physician could review the radiographic studies her family's physician had ordered. Our doctor agreed with their physician's findings and recommendations. Daniel's family requested his care be transitioned from Myrtle Beach to Columbia, and we complied.

Weaver was withheld from all practices that fall. He eventually lettered for three seasons and will forever be remembered for his forty-two- yard field goal as time expired to give South Carolina a 31-28 victory over Ohio State in the 2002 Outback Bowl. It was South Carolina's second consecutive Outback Bowl win over the Buckeyes.

This win might not have happened had Weaver's care not been turned over to our excellent team of physicians at South Carolina.

The University of South Carolina annually followed the policies as most NCAA Division I schools (FBS) and conducted medical screenings of its players following each season, then again prior to the next season. The interval year medical screens were a general review of systems or injuries occurring since the student-athlete's last medical screen. They were required of all student-athletes. I mirrored the practice of my good friend Jeff Monroe, assistant athletic director and head athletic trainer at Michigan State University. Jeff and physicians encouraged each of their football signees to attend the Spring Game, and be screened per their pre-participation medical examination. As soon as the student-athletes officially were "signed" on the early February National Signing Day, a packet of information on the medical process was sent to each player. The packet included a detailed medical information and demographic sheet as part of a comprehensive medical history. This information was returned to Jeff's office and a thorough review engaged. Per NCAA guidelines, the student-athletes were allowed to attend the Spring Game, and prior to the game Jeff and his physicians screened each of the prospective student-athletes. Any medical concerns could then be further studied and any surgical records could be requested.

Our next case concerned a young man we will call George to protect his privacy. He was a defensive player from the southeast who spent most of his first two seasons at South Carolina on the sideline with a shoulder injury that required surgery. Prior to this particular season, George had failed to complete his medical screening. As the story goes, he complained about pain in his testicles and immediately sought care at the hospital closest to the apartment complex where he was living, as this was over a weekend. The emergency room physician examined George and ordered a urinalysis. Based on his findings, the physician prescribed an antibiotic and ordered rest over the weekend. As George was prescribed an antibiotic, it was assumed the patient had some type of urinary tract infection. On Monday, George reported to the athletic training room and requested to see the team physician.

Upon examination, the physician questioned some pathology in the young man's testicle and ordered an ultrasound STAT, defined in the medical community as fast, quick, or immediate. About one hour later, I received a call from George saying he had to have surgery. I was totally shocked, but more stunned by the reason. We learned that George had a spermatic cord torsion, which had now gone for more than forty-eight hours, and now he had a necrotic condition in his testicle. The only resolution was to surgically remove his testicle due to the missed diagnosis. I was livid, as he had been treated by an emergency room physician for something he did not have, and now this young man was faced with a significant surgery due to an incorrect diagnosis.

George had no primary insurance, and since this was not an athletic injury, the university was unable to cover the expenses. (The NCAA has since changed this rule, and institutions can cover any and all medical care for student-athletes during their enrollment). I made a call to a friend in the hospital's administration and quite succinctly promised that if this young man received as much as a single bill for any of this surgery, I would thoroughly explain to him the travesty that had occurred, and further recommend he seek legal counsel.

George still had some concerns, as he was unsure whether his other testicle was functional. Thank goodness, the remaining testicle was functional and he recovered well from this debacle.

And, I forgot to mention: George never saw a bill from the hospital.

Short cuts will get you every time. This is true of sports in general, and more specifically in sports medicine. Sports medicine as we know it is good, sound medical advice applied to physically active people. There are no short cuts to decrease a player's down time. We certainly know if we take short cuts, often this can increase the amount of time it takes for a student-athlete to recover. People often believe that in sports medicine we have short cuts to get people back on the playing field. This quick recovery is the response of patients and student-athletes often because they are so motivated, are in such great shape and they respond well to treatments. However, it takes time for healing which must be addressed when dealing with injuries. We cannot speed up healing, but we can certainly slow it down.

I have always preached that physicians are an athletic trainer's best friend. I truly believe this. There was never a physician that I appreciated and respected more that Dr. Bob Peele. He gave so many years of his life and time away from his family for South Carolina football. He was an athletic trainer's physician.

I developed an appreciation for the specialty of Primary Care Sports Medicine physicians during my days at the University of South Carolina. These physicians were generally trained in emergency medicine, pediatrics, or family medicine. They are trained in non-operative techniques, and are tremendous professionals. The Primary Care physician focuses on the total being, while specialists such as cardiologists or dermatologists or orthopedists view the patient with primarily their specialty in view. Drs. Bill McKenzie, Mark Leski, and Tom Armsey were experienced physicians and a pleasure to work with and were excellent professors to their fellows studying sports medicine. This clinical and educational opportunity provided the best of both worlds in my view. If you are practicing good clinical skills, you are showing the proper way to do a skill. By teaching a skill, you are providing the standard of care you need for your patients. South Carolina was afforded a great fellowship in sports medicine with good education and quality healthcare.

One of our first fellows, Steve Youmans, an avid South Carolina fan, was completing his clinical hours in the athletic training room. He was great friends with our staff and very approachable from the coaches. Everyone loved Dr. Youmans.

Let me give you an example of how coaches sometimes want to cut to the chase and fix everything right now. On September 15, 1991, Sparky

Woods was extremely frustrated with lack of practice time of a key player. At this point, Woods was in his third season as South Carolina's head football coach. Woods was not alone in his frustration. An entire fan base at South Carolina wanted this player back in action . . . yesterday.

Woods reminded me: "You were a pretty good athletic trainer when you were at Appalachian." This really bothered me because we could not explain mechanically just what was wrong with this student-athlete. Why was his knee continuing to be swollen? Our team physician and my staff were focused entirely on what could be done to resolve this injury. We sought counsel of other professional teams, and questioned each and every decision we made. Nothing was working. Little did we know that all the problems with the student-athlete were not mechanical or orthopedic in nature. It was a systemic problem, secondary to a sexually transmitted disease (STD) that had not been effectively treated. Remember, your physician can only treat what the patient presents. There were no reported problems associated directly with a STD in this case. When the STD lies dormant for some time, the bacterial nature of the condition becomes viral and is resistant to antibiotics. It simply has to "run its course" before there is a resolution, proving to us that we often have to look at the entire patient, not just one system.

Dr. Bill McKenzie (Primary Care Sports Medicine) and Dr. Bob Peele (Orthopedic Surgeon) did an excellent job of evaluating this case and finding the exact cause of the problem. It was the perfect example of how sometimes we must exercise patience. That often happens against the push of coaches to find a solution quicker.

Again, a couple of examples of the global view being the key.

When the university's medical school began its affiliation with the athletic department, one of its first residents to rotate through the athletic training room in his final year of residency was Dr. Steven Youmans. He was great friends with our staff and very approachable. Dr. Youmans handled all the general medical needs of our student-athletes, so you can see what his faculty and attending faculty thought of him. He worked so well with Dr. Peele. He did not want to be an orthopedist and Dr. Peele expected Dr.

Youmans to handle general medical needs—which he did. Everyone loved Dr. Youmans.

He did have one special patient, my son David. It was November 6, 1994. On the typical Sunday evening, David attended his functions at Saxa Gotha Presbyterian Church in Lexington, South Carolina. While having dinner with the family, David noted that he had to go to the bathroom to urinate during his choir activity. Being a young kid, and so full of himself, I questioned if he was showing off. He denied it and I dismissed the thought. That night, David had a bedwetting accident. We changed his bedding, bathed him, and he was off to Lexington Elementary School.

That afternoon, I mentioned the problem David was experiencing with Dr. Youmans. He suggested conducting some tests on his urine to see if there was an infection or something else that needed to be dealt with. The next morning, I delivered the urine specimen to Dr. Youmans office. He quickly called and said he needed to draw blood for further tests. I picked David up from school and drove him directly to Dr. Youmans Palmetto Richland Family Practice office. I returned to my Williams-Brice Stadium office, and around 3 p.m., Dr. Youmans came into my office and said we needed to talk.

I was not sure what the problem was, but I could see in his eyes he was very concerned. Dr. Youmans told me David was a Type I diabetic, a diagnosis that would forever change David's life.

Part of the education of a diabetic is to teach the patient and in David's case, his mom and I, how to monitor blood sugar, balance food intake with insulin, as their body no longer produces insulin. This was a tough challenge for everyone. I was totally floored—this was probably the furthest thing from my mind and would have been the last condition or disease I would have thought would afflict David.

The endocrinologists at Palmetto Richland Hospital in Columbia were great. The educational staff they had to work with the families was awesome. November 11, 1994 was our first follow-up visit with David and the team of specialists. He and I drove from the hospital back to my office. Later that afternoon I would fly to Gainesville, Florida with our football team to play the Florida Gators. As we turned left onto Assembly Street in downtown Columbia, there was a crowd of people outside St. Peters Catholic Church. I reminded David, Coach Frank McGuire's funeral was being held there. David had met Coach McGuire in the athletic training room, and he always took time for little kids, and was such a presence among them.

No one could have been better than Dr. Youmans as the supervisor of David's care and introduction to this tough disease.

David would deal with diabetes for the rest of his life. As a parent, I prayed so many times that I wish this could have happened to me and spare him. This is a tough disease, and must constantly be addressed with blood sugar monitoring.

In December of 1998, Coach Lou Holtz became head coach at the University of South Carolina. As I met his family, all his children were adults. One son, Kevin, was also a Type I diabetic. He was an insulin pump user, and quite an advocate.

One day following a staff meeting, Coach Holtz asked to see me in his office. This was never good. The subject could be concern for how I handled a player, a personal medical need, who knows. Very seldom was the chance to meet with him one-on-one a good thing.

This day was different. Coach wanted to know about David—how he was dealing with his diabetes—and was I interested in putting him on a pump. I told him we were actually going through the steps at that time to engage him in insulin-pump therapy. He was to be transitioned to the pump in the coming days. He asked that we keep him abreast of the developments, and I did.

A few days later, the pump orientation took place, and we told Coach about the experience. He was interested, and excited for David. It took some time for David to get adjusted, but it definitely allowed more control of blood sugars with the "on-board" source of insulin. The downside was the constant tethering to the device.

The next day, following a staff meeting, Coach inquired how David was doing with his pump. I told him he was doing well. He also inquired about how well the state's health plan had paid on the pump. We discussed the overall care and treatment of diabetics, and I returned to my office on the west side of Williams-Brice Stadium.

As I walked into my office, my phone rang. It was Rita Ricard, (Rita Boykin). Coach had left something for me. Not sure what it was, I returned to his office and retrieved the envelope he had for me. I opened the envelope to read what it said. Coach would send you a note from time to time to communicate his goals or concerns. This note was different. It was something people don't realize about Coach. Inside this envelope was the co-pay for David's insulin pump. What a nice surprise.

Another area of concern where shortcuts are taken is in regards to education in the use of equipment. No question, the best way to teach people how to use a product is to make them comfortable with the product's use.

As an athletic trainer, I took numerous science and education classes in college. The majority of professional preparation for athletic training students in my collegiate studies was coupled with training in teacher preparation as most jobs included teaching. When I graduated and got into my first job at Lenoir-Rhyne College, Tony Bullock came by to see me. Tony was probably a couple years older than me, and a South Carolina native who had a new company. He wanted to show me a big ice machine, for therapeutic application of ice or cryotherapy. Tony called on us even though we had no use for one at the time. Nonetheless, as time went on, Tony continued to send samples to me of various products and demonstrated the use of some of his items as he made his route through Hickory, North Carolina. Tony explained how the machines worked, and was an excellent teacher of the principles of physical medicine.

One of those items was an electrical muscle stimulator called Medcosonnolator, which was used a great deal in the athletic training room. We used it for pain control and for muscle re-education. Electrical muscle stimulation was a significant modality in 1980. I didn't have much electrical muscle stimulation education in college. Appalachian State had limited modalities, which is unlike today where there are many controls and directives on what must be taught in college curriculums to be an approved program.

When Tony came to see me at Lenoir-Rhyne College, he demonstrated these different electrical muscle stimulation devices. Many times, physicians and athletic trainers—any professionals—are intimidated when a sales person shows them how to use a product because, quite frankly, the professionals are not familiar with the product. People don't like to be embarrassed or feel uneducated. I like to tell people that many times the person who demonstrates a new surgical technique may be a technician, not a medical professional.

From that day forward I believed that the best way to sell people is to teach them how to use a product. The best way to sell is good education. In sports medicine that is certainly true. Tony Bullock taught me a very valuable lesson - one I would use much more than I could ever believe as a young athletic trainer.

When I left the University of South Carolina, I became a resource in various products for several companies. One of those was EMPI, an electrophysiological company that used iontophoresis, low voltage direct current to introduce medicine into the body. A couple of other companies were Sutton Medical, which had an electronic medical records product, and Donjoy, which provides braces to the orthopedic community. I have also been providing educational seminars on behalf of Biodex relative to concussion management, and 3M Casting and Splinting Seminars.

I tell these companies very quickly that I will not be a sales person. The minute I become a sales person, I lose my credibility as an educator. Once you cross that road, you can't go back. I treasure my ability to teach concepts and apply good, sound educational concepts to clinical athletic training and clinical sports medicine. I was trained early in my career that education is key.

From a business perspective, to be effective in sales, a company must educate all levels of the decision-making process. Though I do not want to be a sales person, I certainly believe much can be learned from the sales process.

In 2008 I made a decision to conduct some of my educational seminars as part of an insurance company, AssuranceAmerica. Bud Stumbaugh was the head of this company, and was introduced to me. Bud was the consummate insurance salesman. When you met with him, you had better be prepared as he could sell ice to an Eskimo. One of the most valued lessons I learned from Bud and his team at AssuranceAmerica was to make sales calls to all levels of an organization. For example, when you are trying to take a concept to an athletic department and get the agency to embrace "cost containment strategies," this needs to be taught or portrayed to the athletic trainers as they will be closely dealing with the claims activity; the business office as they are associated from the expenditure side; the risk manager as they see the value of minimizing the loss; and finally the senior administration as they see the value of the total reduction of risk.

I will always be indebted to Bud Stumbaugh for his leadership abilities and lessons taught.

It is always the athletic trainer's goal to provide the best of care to student-athletes. Any equipment or service that may enhance performance is provided. In the spring and summer of 2004, flu shots were ordered and the vaccine was offered to student-athletes at South Carolina as was consistent from year to year. There was much concern then about the flu virus and the ongoing vaccine shortage.

The vaccines were distributed primarily to those student-athletes who traveled quite a bit in the fall and winter because they were exposed to more viruses than others. I knew there was going to be a shortage of the vaccine that year, so I first scheduled immunization for our men's basketball team, due to its suddenly approaching international travel. When our team of physicians administered the waivers and vaccines to the players following one practice, it just happened to be on the same day of elevation of the scarcity of the vaccine. Vaccines were only to be provided to infirmed, the elderly and those who had significant risk factors.

We had already immunized these players when the media began asking questions of men's basketball coach Dave Odom. He said his belief was that his players were in a high-profile situation and needed these shots. The university used no state funds to operate athletics, so though purchased under the umbrella of state contracts, etc., discounts were applied to purchase these vaccines. Still, it just did not wash well with the public that these student-athletes were getting immunizations while elderly and infirmed were being shut out. Three vials of ten vaccines were secured to immunize the student-athletes and support students (managers and athletic training students). What made a bad situation worse was the remaining vaccines from the vials were also used to immunize full-time staff members and their spouses. We should not have used athletic department funds for such a practice; and the timing could not have been worse. Mike McGee did not understand this scenario when I reported it to him.

The athletic training program is becoming more fractured today as the department enjoys growth. In 1990, I was challenged by King Dixon to bring a unified standard of care and services to all student-athletes. I was proud of the level of care we provided from that year forward, but more proud of the consistency among my staff in the care provided. In 1990, we had athletic training rooms at the Williams-Brice Stadium (football and cheerleading), the Spring Sports Center (baseball, track, tennis, and soccer), the Physical Educations Center (volleyball, women's basketball, swimming and diving) and Carolina Coliseum (men's basketball). By the time I departed in 2007, we had all of the above with additional athletic training rooms at the Carolina Coliseum for women's basketball and volleyball; athletic training rooms for men and women's basketball at the new Colonial Center; and an athletic training room at the new baseball stadium. This facility served baseball and softball. It is almost impossible to oversee all these sites with consistency of care to all student-athletes.

The University of South Carolina is not the only institution moving from a central theme to decentralized facilities for each sport. This is true not only for athletic training but academics, strength and conditioning, and athletic equipment. It is just fiscally challenging to staff and equip each sport on an individual basis.

Shortcuts never work. Just like the quick immunization of a basketball team without waiting normal times, we try to quick-fix things in college athletics too many times.

Eric Sullivan was a rising junior during the 1993 football season at Appalachian State. He had some dizzy spells with summer conditioning, and our staff quickly referred him to see our primary care team physician. With his examination and battery of tests, the physician referred this young man for a cardiac consultation due to an abnormal heartbeat or atrial fibrillation.

Eric was scheduled to see a specialist for a cardiac ablation. This was a procedure for the treatment of the irregular heartbeat, and involved refining the firing pattern of nerve fibers in the heart. Dr. Warren Jackman was one of the lead researchers in the country, and that is whom we sought for Eric's evaluation and recommended plan of action. The progressive cardiologists were mapping the heart electrophysiologically and then treating the defective electrical shortcuts.

Based on his findings, Dr. Jackman was confident of the need for a cardiac ablation. However, we had to get to Oklahoma City, Oklahoma in a very timely manner as he was embarking on a two-week family vacation. We did not make the deadline. While this seemed so critical to the administration and coaching staff, it did give this young man and his mother time to discuss the implications and subsequent risks of this procedure. This was not an outpatient orthopedic procedure. It involved invasive mapping of his heart and subsequent ablation of nerve fibers to stop the short-circuitry which was causing his abnormal heartbeat and dizziness with activity.

I learned a valuable lesson that day. Sometimes it is best to let things run their normal course. The time Eric and his mother had to discuss this situation was so valuable. His cardiac problem was assessed by the physician; communicated to Eric and his mom; and he was able to decide his treatment plan and proceed according to their wishes.

Dr. Rod's Treatment Plan

EMERGENCY ACTION PLAN

INJURIES ARE CERTAINLY INEVITABLE, and these emergency situations can arise at any time during athletic events. Coaches and Sports Medicine staffs must work together to plan out the "course of action" in the event of injury. Such a plan helps ensure the best care will be provided.

Through careful pre-participation physical screenings, adequate medical coverage, safe practice and training techniques and other safety avenues, some potential emergencies may be averted. The incidence of injury is inherent with sports participation and the development of a good Emergency Action Plan facilitates proper management of the emergency situation.

Successful Emergency Action Plans have three basic components: emergency personnel, emergency communication, and emergency equipment.

Emergency Personnel

With athletic association practice and competition, the first responder to an emergency situation is typically a member of the sports medicine staff, most commonly a certified athletic trainer. In professional sports, a physician may not always be at practice. All high schools are not afforded the luxury of a certified athletic trainer. Recreational sports teams certainly do not have medical professionals at practices; but the need still exists for a proper plan of action to be followed in the event of injury.

In colleges, the first responder in some instances may be a coach or other institutional personnel. Certification in cardiopulmonary resuscitation (CPR), first aid, prevention of disease transmission, and emergency plan review is required for all athletics personnel associated with practices, competitions, skills instruction, and strength and conditioning. (NCAA, 2010a, 2010b)

Emergency Communication

Quick, decisive decisions can only be made with good communication. The Emergency Action Plan requires thorough planning and communication is a major tenant. Athletic trainers and emergency medical personnel must work together to provide the best possible care to injured athletes. In the event emergency medical crews are not on site, then they must be called. If a landline is not available, a mobile phone should be utilized. The communication should include:

- Call to 9-1-1 (if available)
- Provide:
  ○ Name, address, telephone number of the caller
  ○ Number of athletes
  ○ Condition of athlete(s)
  ○ First aid treatment initiated by first responder
  ○ Specific directions as needed to locate the emergency scene (important to have)
  ○ Be prepared to answer additional information as requested by dispatcher

Emergency Equipment

All necessary emergency equipment should be at the site and quickly accessible. Personnel should be familiar with the function and operation of each type of emergency equipment. Equipment should be in good operating condition, and personnel must be trained in advance to use it properly. Emergency equipment should be checked on a regular basis and its use rehearsed by emergency personnel. The emergency equipment available should be appropriate for the level of training of the emergency medical providers.

Transportation

Emphasis is placed at having an ambulance on site at high risk sporting events. EMS response time is additionally factored in when determining on site ambulance coverage. The institution should coordinate on site ambulances for competition in all sports. Ambulances may be coordinated on site for other special events/sports, such as major tournaments or regional or championship events. Consideration is given to the capabilities of transportation service available (i.e., Basic Life Support or Advanced Life Support) and the equipment and level of trained personnel on board the ambulance. In the event that an ambulance is on site, there should be a designated location with rapid access to the site and a cleared route for entering/exiting the venue.

Venue-Specific Emergency Action Plans

The importance of being properly prepared when athletic emergencies arise cannot be stressed enough. An athlete's survival may hinge on how well trained and prepared athletic healthcare providers are. It is prudent to invest athletic department "ownership" in the emergency plan by involving the athletic administration and sport coaches as well as sports medicine personnel. The emergency plan should be reviewed at least once a year with all athletic personnel, along with CPR training.

The best plans are those embraced by an entire department or company. Part of the emergency action plan is the quarterly review and practice of plan implementation to guarantee all employees and participants are engaged.

CHAPTER 2

SPORTS FACILITIES

These days, just about any place you turn in college athletics you see tremendous growth. Student-athletes are bigger, faster, and stronger across the board. Coaches are better schooled in the intricacies of their sports, and there are enough coaches to give individual attention to every student-athlete. Administrators are educated for the sole purpose of entering college athletics and no longer are retired coaches with little background in running a department.

Then there are the athletic facilities on college campuses. Football stadiums are larger and more fan friendly. Multi-million dollar baseball stadiums are being built across the country. Newer and better soccer complexes, tennis courts and swimming pools are sprouting up everywhere.

Athletic training facilities have experienced the same expansion and growth. It is worth tracing my route through college athletics to fully appreciate and illustrate the boon in training facilities over the past four decades or so.

The athletic trainer's job description generally includes the words "prevention, care, and rehabilitation of athletic injuries." This was true at all three jobs I held in collegiate athletics. In addition, I was assigned responsibilities coordinating athletic team travel logistics during much of my career. This included team meals and general oversight of menus with the dining hall for student-athletes, or more commonly called our training table.

I loved to have David and Ryan accompany me to the stadium anytime they could. They loved to be around the players, and it generally was a good place for them. I reminded them that the things they saw and heard, needed to remain there. They would be exposed to some things that were not good, but I did think it was still good for them to be exposed. I reminded them "what goes on the road, stays on the road."

During two-a-day practices, it was common for coaches to request meals to be catered at the Williams-Brice Stadium facilities. This was certainly the case with Coach Brad Scott's tenure. The department's administration was sensitive to costs, and catering was expensive. To facilitate everyone's needs, I would often arrange for one of my students to pick up the contents of a continental breakfast from our training table —thus keeping costs down while meeting the expectations and wishes of the coaches. I would always try to find a student athletic trainer who had good people skills, and could make things happen. During the late nineties, none was better than Greg Harmon.

Greg would drive over to the training table and pick items up. He only had to be instructed one time. Greg was one of my favorites, still to this day. My favoritism of Greg led to much chiding from his classmates, but did not seem to bother him.

David and Ryan were both big fans of not only Greg, but many of our athletic training students and graduate assistant athletic trainers over the years. Ryan loved to come with me to summer practice before he had to go back to school. He would ride with Greg and help him pick up breakfast for the team.

One day, Ryan was riding with Greg. They were using the athletic department's Chevy van, and Greg noticed Ryan did not have his seatbelt engaged. Greg chastised Ryan for not wearing his belt, reminding him "if your Daddy sees that, he will yell at both of us." With a cute little smirk, Ryan responded to Greg "what goes on the road, stays on the road."

I guess I had shared that one time too many!

Case in point: during my tenure at Appalachian State University from 1985-1990, I traveled with both the football team and the men's basketball team. In 1986, we were scheduled to play basketball in the Charlotte Coliseum. It had been built as a state-of-the-art complex with luxury boxes and a large eight-sided video scoreboard. The facility included twenty-four thousand seats; it was not only the largest venue in the National Basketball Association, but the largest basketball-specific arena ever to serve as a full-time home for an NBA team. Some thought the Coliseum was too big, but owner George Shinn built the facility in the basketball crazy Charlotte area in the middle of Atlantic Coast Conference basketball.

The arena was home to the Charlotte Hornets prior to Shinn's move to New Orleans, Louisiana. The arena was also used for a variety of collegiate basketball events over the years, hosting the 1994 Men's Final Four in addition to many NCAA Tournament regionals for men's and women's college basketball. It was the site of eight ACC men's basketball tournaments and the 1989 Sun Belt Conference men's basketball tournament.

The facility, as grand as it was, was obsolete by its twentieth birthday. When NBA basketball returned to Charlotte in the form of the Charlotte Bobcats, a new facility was being built downtown. The revenue today is in seat licenses, suites, and the amenities associated therein.

It is interesting to travel around the country and see the transition to the newer, more modern facilities. The new Yankee Stadium, Cowboys Stadium in Arlington, Texas, and even the Raymond James Stadium in Tampa, Florida were all built for the comfort of the fan. The stadiums were designed completely for the convenience of the participant. No more are the concession stands serviced from the walkways, rather, service access is away from the walkways. The stadiums are built with ample suites for revenue generation, and premiums seats are the norm.

From the day I returned from Greensboro, North Carolina, in the late days of July, 1972, I started an annual tradition of setting up the athletic training room for the upcoming fall preseason football practices. Granted, my expectations that year paled in comparison to what I would embrace in later years with the completion of my undergraduate education and mastery of the Board of Certification's Athletic Training examination.

Remember, air conditioning was not a household feature in those days. The athletic training room was in the hallway outside the head football coach's office. Across the tiled hallway was the football locker room, replete with its all-so-familiar aroma. The first day Tony Hopfer and I viewed the facilities we found whirlpools that had not been emptied or cleaned the last time they were used! The wall of windows provided excellent exposure to the sun's rays to the two treatment tables. The vinyl covering was brittle and torn, and badly in need of repair.

An inventory of supplies did not take long. Three plastic jars of Cramer salt tablets, five-thousand count each. Two packs of ammonia capsules, five ampules each. Three boxes of band-aids, twenty-five bandages each. Seven, four-inch elastic bandages, three in need of a washing machine. Two, ten-gallon coolers for mixing electrolyte solution for practice. Two, one-gallon containers of Cramergesic, the balm you may never have heard of, but any student-athlete can identify its familiar scent.

Just as we had been instructed the days prior in Greensboro at the North Carolina Coaches Association's Student Trainer Clinic, we began cleaning the room and finding a proper place for all items. We wanted to create a sense of pride among our classmates/teammates with the athletic training room, one they could enter and feel comfortable in receiving care for their injuries.

Tony and I took pride in our facility. It might not have been as large as the athletic training rooms I entered in coming years, but it was just as important. We asked the coaches for money to cover and paint training tables, and paint cabinets. The coaches knew we were eager and excited to do our work, and they threw us a carrot with financing to cover our basic needs.

Shortly after I left high school for Appalachian State University, many high schools in North Carolina employed the services of full-time certified athletic trainers. North Carolina was one of the first states to embrace the concept due to the influence of Dr. Al Proctor and his outreach and networking with state legislators and secondary school administrators.

Proctor cast a long shadow on the North Carolina program with his work in the Sports Medicine Division with assistance from Warren Ariail, Phil Callicutt, and eventually Robbie Lester. Proctor passed the baton to Lester in 1988, and Robbie continued to lead the division until he returned to Bowman-Gray School of Medicine in Winston-Salem, North Carolina, to complete his training as a physician's assistant. North Carolina high school student-athletes were never in better hands.

Appalachian State University is located in the Blue Ridge Mountains of North Carolina and has one of the highest elevations of any university east of the Mississippi River. Appalachian State opened its doors in 1899 under the name Watauga Academy as an institution to educate teachers in northwest North Carolina. On March 9, 1903, the Appalachian Training School for Teachers was established and opened seven months later with three hundred and twenty-five students.

Appalachian Training was transformed from a single-purpose teacher's college into a multipurpose regional university and Appalachian State Teacher's College became Appalachian State University in 1967. Five years later, Appalachian State was incorporated into the University of North Carolina system.

Appalachian State was one of the initial two athletic training schools in North Carolina. Athletic training education in those days was based in education settings, and was not embraced in allied health as is common today.

The athletic training and physical education influence at Appalachian State was strongly influenced in those days by Professor Roger Thomas, who brought many of his practices and theories in physical education and muscle physiology from Springfield (Massachusetts) College. Springfield College has long been representative of physical education dating to its early roots and affiliation with the Young Men's Christian Association (YMCA). "Doc" Thomas was the consummate educator who preceded my mentor, Ron Kanoy, as Appalachian State's athletic trainer.

"Doc" Thomas' physiological influence was great. He taught his physical education and athletic training students "the most complete modality was exercise." This was probably his primary tenant, and it is one that really stuck with me. I have used that in my clinical practice over the years. Athletic training students today need to hear his lecture, as many try to treat with machines and forget the importance of exercise.

The basement of the Broome-Kirk Gymnasium had the strong appearance of the physical education facilities of the 1900s. The stark gray walls, terrazzo tiled floors, high ceilings and vast facilities mirrored those of other colleges across the country. The drab appearance made it look like a prison. The color scheme and lack of acoustics gave it the look and sound of an airport hangar.

Access to the gym from Faculty Street meant crossing one of several bridges traversing the famous Kraut Creek. Boone Creek is known locally as Kraut Creek because of the smell that wafted across town from a Boone sauerkraut plant.

Furnishings in the athletic training room were limited, at best. As great as Thomas and Kanoy were in their field, they were not progressive in the selection of therapeutic modalities—ultrasound, electrical stimulation, exercise modalities, and diagnostic devices—for use on student-athletes and for the education of athletic training students.

The spaciousness of the facility allowed for five separate rooms with the back room closest to Kraut Creek used for taping. There were six taping tables that were thirty-six inches high, twenty-four inches wide and thirty-six inches long. Tables like this were fairly common in athletic training facilities for pre-practice taping.

The next two rooms were more centered on treatments with six-foot long tables, thirty-six inches high and thirty inches wide. The tables were strategically placed along the walls. They were accessible by both Hydrocollator cold packs and Hydrocollator hot packs. A freezer also was close by with ample supply of frozen ice cups for "ice massages." In later years, we got really fancy and applied a tongue depressor to the cups to build in a handle for ice massage treatments.

The final treatment room was for hydrotherapy. There were two "low boy" whirlpools in addition to the smaller extremity whirlpool. The room also included a crushed ice machine and a tub for sitz (soaking) baths. One of Kanoy's favorite rituals was cleaning up the athletic training room on

Friday and making homemade ice cream afterward. The crushed ice was perfect for this activity. As nice as the ice machine was for our Friday ritual, it was a source of auditory clutter the remainder of the time.

Another room served as an office where both Doc Kanoy and his graduate assistant had a desk. My senior year in college, a female assistant was hired. Pat Buchanan was a very quiet assistant, much like Kanoy. She continued at Appalachian State until she returned to school to complete her physical therapy degree. Though athletic training was quickly becoming a co-educational profession in 1975, our athletic training room was adjacent to the men's locker rooms, and directly accessible with doors. No barriers protected females from the contents of the locker room.

My classmates and I spent many hours daily in the athletic training facility. Jim Parker was a freshman with me in 1975. Jim grew up in Troutman, North Carolina and had attended South Iredell High School. We joined a staff of other students, many of whom continue today in athletic training. Michael Smith was two years my senior from Salisbury, North Carolina. Today, he is the athletic trainer at York Comprehensive High School in York, South Carolina. Other athletic training students included Steve Correll, Tony Sutton, Larry Swisher, Alex Brown, Chip Buckwell, Alan Russell, Mark Laursen, and Patti Pleasants.

Appalachian State played its home games in Conrad Stadium, which was nestled on campus in a stately setting along the mountainsides. When I visited Boone and Appalachian State in the summer of 1974 with my family, I was so intrigued with the setting. I knew that was where I wanted to attend college.

For a young school athletically, Appalachian State had much tradition. Conrad Stadium was opened on September 15, 1962 and was originally constructed with ten thousand permanent seats. The stadium was the first venue in the Carolinas to install artificial surface with Tartan Turf. Appalachian State and Elon first played on the new surface on October 3, 1970. The seating capacity was expanded to eighteen thousand following the 1978 season. On September 22, 1979, Conrad Stadium was the setting for ESPN's second televised college football game. The stadium was renamed on September 3, 1988 in honor of Kidd Brewer, one of the most successful head coaches in Appalachian State football history and a colorful part of North Carolina history.

During the summer of 1975, Appalachian State installed new AstroTurf. This second generation product was a nylon carpet woven just like commercial carpets. It was applied over a one-half inch closed cell foam pad, which provided the cushioning for the surface. The pad underlayer was glued directly to an asphalt base that was placed over a graded surface with a traditional football field crown. The crown was important in those days to facilitate drainage of rain water. The need for incorporation of a crown would be minimized in coming years with the installation of drainage concepts into padding.

AstroTurf, as abrasive as it proved to be, was so important for Appalachian State due to the harsh winters and frozen turfs associated with spring in the mountains. Grass fields were not durable in Boone, and the addition of the AstroTurf field provided a good footing surface for not only football practices and games, but also a superior surface for Appalachian State's nationally prominent men's soccer team, which also practiced and played at Conrad Stadium. Scheduling was a challenge because Appalachian State's "Band of Distinction" also needed practice time on the field. The beauty of the challenge was the lights that allowed more time for use by these teams, the band intramural activities also benefited from the structures.

The field house in the north end zone of Conrad Stadium was one-quarter of a mile up Stadium Drive from Varsity Gymnasium and the adjacent Broom-Kirk Gymnasium. The field house was used as a locker room facility for the football team. It had a porch across the front that faced the stadium. As you entered the field house from the porch, the Mountaineers' locker room was to the right, or east, and the visiting team was to the left, or west side. During the week, the Mountaineers' underclassmen dressed in the visitors' locker room to prepare for practices. A taping area was located between the locker rooms. The taping area was very small. This field house would be expanded some three times from its footprint in 1977, and the renovations included adding offices and meeting rooms to the second story.

My residence was on campus for my first three years. My freshman year I was in what we called Eggers Convent. The dorm's ninth floor was for those of us whose parents selected the "no visitation" option. I was able to change this for my second year when I shared a room with Mark Frazier in the old Justice Dorm, which was strategically located halfway between Broom-Kirk Gymnasium and Conrad Stadium. My roommate my senior year was John Keeton, a tight end on the football team and one of the most colorful guys on the team. It was never a dull moment with John. Following college, he continued with Army ROTC training at Appalachian State and embarked on a twenty-year military career. Today, he is a successful jet pilot and flies for NetJets. He and his family live in the Pensacola, Florida area, and we have rekindled our talks from college.

As a student athletic trainer, I had the opportunity to be good friends with many student-athletes. The list is too long to include here. I have fond memories of those days, none greater than my first airplane ride with the football team in October, 1976. We played a game that season at Ball State in Indiana, which meant the team took buses some eighty miles down the mountain to Winston-Salem. The plane ride was scary for a lot of us, including a couple of players from Goldsboro, North Carolina, Emmitt Hamilton and Devon Ford. They were clinching the armrests when Mike Smith, another student athletic trainer, joked to them about the plane's shaking wings outside his window. Smith was the team clown or funny guy, and we continued to laugh about this for years. While the trip was a good experience, the game left much to be desired as we lost on a rainy, dreary day, 20-7, in front of our smallest crowd (just over thirty-three hundred) in years.

My college career was strongly rooted in the bowels of Broome-Kirk Gymnasium, the taping area of the athletic training room at Conrad Stadium and later Kidd-Brewer Stadium. My senior year, as the head student athletic trainer, I was afforded the responsibility of travel with the men's basketball team. Bobby Cremins was the young coach, and everyone knew he was destined for greatness. The 1979 team won the Southern Conference tournament championship and received an automatic bid to the NCAA tournament where we lost to LSU, 71-57, in Bloomington, Indiana.

Appalachian was a great setting for the beginning of a great career.

My first day at Lenoir-Rhyne College was met with great optimism, excitement, and anticipation. The college had never had a full-time certified athletic trainer before my arrival. I recognized immediately that I had a tremendous challenge educating not only the student-athletes about best practices for athletic training, but also an administration that did not know the job of an athletic trainer. Hanley Painter was Lenoir-Rhyne's athletic director. He had a long history at the school as a player, an assistant coach, head coach, and athletic director. Coach Painter was a colorful person who often was short and to the point in his comments. One of my first encounters, he told me "Walters, a few things to remember: Make sure your expenses are accurate, and always be loyal."

Coach Painter was best friends with Dr. Benny Goodman, the school's long-time team physician. Dr. Goodman was a family practice physician at the Medical Arts Clinic in Hickory, North Carolina. He was a tremendous physician, and certainly got me well on my professional way with developing both friendships and respect for team physicians.

The athletic training room at Lenoir-Rhyne was a facility challenge. I was greeted in the athletic training room my first day by John Worley, an upperclassman with an affinity for the profession. John was reared in the area and was a high school football player at nearby Hickory High School. Upon graduation, he returned to his alma mater as a teacher-coach, and Was the school's athletic director and head football coach. I certainly was not surprised at John's success as a leader of young people. He had such a presence among people. We need more Worleys in this world.

John was receptive to helping me set up the athletic training room, which was sparse in equipment and contents. The two, school-built treatment tables were sturdy, and very heavy. The room was about twenty-five feet square, which was only good when we went to request that it be painted. As you entered the facility, a sink was in the back left corner. There were two whirlpools along the back wall. The two treatment tables were on the right side along the back wall and the supply counter was found along the right wall. It was small, but we had it painted, scrubbed it from corner to corner, and it served its purpose well.

The football staff room was actually in a Shuford Physical Education building classroom. It was not a secluded work environment. It was just a place coaches met and watched film. This was the same facility that housed the athletic training room, conveniently located central to all student-athletes.

I was the only athletic trainer, and we had a few athletic training students. One of the students, Kevin Jones, was hired by Gardner-Webb College (now University) following graduation from Lenoir-Rhyne. Gardner-Webb made a great hire, and Kevin continues his work there today. Other students included Drew "Wood" Hood, who was a golfer from Philadelphia; LeeAnn McCall; Cindy Davisson; Amy Robbins, also a Hickory High graduate; Ervin Williams; and Bill McBrayer, who now is the human resources/safety/health and environmental manager at Lexington Home Brands in Hildebran, North Carolina.

Ervin "Big E" Williams was one of my favorite students at Lenoir-Rhyne. He came to us from Louisburg (NC) Junior College. He quickly grew to be loved by all of us. As close as he and I were during my tenure, "Big E" was even more attached to Keith Ochs, our athletic director. Upon his 1987 graduation, Williams returned to Louisburg Junior College as the intramural director and was an administrative assistant to the women's basketball team. He left Louisburg in 1997 for the University of Nebraska where he joined the women's basketball staff as director of operations and continues today as an event management specialist.

President Albert Allran and the Lenoir-Rhyne College community were supportive of our program. By my fifth year, we had a very nice collection of therapeutic modalities, improvements to the facility, and all coupled with the gifts of an Orthotron isokinetic knee machine and beautiful oak treatment tables that my friend—orthopedic surgeon and team physician Dr. Alfred Moretz—built while allowing me to watch him work his magic.

Whenever I talk with Ervin Williams, Bill McBrayer or John Worley, we reflect on the good days we shared at Lenoir-Rhyne. Like so many colleges and universities, its facilities are much improved today, but we all agree we shared some great memories in that small athletic training room in Shuford Gymnasium.

The summer of 1985, while heavily engaged in my doctoral course work at Middle Tennessee State University, Appalachian called and invited me for an interview for the head athletic trainer's position. I flew back to Hickory, North Carolina to visit my wife. The interview gave me a free trip home. I was scheduled to visit with the administration and football coaches regarding a job opening at my alma mater, Appalachian State. I was really excited. I was the first of three candidates to visit. I knew it was up to me to set the bar or suffer the spoils. I really wanted this job. I loved athletic training, even then. As much as I loved Lenoir-Rhyne College, I knew there was only so much I could do there. It was time to move on.

As I drove up Highway 321 from Hickory toward Blowing Rock and Boone, the temperature outside dropped steadily. The sight of the mountains was a welcome memory. As I drove onto that beautiful campus, not much had changed in the five years since I graduated with my masters and bachelor degrees. A few new restaurants had popped up. The Student Health Center had moved to the center of campus. I was greatly anticipating a visit with Dr. Evan Ashby, the director of Student Health who remained an advocate for athletic medicine. As a key player in the American College Health Association, he understood student health.

I turned left onto Rivers Street. I passed the Broome-Kirk Gymnasium where I had spent countless hours in the athletic training room, the adjacent classrooms, and the labs of my professors. Dr. Vaughn Christian had challenged me so much in his classes, and I was so appreciative of that now because I felt prepared to deal with many new challenges. My mind was going one hundred twenty miles per hour with some great memories.

My interview was scheduled for the Owens Field House, which was the renovated version of the old field house from my college days. I approached the stop light at Stadium Drive, and planned to turn left. I took a deep breath as so many great memories began to flood over me. The pond was still on my right with the dozen or so ducks there tending to their own agendas.

Among the changes were personnel. Jim Garner was now the athletic director and Roachel Laney was an associate athletic director. The head football coach was Sparky Woods, who was unlike any other coach in that he truly believed in what he was doing. He had a staff with similar beliefs and values, and was committed to the institution and to the student-athletes. He was revered in Boone, so I had a feeling there were good times ahead for Mountaineers' fans.

Following the interview, I returned to classes at Middle Tennessee State University where I was working in the second year toward earning a doctorate in Physical Education. The offer came shortly, and I was excited about the move to Boone.

I was initially impressed and amazed at the improved facilities at Appalachian State. My office was in the same area where I completed my undergraduate and graduate studies. It included plenty of challenges that every athletic trainer faces in July and August. That includes the completing of all insurance claims for student-athletes who had sustained injuries, as well as receiving medical supplies that had been ordered for the upcoming academic year. I knew the ordering would be in great shape, as Ron Kanoy was a tremendous businessman, and frugal in both spending and ordering.

Cindy Thomas was in her second year as the assistant athletic trainer. She replaced Pat Buchanan, who departed to study physical therapy. Thomas was a tremendous educator, and was very popular with athletic training students. Cindy Thomas had really helped launch Appalachian's recognition as a prominent athletic training educational program. I was ready to try to take the healthcare from where Doc Kanoy had built it. Athletics were really starting to move, and the administration challenged me to be a part.

The cavernous Broome-Kirk Gymnasium athletic training room needed to be brought into the latest century. It was stark. We installed a set of cabinets purchased from First Plaza Orthopedics in Hickory, and they proved to be a tremendous addition to the facility.

With the influence of Cindy Thomas and Craig Denegar, the new athletic training clinical coordinator, Appalachian State had grown leaps and bounds in facilities and equipment for the clinical areas. We had to upgrade the equipment to meet educational competencies and expectations as created by the National Athletic Trainers' Association.

It also helped matters that the athletic training program was attracting many solid students, many of whom remain in the business today. The athletic training program was not only one of North Carolina's first academic programs, but one of the best overall programs in the nation. The lineage of students was significant: Phil Hedrick, now at North Carolina State; Kent Atkins, now at Lander (SC); Alan Freedman, Stony Brook (NY); Liesel Lindley, Plymouth State (NH); Jeff Parsons, who was a graduate assistant and later an assistant athletic trainer at South Carolina who is in drug sales in Lexington, South Carolina; and Ron Reagan, now in medical sales in North Carolina.

The Appalachian State athletic program was growing. The athletic director had hired Tom Apke from the University of Colorado. Following his stint at Appalachian State, Apke ventured into television broadcasting for college basketball. Today he sells real estate in Charlotte. Apke was joined by a celebrity staff that included Ralph Patterson, now vice president for advancement and Lander (SC) University Foundation executive director; Jimmy Dykes, who moved from graduate assistant at Appalachian State to ESPN basketball commentator; Floyd Kerr, now athletic director at Morgan State (MD) University; Buzz Peterson, former graduate assistant who has served as head basketball coach at Appalachian State, Tulsa, Tennessee, Coastal Carolina and now UNC-Wilmington; Chris Ferguson, an assistant basketball coach at Oklahoma State University; and Todd Sandstedt, a special agent with the FBI. The sports information director was the ever-colorful Rick Covington, who claimed to work more hours than any communications person in the country.

As with many athletic trainers in college athletics, I handled travel for the football team at Appalachian State. Those duties included setting up charter buses, hotels, and meals for road trips. I worked with David Bibee, an assistant head coach who provided me with the team's needs regarding meetings, arrival times at the game, etc. To meet budget, I attempted to squeeze as much out of a dollar as possible.

Appalachian State had better finances in those days than many of our Southern Conference opponents. The administration funded the coaches as full-time employees and hired graduate assistants to teach classes. The graduate assistants worked under teacher-coach agreements with the state of North Carolina and taught six hours per semester. Release time was granted for coaching duties. This was a similar practice used in the larger Atlantic Coast Conference and Southeastern Conference, and it showed how our athletic director, Jim Garner, did his best to run our program like those guys.

To help coaches attract student-athletes to Boone, North Carolina, Jim Garner, the athletic director allowed coaches to offer Pell-eligible student-athletes to maintain their grant money. In the past, any financial aid had been applied against the scholarship value. The pattern previously—and at other schools—was to apply Pell Grant money to their financial bill with the university and minimize the payout by the school. By letting the student-athlete retain this amount, the basketball and football programs at Appalachian State had a tremendous leg up on the competition.

Garner and his administration also funded the travel, equipment, and support staffs, unlike any of the conference opponents. The only NCAA Division I-AA program that was close to us in those days was Marshall University, which eventually moved to Division I-A in football.

Football practices were fun at Appalachian State. Well, they were as fun as they could be. We were beginning to field winning teams that included Southern Conference championships in 1986 and 1987. The predominant color in the Mountaineers home uniform was "black," so our "Black Saturday" was a fun time with fans wearing the color in the stands. We had outstanding players, including Dino Hackett, Mickey Ray, Tim Sanders, Todd Peyton, Derrick "Big Sexy" Graham, and John Settle, to name a few. There were many good players and they were the reason Appalachian was on the verge of helping coaches take the program to the next level. Any coach will tell you, coaches don't make good programs— good players make good programs.

Practices were held on the carpet in Conrad, now Kidd-Brewer Stadium. Coach Woods and his staff strategically carved out the turf to efficiently use every square inch. We did not have much sideline space for setting up breaks, so it was a common occurrence to take a couple of students to the concessions stands to set up breaks. We accessed the ice from the concession stand and set up water and Gatorade.

I always have been a huge fan of nacho chips. During the fall days when the temperature started to approach the forties, I often returned to the practice field from the concession stand with one of the large pockets on my sideline overcoat stuffed with nachos. Jim Jones, our business manager, always had a box left on the counter, and I am confident he did not mind me paying my students for their hard work with a few of his good nacho chips.

Working in North Carolina proved to be a tremendous honor and responsibility for me. Purchasing in the North Carolina system was not without challenge. The state had the toughest, shrewdest purchasing and procurement system. Officials from the state auditor's office came to the athletic training room every July to review our inventory. They wanted to account for every band-aid, not every box of band-aids. Their policies were relentless. Purchases during a fiscal year had to be received and accounted for during the actual fiscal year. This is a sound accounting principle, but I promise it is one not adhered to by universities, especially outside of North Carolina.

A few months later, when I was hired at South Carolina, we followed state procurement requirements, but the rules were relaxed as the athletic department did not receive state funds for operations. When we ran out of tape in May, the business office instructed me to go ahead and order the tape, and it was paid for in July under the next fiscal-year budget. Never would that have occurred at Appalachian State. Further, such practices would have been rewarded with a trip to Raleigh to the state prison! That was only one of many different practices I would encounter with my upcoming move to Columbia—some better than others.

Upon beginning work at South Carolina, I sensed a tremendous amount of responsibility—and urgency—staring me in the face. I had given two-week notice to Appalachian State, and agreed to work one week. The second week was waived because students were on spring break.

I arrived in Columbia on the evening of Sunday, March 4, 1990 to begin work the next day. I checked in to the Marriott hotel, which had been arranged as my housing until the home we had purchased was built. I knew I would be in the Marriott for a minimum of ninety days while my family remained in Boone. It was tough being away from my family, but I knew I had a ton of work ahead of me as the Gamecocks prepared for spring football practice.

Jim Shealy met me that Sunday evening and issued me my keys. Jim was more than the equipment manager at South Carolina. He was a good friend. He was one of the most loyal people I have ever known. I am proud to call Jim a friend to this day. He has been so good to me through the years. Once I left the university, he kept a watchful eye on David, and even hired him. Heck, he even hired my Clemson Tiger, Ryan, for work in the summer!

As I walked into the football complex at Williams-Brice Stadium from Gate 5, where I would be parking for the next seventeen years, I reflected to the fall of 1975. That is when Appalachian State played a football game in Columbia against my new employer. In those days, the visiting team entered Gate 5 and drove under the stadium to the visiting team locker room at the northwest corner of the stadium where it unloaded equipment. Eight years later, in 1983, that driveway to the stadium would be part of stadium renovations that included expanding the equipment room, locker room, coaches locker room, meeting rooms for each of the assistant coaches, and a huge weight room.

Upon entering the complex as the new head athletic trainer, we turned left to the spacious football locker room. This locker room was impressive because of its cleanliness, thanks to Herbert Kit, who completed the laundry each day, then ended each workday by vacuuming the "red carpet area." The temperature in the locker room was sixty-five degrees. It always seemed cool in there, which was amazing since the facility is beneath the stadium grandstands and was never constructed with adequate insulation. As I headed on to the west, I was facing the double doors that opened into the athletic training room.

This room was roughly twenty-five hundred square feet (twenty-five feet deep and the width of the locker room of one hundred feet). To the left were a half-dozen, six-foot treatment tables. There at the end was my office, totally encased in glass so I could see all the happenings in the clinical area. Across from my office was the hydrotherapy area with four whirlpools, and an ice machine adequate to meet our needs for practice and clinical treatments. To the right was the rehabilitation area complete with the Cybex machine, an isokinetic testing and exercise device. Between each of the treatment tables was a small table with a modality for ultrasound, electrical stimulation, compression, etc. There was a large Hydrocollator steam unit in the athletic training room that would be used at great length by my staff and the players.

The athletic training room had a fully functional X-Ray machine, though we would have to replace the generator shortly. The university's administration was supportive of our facilities, especially when it was for the healthcare of student-athletes. This was a tremendous adjunct for our medical staff. South Carolina had orthopedic clinics three days per week in the athletic training room.

As I turned away from my office, I looked down the hundred-foot length of the training room and had complete view of the facility. The taping area was massive. The "Gamecocks" script over the taping tables was of artistic quality. This was truly a "big-time" facility. It was unlike any facility I had seen. Too bad my bubble would burst when I began a tour of facilities around the southeast, particularly in the Southeastern Conference.

As I exited the football locker room and ventured down the "red carpet area," Jim and I entered the assistant coaches' locker room. There was a cot, a locker, a stool, and a desk chair at the locker area of each of the nine assistant coaches, the weight-training coach, and the head athletic trainer. In each of the lockers were all the coaches' workout gear, practice gear, game gear, and appropriate shoes. Jim and his staff took great pride in taking care of the assistant coaches. Each coach had a number, as did the players. My number was "207," and that number appeared on the bottom of each of my socks, in the neck of my shirts, everywhere. Each equipment manager has his or her means of monitoring equipment and assigning it to you. Jim's was quite extensive.

Jim continued his work at South Carolina until 1999 when he was promoted to stadium manager. When he arrived as head coach, Lou Holtz reached out to his former equipment manager at Notre Dame, Chris Matlock, who came to South Carolina and continues as its equipment manager today.

The trend in 1990 was centralization of facilities. The South Carolina administration impressed upon me that I was the head athletic trainer.

It wanted one policy, one procedure, and all student-athletes would be handled accordingly. This was difficult on the staff as it had been at South Carolina quite some time. However, they all worked to meet the needs and requests of the administration. I attempted to sell concepts to the staff, and get it to embrace the change. These were not "my ideas" but "our ideas." Again, it was the goal to get rid of the team empires that were growing, and attempt to provide one standard.

As I reflect on South Carolina's facilities, a lot has changed since my arrival there in 1990. In those days, we practiced football each and every day on the present soccer practice fields more than a mile from the stadium, making every practice a road trip for the athletic training staff. We carried all practice supplies for the equipment room and athletic training room in addition to ice and Gatorade for breaks. When the practice fields were moved to the present site at the National Guard Armory on Bluff Road, the coaches and student-athletes were happy. No one was happier than me.

I joked with my long-time supervisor, Dr. John Moore, many times about facilities. Mike McGee was an iron-fisted administrator who did not like to spend money. He was fiscally the tightest person I ever worked with. We did more studies for redoing the athletic training areas, and I eventually told John that "if we would save the money from feasibility studies and spend it toward reconstructing our facilities, we would be much closer to completion!" McGee was supportive of improvements and equipment for rehabilitation (Biodex) and an X-Ray generator for our orthopedic clinics in the athletic training room.

The program for athletic training at South Carolina was very large. We had an undergraduate program that Malissa Martin started in the late 1980s. It continues today, but pales in comparison with the undergraduate program at Appalachian State. In 2004, South Carolina launched an outreach graduate education program for athletic trainers, a two-year program that educates more than twenty students in the two-year program. This serves as a great staff of students to assist the athletic training staff and also provides service to schools or programs in the areas that do not have athletic trainers.

I always felt we did a good job with hiring graduate assistants. Some of the graduate assistants I worked with prior to this system were assigned to work football all year, and were treated as full-time employees relative to work expectations. I had to remember they were also taking a load of classes to complete their graduate degree within a twenty-four month period. The assistants included Kent Atkins, Eric Oliver, Lee Gray, John Singerling, Chip Wise, John Krovacs, Brett Hoffman, and Jarod Grace. It was easy to attract graduate students to the University of South Carolina to work football. It was a little more difficult to attract them to work cheerleading or some of the less popular sports. Due to that, I setup a rotation system where they went from a training ground in athletics learning our philosophy and procedures during their first year and they would then be rotated to other sports within the outreach program. The program has grown, and today produces upward of twenty graduates annually.

Some of our students had more popular careers than others. Scottie Patton was off to good things quickly after he left South Carolina. Scottie began his professional work following his days at South Carolina with tenure on hall of fame athletic trainer Lindsey McLain's staff with the San Francisco 49ers; and then was an assistant with Rick Burkholder's Philadelphia Eagles staff; before moving to New Orleans to head up the athletic training staff with the Saints, where he was part of the 2010 Super Bowl championship. About the same time Scottie was at South Carolina, so were two students who were classics with Brainard Cooper. The first, Dave Groeschner went directly to Major League Baseball. He was the head athletic trainer with the Chicago Cubs and also the San Francisco Giants, where he too won a world championship in 2010. Mark Littlefield, also a Cooper disciple, has enjoyed a storied career in professional baseball with the New York Yankees. Mark has worked in Tampa, Florida directing all medical services for the Yankees as their minor league medical coordinator. In January of 2012, he was promoted to the assistant athletic trainer position moving to the big leagues as Steve Donoghue's assistant in New York.

I have traditionally been against providing graduate assistants to perform athletic training duties because it circumvents a school hiring a position and committing to such a program. Now with the graduate and undergraduate program, South Carolina has a significant number of graduates annually. From this program, we hired a couple of early graduates in Kerry Gordon and Danny Cobble. Gordon worked with the track and field program before being lured in 2008 to work for Cirque du Soleil in Las Vegas. Cobble was hired to assist Bill Martin with the South Carolina football program in 2006.

Graduate assistants in football were important hires in the 1990s. The most popular with my boys was the run of graduate assistants including Lee Gray and John Singerling in 1994-1995. The next crew included Chip Wise and John Kovacs. Wise had gone to Michigan State where he was a classmate of Singerling. Both Wise and Singerling had worked as summer interns in the NFL. Wise and his family live in the Scottsdale, Arizona area where he is director of business development with Navigant Consulting. Singerling has been with Palmetto Health in Columbia, South Carolina since 1996 and became president of Palmetto Health in October, 2010.

While Jeff Parsons came to South Carolina as a full-time assistant with football, we moved him to men's basketball in 1993 where he worked until 2001. Jeff was a great staff member. I knew him well as he had worked with me at Appalachian State University as a graduate assistant. Jeff was my first staff hire at South Carolina and worked as my assistant in the football athletic training room. I see Jeff quite often and he and Jennifer still live in Lexington, South Carolina along with their two boys.

Kris Mack (Mack-Ficken now) joined my staff in the early 1990s. She had worked at Vanderbilt, where she obtained her master's degree. She was a great teammate. One of her graduate assistants was Nikki Lukas (Harman), who later was hired to replace Mack when she left South Carolina for a staff position at Stanford. Other staff members included Sue Biles, Tara Lein (Chase), and Jennifer Bednar (Herod), who also had worked under Mack as a graduate assistant.

You are always proud of your students. One student, Robbie Stewart, left South Carolina to complete his undergraduate studies at Clemson. Today, Stewart works with former South Carolina assistant coach Rick Stockstill at Middle Tennessee State. Stewart is an outstanding professional and a great example to his students at Middle Tennessee State. He once made a "heads-up" call on a student-athlete in quickly recognizing a potential life-threatening situation. It gives you pride to see such acts by your associates.

The last story on students is about Rebecca Seibert. She came to the program in 2005, transferring from Liberty University. Seibert was an athletic training student and was sent to football for her clinical assignment. She was the first person in the athletic training room daily in an attempt to learn as much as she could. She listened to each and every word from Bill Martin and then-graduate assistant Danny Cobble. Seibert was assigned as the athletic training student to assistant coach Madre Hill. Our equipment manager, Chris Matlock, had David Walters assigned to him as a student equipment manager. My son and Seibert began to date during South Carolina's trip to the Independence Bowl in Shreveport, Louisiana in December 2005. The two continued to date through college. Rebecca received her undergraduate degree at South Carolina and her master's degree at Virginia before becoming an athletic trainer at Pelion High School in Lexington, South Carolina. The two were married in March, 2010. David graduated from South Carolina in May, 2010. They made us all very proud June 9, 2011 with the birth of our first grandchild, Grace Christine Walters.

Everyone talks about the great fortunes and love associated with grandchildren. Truer words have never been spoken. When Grace comes into our home, she brightens up every time she sees Susan or me. Her parents, David and Rebecca, are really good parents. She loves her mom and dad to death. She is the epitome of a child. We told David and Rebecca to be prepared if they have more children, as there is no way another can be as good as Grace.

During Mike McGee's tenure as South Carolina athletic director, when I was given extra duties as director of drug testing I requested administrative support in light of staff additions. Sandra Schmale, whose daughter, Krisdee, was working in Coach Lou Holtz's office as an intern, was hired. This was a great addition for me. Schmale shielded me from calls, scheduled and balanced my daily appointments, and was a big help with the volume of work that came across my desk while coordinating healthcare of four hundred-plus student-athletes. Our staff had grown to eight athletic trainers as well as ten graduate assistants. Healthcare at South Carolina was a big job and bigger challenge.

I am proud of what South Carolina has today. Athletic Director Eric Hyman did an excellent job to bring facilities in line with South Carolina's Southeastern Conference opponents. A seat-licensing program and increased television revenues from the SEC more than cover the downturn in turnstiles at South Carolina football games. I do not recall many football game days at Williams-Brice Stadium that did not have sellouts, even during the lean years of Brad Scott's last season in 1998 or the winless first season of Coach Holtz in 1999. (Hyman resigned from South Carolina on June 29, 2012 to assume the athletic director position at Texas A & M.)

Williams-Brice Stadium has a glitzy appearance today. Renovations to the players' locker room, the players' lounge (now located in the old athletic training room), the new athletic training room (located in the old weight room), the HydroWorx hydrotherapy area, all provide first-class equipment for the student-athletes. My first walk into the facilities was breathtaking. It was amazing to see the transformation that had taken place. Traveling around the country, I am exposed to some first-class facilities. There are not many better in the country.

I am impressed with the job done by John Kasik, South Carolina's director of sports medicine. He has a difficult job of balancing healthcare of the student-athletes within the confines of the NCAA, the wills of the coaching staff, and the budgetary constraints provided by the athletic administration.

It always was my contention that the NCAA should allow any and all "medical or accident costs" incurred or associated with practice, conditioning, or games to be covered by the institution per NCAA bylaw 16.4 "Medical Expenses." It was not my decision regarding which medical expenses should be covered, as it was legal and permissible to cover them all. In my opinion, it is imperative that the athletic administration determine what is covered within its mission statement. This is difficult for many institutions, but it is needed today.

Perhaps the hottest item on facilities' plans today is indoor football practice facilities. Coach Mack Brown referenced this recently at Texas, where he believed an indoor facility allows greater latitude in practice time during summer workouts. The radiant sun in south Texas is evident, and the ability to practice indoors is a significant advantage for such teams. Further, during the season, inclement weather can be avoided by going indoors.

As I mentioned, the athletic training staff at South Carolina is being provided with first-class facilities. Football's facilities are second to none. The baseball team now plays in a beautiful new stadium. The men's and women's basketball teams have competed in the eighteen-thousand-seat Colonial Center for a decade.

An ongoing capital campaign for facilities includes a new tennis complex, a new track complex, and a renovated softball stadium. None of these teams brings significant dollars to the athletic department, but is still being handsomely rewarded. The recent opening of the Dodie Academic Center for athletics reminds all South Carolina fans why student-athletes are at the school.

Dr. Rod's
Treatment Plan

TAPING CONCEPTS

HISTORICALLY, ATHLETIC TRAINERS USED various methods of tape to protect the ankle. In the sporting arena, athletic trainers tape the acutely sprained ankle to control excessive motion. This practice often includes prophylaxis treatment. Athletic trainers seek techniques to enhance performance. By enhancing proprioception and function, performance improves. Lohrer reported ankle taping as an efficient method to protect the ankle joint from possible injury.

Concerning function assessed by the parameters of balance, agility, or speed, no studies reported improved function from athletic taping, bracing, or wrapping. Several authors reported taping not a deterrent to performance. Recently, various devices have evolved to brace against the extremes of ankle motion. Athletic trainers use white, non-elastic tape to limit ankle motion and protect the acutely sprained ankle. During recent years, elastic tape has emerged for use on the ankle. This use offers compressive characteristics and the ability to enhance proprioception with taping.

Ankle taping decreased agility performance as compared to studies with subjects with no protection or using laced ankle stabilizers. Proponents of prophylactic taping claim usage not to impair function, force production, or limit ankle motion as decreased ankle motion supported the joint against forces during activity. Ankle taping tested superiorly to elastic tape procedures or ankle wrapping. Taping was reported to become virtually ineffective after periods as short as forty minutes.

Tape loosened with exercise, maintaining minimal support. Ferguson discouraged taping due to the mobile nature of skin. Also, the concern of moisture beneath tape, disuse atrophy of muscles supporting the ankle, and the lack of emphasis on conditioning to prevent ankle sprains supported his concerns.

High top shoes have been studied as a means to reduce injury while no strong relationship was found between shoe type and ankle sprains. In two separate studies, subjects with low-top shoes and lace-up ankle braces and high-top shoes combined with prophylactic taping sustained fewer injuries. Orthotic braces used in the treatment of acute grade III lateral ankle ligament injuries produced no statistical differences from patients treated with cast-immobilization. Bracing combined with taping effectively restricted motion though limitations decreased force production and total work. Paris found no significant differences in speed, balance, and agility between braces or ankle taping.

Around 2001, cohesive products were invented. These products incorporate the protective ability of pre-taping under wrap with a product that "grips" the skin and provides excellent support. In lab studies, the self-adherent cohesive tape maintained range of motion restriction both before and after exercise. Conversely, the white cloth tape lost some of its restrictive properties after thirty minutes of exercise.

CHAPTER 3

WHEN PREPARATION MEETS OPPORTUNITY

"Luck is what happens when preparation meets opportunity."
—Seneca

There is no more beautiful setting for college football than Appalachian State University. On one particularly glorious day in the summer of 1985, I stood on the balcony of the Owens Field House in the north end zone of what was then called Conrad Stadium in Boone, North Carolina. The view of the stadium is stunning with the thick, green maple trees, rhododendron, and evergreens of the Blue Ridge Mountains serving as a backdrop. The view was even more sensational for me that day because I felt like I was standing on top of the world. At age twenty-seven, I had been hired as one of the nation's youngest athletic trainers. As I stood there on that balcony with Sparky Woods, also a young man in the college football coaching profession at age thirty-one, I could not help but think that underdogs occasionally do taste success. From my teenage days I dreamed of the day I could head an athletic training staff for a university. Never in my wildest dreams did I believe I would accept such a position just five years out of college and at my alma mater.

Not many junior high school students have an idea about what kind of professional career they would like to pursue. That path came into clear view for me one school day in my hometown of Fayetteville, North Carolina, when a notice appeared on the Alexander Graham Junior High School bulletin board under the headline "Be an All-Star Trainer." The poster was intriguing, to say the least, and I immediately informed my parents of the upcoming camp that was advertised, and Mom went to work researching information.

She found the student-trainer camp coincided with the annual East-West All-Star Games and North Carolina Coaches Association meeting in Greensboro, North Carolina. These all-star games began in 1949 and continue today. For many years, a basketball game was played on Tuesday night and a football game on Thursday night. In later years, an all-star soccer game was added. The student-trainer camp was held every year beginning on Tuesday afternoon and concluding after the football game on Thursday.

My first camp was held in 1972 on the University of North Carolina-Greensboro campus and was hosted by Al Proctor, soon to be Dr. Proctor as he would be completing his doctoral studies at North Carolina State University. At that time, he was the head athletic trainer at North Carolina State. A buddy of mine, Tony Hopfer, accompanied me to the camp. We rode a Trailways bus from Fayetteville to Greensboro. The ninety-four mile trip took almost three hours. As soon as we checked into camp, we discovered a plethora of prominent people in the profession in attendance. My counselor was John Joseph, the athletic trainer at Pembroke State University (now UNC-Pembroke). We also met Zack McNeil, who remains the head athletic trainer at Scotland County High School in Laurinburg, North Carolina; Ronnie Barnes, a student athletic trainer at East Carolina University and later with the New York Giants of the NFL; and Alex Brown, who was at Northern Durham High School and later headed to Appalachian State University.

It was quite an experience for a rising sophomore. We learned the basics of athletic training: prevention, care, and rehabilitation of athletic injuries. There were labs for ankle taping, classes on treatment of heat illness and wound care. We covered the basics of ice, compression, and elevation or I-C-E, for acute injuries. The common treatment has long been recommended for acute injuries to minimize bleeding, pain, and swelling associated with injuries. It scares me today to think about the responsibilities these student-trainers had in those days.

My instructors were Bubba Porche of Tulane University, Steve Moore from Tennessee Tech, and Warren Ariail of Wofford College. Ariail had served as an athletic trainer at Wake Forest University, Indiana University, Iowa State University, with the New Orleans Saints and Miami Dolphins in the NFL, and with a couple of teams in the Canadian Football League. In the late seventies, Ariail worked with Dr. Al Proctor in the Sports Medicine Division before returning to his wife's home area in Gaffney, South Carolina. There, Ariail worked at both the Cleveland County Sports Medicine Clinic in Boiling Springs, North Carolina and also served as an associate athletic director at Gardner-Webb College.

The experience was beyond compare for a young student and served as convincing evidence that I wanted to pursue a career as an athletic trainer. Those camps were my initial education in the field. By Christmas 1972 I sought any reading material one could find on athletic training, and requested books on the subject as gifts. Unfortunately, my parents could not find anything. Today there are entire sections of bookstores devoted to athletic training. My, how times have changed.

Naturally, I worked as a student athletic trainer throughout my high school days at Terry Sanford High School in Fayetteville, North Carolina. My primary work was with the football and basketball teams and I could not have asked for better guidance than from coaches Len Maness and Macky Hall. Both were outstanding examples of solid mentoring of student-athletes, including the likes of Rusty Clark and Vann Williford who eventually became basketball stars at the University of North Carolina and North Carolina State University, respectively. Coaches Maness and Hall were awfully good to me and my compadres, Tony Hopfer and Allan Glenn. The coaches allowed us to care for their players' injuries. There was such great pride in the training room at Terry Sanford High and we constantly had to check ourselves to make certain we did not exceed our boundaries.

During my sophomore year I received a letter from a state of North Carolina agency. A Sports Medicine Advisory Commission was being formed by North Carolina Governor Bob Scott in the wake of the death of Bill Arnold, a University of North Carolina football player. Arnold was an offensive guard from Staten Island, New York, who was entering his junior season when he collapsed and died on a Chapel Hill practice field from heat stroke.

His death, while tragic, led to several changes in athletic training at UNC, according to a 2002 www.tarheelblue.com story. Among them were:

1. The Sports Medicine program is now administratively housed within the Student Health Service rather than the athletic department;
2. Medical personnel such as athletic trainers now report to medical supervisors rather than non-medical staff, such as coaches.
3. An increase in certified athletic training staff, some of whom are both dually credentialed as physical therapists and athletic trainers.
4. The establishment of an athletic training program with both undergraduate and graduate degrees.

Governor Scott formed the Sports Medicine Advisory Commission within the Department of Education. Dr. Craig Phillips was the state superintendent of education, and he was very emphatic about his concerns for health and fitness in the schools. He embraced the commission and appointed Dr. Proctor as the head of the Sports Medicine Division. It was Dr. Proctor's charge to develop a program to protect sports participants within the state's public schools while instructing coaches and educators about sports injuries.

Part of the new Sports Medicine Division was a Sports Medicine Advisory Commission. Included on the commission were three athletic trainers, three coaches, three principals, three physicians, three physical education teachers, and three state legislators. The student athletic trainers, besides myself, included Ronnie Barnes from East Carolina University and Alex Brown from Northern Durham High School. We were permitted to miss school for an entire day, three or four times a year, to go to Raleigh for our meetings in the board room of the state superintendent of schools. It proved to be a tremendous opportunity to serve on a commission that helped shape the future of athletic training in the state. The athletic trainers on the commission certainly have enjoyed some great careers.

Barnes today is the head athletic trainer and vice-president for medical services for the New York Giants in the NFL. Barnes remains one of the most respected athletic trainers in the National Athletic Trainers' Association. He won the 1996 NATA Distinguished Athletic Trainer Award, and in 1999 was inducted into the NATA Hall of Fame. He was twice voted national athletic trainer of the year by the Professional Football Athletic Trainers' Society. He was a member of the NATA board of certification, past president of the NATA research and education foundation and a recipient of the Tim Kerin Award for excellence in athletic training. He and his staff also won the Ed Block Courage Award in 1999 as the NFL athletic training staff of the year.

During one session in the spring of 1973 at the state capitol of Raleigh, North Carolina, Barnes told me about the National Athletic Trainers' Association and I soon completed my application. In 1973, student athletic trainers needed a sponsor to join, and Rod Compton was mine. Compton was the athletic trainer at East Carolina University where he was the consummate educator. He won the Distinguished Educators Award from NATA in 1989, one of the highest honors in our profession. Compton died in 2009. He was a visionary in athletic training education, and was leagues ahead of his peers.

About that time, I began to think seriously about where I wanted to attend college and further my education as an athletic trainer. I really liked Appalachian State University, a relatively small school with nine-thousand students at the time. It was located in the mountains of North Carolina and only a four-hour drive from my home in Fayetteville.

During the summer of 1974, our family ventured to the Smoky Mountains of North Carolina for our family vacation. While there, we visited the Appalachian State campus and I first met Ron Kanoy, Appalachian State's athletic trainer. He was a great influence on my decision to attend the school. In the spring of my senior year of high school, I received a letter from Kanoy offering me a position as a student athletic trainer.

My high school education was very challenging. Terry Sanford Senior High School was very much a college preparatory high school. The vast majority of my senior class attended college, and many of my friends and classmates were honored as National Merit finalists, Morehead scholars, etc. The faculty was great, and I have so many fond memories of the classes.

I truly enjoyed school. Recently I ran into one of my favorite teachers, Mrs. Connie Koonce. Mrs. Koonce taught Trigonometry, Calculus, and Algebra II. She was everyone's favorite.

I do recall my visit to the guidance office to obtain the mandatory school endorsement for my application to Appalachian State University. I had above average grades, but they were not on the level of those students competing for the coveted Morehead scholarships at Chapel Hill, North Carolina. The guidance counselor suggested I investigate a trade at the local technical school in lieu of applying at Appalachian State University. She was very sincere in her recommendation. I requested she allow me to try for admission.

I am glad I did, as I was accepted. I am glad the guidance counselor did not convince me to go another route. It was my goal to pursue a degree in athletic training, and I certainly have enjoyed this career path.

I always enjoyed dressing professionally. As a young man, my dad imparted this habit in me. Being clean, neat, and professional was taught from an early age.

Clothes have always been a favorite of mine. Dr. Bob Peele is one of the most colorful and "southern gentlemen" dressers I know of in the state of South Carolina. With all the time we spent together working with student-athletes, his taste in clothes also wore on me. I too developed an appreciation for nice clothes.

It is fitting that some of my fond memories of haberdashers are Chad Frick, Michael Meeks, and most recently Tom Blackburn. These gentlemen have helped me select clothes from their shops, and certainly understood my Cadillac tastes and Chevrolet budgets. Most recently, my wardrobe has migrated from suits and ties to business casual. Tom has helped me more than adequately stock this wardrobe. Like Chad and Michael, Tom has been more of a friend than advisor, and his taste is certainly appreciated.

During my later days of working with the football team at the University of South Carolina in the mid-nineties to 2006, it became my habit to wear a dress shirt and tie on the sideline. Other athletic trainers have adopted this wardrobe, and I always felt it was a professional look. Some like shorts and golf shirts, I liked ties. I have always tried to present a professional image of athletic trainers, even before my board of directors tenure with the NATA.

Another friend always helping me out is Jan Roland, my barber. Jan and I have a standing appointment every two weeks, so I can avoid the "just got a haircut" look. She also does a great job of keeping the gray color of my hair just right. Only Jan could balance this!

Part of being a student athletic trainer at Appalachian State was reporting to preseason football practice in early August. I jumped right in and was accepted by the staff, which consisted at the time of a head athletic trainer, a graduate assistant and eight or nine students. Kanoy, whom everyone called "Doc," was a tremendous influence on his staff, a great family man. "Doc" was very quiet and unassuming. He was a seasoned professional and even-keeled in his decision-making as well as his work.

My first day on campus, we checked into my dormitory with my parents lending a hand. We were introduced to Coach Jim Brakefield, the Appalachian State head football coach. He made an immediate impression on my parents when he let a dorm counselor know that some rooms were not up to standard. He was assessing the dorm for cleanliness, safety and health of every student. Coach Brakefield did not win any championships in his eight seasons as head coach from 1972 through 1979, but it was not because he did not pay attention to details.

There was no bigger day in my professional career than in May of 1997 when I spoke at "Doc" Ron Kanoy's retirement ceremony in Boone, North

Carolina. The evening was a toast to my mentor at Appalachian State and the turnout of his friends and former students was a tremendous testimony to his illustrious career. This was a neat opportunity for me to see so many associates and former classmates I had not seen in years. I was never able to attend such functions.

From the outset I was absorbed with being a student athletic trainer. I spent an inordinate amount of time in the athletic training room. I was in love with the craft and could not get enough of it. Between classes I would run back to the athletic training room to assist the staff with treatments or other duties they needed help with. I was fortunate enough to work with the football team every season, and then was assigned to rotate through all other sports. I quickly found out the desire to work with some sports was not as great as others. Wrestling never was a favorite of mine, perhaps because it takes a special kind of individual to participate in that sport. Nonetheless, I appreciated the different challenges wrestling—and gymnastics—presented to an athletic trainer.

Football was my favorite sport, no doubt. Appalachian State had a young staff of assistant football coaches, including the likes of Fisher DeBerry, who coordinated the defense and coached the defensive backs, offensive coordinator Buddy Sasser, and linebacker coach Roachel Laney. I had the great fortune of riding along with coaches on Friday night trips to watch high school prospects, often twisting through the back mountain roads into Tennessee while listening to the Grand Ole Opry on the radio. That is where I developed a lifelong love of country music.

I often attended Sunday morning services at the Boone United Methodist Church, and the DeBerry family would invite me and teammates to their home for lunch. We often would see the coach and his family in the Appalachian cafeteria. His family was around the football team all the time, setting a tremendous example of family-first and parenthood.

DeBerry left Appalachian State in 1979 to become the quarterbacks coach at the United States Air Force Academy. He assumed the head-coaching duties in 1984 and remained there through the 2006 season. His success at Air Force Academy was remarkable. Air Force was ranked a high of fourth in the national polls during the 1985 season. His teams won Western Athletic Conference championships in 1985, 1995 and 1998 and played in twelve bowl games. DeBerry gained much national acclaim during his Air Force days, but he still had time for old friends.

In the spring of 2006 when I was at the University of South Carolina, I received a telephone call from Coach DeBerry. He requested a basketball signed by South Carolina men's basketball coach, Dave Odom, to present to an ill friend in nearby Orangeburg, South Carolina. DeBerry called on Thursday and I was prepared to deliver the ball on Monday. Unfortunately, the gentleman died over the weekend. Following the funeral, Sandra Schmale, my administrative assistant, contacted the family and sent the ball to them. Sandra was very attentive to details on tasks such as this. She always made me look good.

Coach DeBerry insisted that our family visit the Air Force Academy campus during the summer before our son Ryan's senior year of high school. Coach had learned of Ryan's interest in studying engineering, and he told me there was not a better place for him to study than the Air Force Academy. He insisted we stay at his home with him and his wife, Luanne. Each morning during our stay, DeBerry pulled out his Bible and held a devotion at breakfast. He was a man who came straight from the heart in everything he did as a coach and as a person. Coach was the real deal.

If anything ever got in his way, it was his honesty, and that is a great way to be. I have kept in contact with DeBerry over the years.

The lineup of coaches and administrators who passed through Appalachian State while I was a student there was quite remarkable. Another of those coaches was Bobby Cremins, who got his start in basketball coaching at age twenty-eight in 1975 when he took charge of the Appalachian State program. From the get-go, Cremins knew how to build a program, having learned his craft as a player at South Carolina under the legendary Frank McGuire. His first team was led by a very vocal guard from Shelby, North Carolina by the name of Alvin Gentry. Today, Gentry is a head coach in the NBA. He has been a tremendous success and shows off the talents of another Appalachian graduate.

By his third season, Cremins had won a Southern Conference championship and he followed that the next year with an appearance in the NCAA tournament. Cremins was straight-up New York City and his Bronx accent provided quite a contrast to the Southern drawl practiced in the mountains of North Carolina. Cremins was an astute coach. He might not have been book smart, but he was an intelligent and shrewd person. He was a keen observer of people and the game of basketball and knew how to use his personality to work for him in teaching the game. His players loved him and loved playing for him. From Cremins, I witnessed first-hand a coach with unparalleled respect from his players. His rapport with his players, coaches, support staff and administration was something to be emulated.

As I set out to do when I left Fayetteville for school in Boone, I earned my Bachelor of Science degree in physical education with a minor in athletic training and education in 1979. That summer I began working on my Masters of Arts degree in physical education and graduated in August of 1980. I immediately began looking for full-time employment. I quickly found to be true the axiom "it's not what you know, but who you know." I simply did not have necessary contacts to land jobs directly out of school, even though I applied at Clemson University, the University of Miami and North Carolina State University. My goal was to land a job with an NCAA Division I program and I initially wondered if that would ever happen. I believed I had a chance at a job with North Carolina State, but that school instead hired young Jim Rehbock, who remained there for many years including the 1983 run to the national basketball championship under Coach Jim Valvano.

I failed to get an interview with Clemson University or the University of Miami. Admittedly, I was forced to reset my sights, and entertained a couple of job offers from North Carolina high schools. Cary High School first offered me a job to teach elementary education as well as work in athletic training. I had also interviewed with Westover High School in Fayetteville, North Carolina. I was not very confident at the time with my job prospectus, but everything would eventually work out.

About that time, I learned of a new position at Lenoir-Rhyne College (now Lenoir-Rhyne University) in Hickory, North Carolina. I was selected for an interview, only to learn the position was combining athletic training duties with supervision of the college's intramural sports programs; in addition to teaching two courses each semester.

In May of 1980 I accepted a job to be the athletic trainer at Westover High School in my hometown of Fayetteville. Ten days later, I received a call from Dr. Keith Ochs, to offer me the job at Lenoir-Rhyne. I turned down the offer as I did not want the dual responsibility of being an athletic trainer as well as being director of the intramural department. Lenoir-Rhyne made a counter offer by promising that if I remained at the school for a second year it would remove the intramural department responsibilities from my job duties. I accepted.

Dr. Ochs served as Lenoir-Rhyne's supervisor of physical education and athletics when I arrived and he proved to be a second father to me. He taught me how to be an administrator. He taught me how to be an educator. He led by example. He taught me how to deal with people. He taught me how to care for student-athletes. For those reasons, Lenoir-Rhyne was a special job. The hours of work at Lenoir-Rhyne were not nearly what they were as I moved up the ladder of college athletics. The headaches were not as great. I soon found out: the bigger the challenge, the bigger the reward; the bigger the responsibility, the bigger the headaches.

At Lenoir-Rhyne, if I did not have money in my athletic budget, I could get it out of the physical education budget. For example, if I needed splints or some other training equipment for football, I could purchase what I needed and use them in First Aid classes.

Following my first year, the school was true to its word. They made me head athletic trainer with no more intramural responsibilities. That spring, I also was allowed to attend my first professional meeting where the institution provided funds for travel and registration. I attended the NATA professional educator's conference in Nashville, Tennessee in February of 1982. I drove from Hickory to nearby Charlotte and boarded a Piedmont Airlines flight for Nashville. No one on that flight was any prouder than I was, as I thought I had really arrived. The conference was right up my alley, being in the home of country music.

After three years I was promoted to assistant professor. As part of the promotion, the Lenoir-Rhyne administration encouraged me to initiate academic studies toward a terminal degree. The school provided financial assistant to encourage me to make the first step. I began work on my doctorate degree during the summer months in 1984 at Middle Tennessee

State University in Murfreesboro, Tennessee. I selected Middle Tennessee because I could satisfy my residency requirement over three consecutive summers and thus continue my full-time work at Lenoir-Rhyne. I stayed at Lenoir-Rhyne five wonderful years. I was able to complete the bulk of my course work by 1986. My dissertation and comprehensive exams followed in 1986-1987 and I graduated in May of 1988.

I was on my way to realizing my dream of becoming an athletic trainer and to show than an underdog can make it to the big stage.

While at Lenoir-Rhyne in 1985, one of my physicians, Alfred Moretz, John Goodrich, a physical therapist, and I were working to develop sports medicine concepts for the Catawba County schools. Moretz completed his residency in orthopedics at the University of Oklahoma and was a team physician at Del City High School near Oklahoma City. We planned a trip to Oklahoma to visit with the sports medicine physicians at the University of Oklahoma. It was also our plan to visit with Henry Manning, a legendary high school coach there.

During our trip in 1984, we also visited the University of Oklahoma and drove down to Ada to visit my Appalachian classmate, Alex Brown. I also had the fortune to meet Dr. Don O'Donoghue, one of the fathers of sports medicine and former team physician at the University of Oklahoma. Dr. O'Donoghue was retired at the time and his office was located inside the medical library.

Our visit to the athletic training room at University of Oklahoma was hosted by Scott Anderson. He was an assistant athletic trainer from 1980-1987, and served as the head athletic trainer at Tulane University in New Orleans from 1987-1996. Scott returned to Norman, Oklahoma in 1996, and continues in that role today. He is a silent leader of the athletic training professional and has been very instrumental in education of coaches and healthcare teams specific to sickle cell trait screening and modification of conditioning program for positive findings.

Roughly eight months after our Oklahoma trip, Alex Brown and I were talking on the phone; catching up as athletic trainers do. He was preparing to walk out to practice, and I had a quick question for him. Alex was not one for small talk, and said he needed to get out to practice as stretching was due to start soon.

"There's a storm coming up," he said, and the phone clicked. Boom. "Sure enough, I better go." Little did we know a bolt of lightning had struck one of his players while he was stretching before practice. It was a sad day out there, as no one should have to deal with the death of a player.

In 1984, I met at Max's Mexican Eatery on U. S. Highway 70 in Hickory with Appalachian State athletic department officials. They included athletic director Jim Garner, associate athletic director Roachel Laney and head football coach Mack Brown. I am not the least bit surprised at Brown's success. What a charismatic personality. He would lead Texas football to prominence and to the 2006 national championship. But the gist of the meeting was to gauge my interest in returning to Appalachian State, which was adding a new position as assistant athletic trainer, one to coordinate educational and clinical care aspects of athletic training. I was interested.

My interest died as soon as it bloomed when I arrived on campus for my interview. It did not take much time for me to see the changes taking place in that beautiful mountain town of Boone. Appalachian State had changed a lot since I had graduated, and I did not think I needed to throw myself and career into the mess that was transpiring. Only the following year, when the much-respected "Doc" Kanoy returned to full-time teaching, was I ready to return to my alma mater as this would give me total control of the athletic training program. I was twenty-seven and wide-eyed as anyone that age would be to step into a head athletic trainer position at a school like Appalachian State.

When I got to Boone for my anticipated interview (I had to return from Murfreesboro, Tennessee, where I was in my second summer of doctoral course work), Mack Brown had moved on to Oklahoma and his offensive coordinator, Sparky Woods, had been promoted to the head coaching position by athletic director Jim Garner. Woods also was young, but at age thirty-one he already was such a dynamic person. He welcomed me to Appalachian State during my interview and really put on a sales pitch like he might with a high school football recruit.

As I stood on that balcony with Woods in the summer of 1985 I began to realize a dream of mine since the first time I saw that brochure on Coach Caudill's bulletin board outside his office in the gymnasium of Alexander Graham Junior High School.

One of the highlights of my days at Appalachian State and the University of South Carolina was the many clinics and educational opportunities I was part of. I always loved to travel. In additional to attending professional meetings, visiting with other professionals is a great way to strengthen one's base of knowledge and learn new techniques. I have always felt one needs to travel to see what other institutions or professionals are doing. You need to see how they do what they do in their clinical setting. My travels were good for me as it showed me how our program compared to our competition. Many of these trips would validate how far behind the University of South Carolina was during my tenure.

In July of 1989 I was invited by Fred Hoover at Clemson University to participate in a student trainer clinic sponsored by Cramer Products. Also joining us to conduct the clinic were Mary Neal Broos, the athletic trainer at Guilford College in North Carolina, and Robbie Lester, athletic trainer in the Department of Public Instruction in Raleigh, North Carolina.

Cramer Products has long provided sports medicine and athletic training supplies to college programs. Chuck and Frank—the Cramer Brothers—helped found the National Athletic Trainers' Association and have invented numerous products that became vital to athletic training. While at the University of Kansas, the Cramer brothers saw the need for certain products such as liniments, which were frequently used in track and field; as well as Cinder Suds, a foaming agent used on abrasions when student-athletes fell on the old cinder tracks and had cinders imbedded in their hands and legs. Cramer also produced a textbook titled *Athletic Training in the Seventies,* which was a three-ring notebook many students used to develop their athletic training skills.

These athletic training seminars were great because they provided a chance for participants to pal around with peers, discuss issues in the profession and educate young students. It was important to share knowledge with students and seek out potential employees.

One of the highlights of this particular Cramer Student Trainer Clinic was running into the legendary Frank Howard. He was part comedian and part coach during his thirty seasons as Clemson head football coach, concluding in 1969. On this day, Howard was sitting in the athletic training room and I had heard so much about him. It was difficult to keep a straight face when he talked because tobacco juice was running out of the corner of his mouth. He was quite the character, a guy who once was asked what he thought about adding crew as a sport at Clemson and responded: "I'm not in favor of any sport where you sit on your butt and go backward."

After five years at Appalachian State I had grown to love that job as I had my position at Lenoir-Rhyne. I thoroughly enjoyed working with the fine faculty and staff at Appalachian State. Athletics was booming. We had great coaches. Tom Apke was the men's basketball coach and his staff included Ralph Patterson, Todd Sandstedt, Floyd Kerr and Chris Ferguson. They all went on to fine careers. The Faculty Athletic Representative for Appalachian, Dr. Tom Bohannon was a key player in seeing that Appalachian was a fun place to work. Dr. Bohannon headed up our institutional research office, and was a most respected faculty member. Our university chancellor, Dr. John Thomas, was a member of the NCAA's President's Council. Appalachian was a great place to work. Our athletic director was not there by chance, and he made Boone a fun place to work. Boone, North Carolina was on the national sports map as the Mountaineer programs were growing by leaps and bounds.

In early January of 1990 I placed a routine call to Sparky Woods, who had moved from Appalachian State University to be the head coach at the University of South Carolina beginning with the 1989 football season. The call was merely to catch up on a few things since we had developed a strong relationship during his Appalachian State days. We were good friends and often roommates for road games during the 1985 through 1988 seasons.

One of our favorite traditions during road games, after we checked all the players into their rooms, was for Sparky and I to catch up and talk about life and football to all hours of the night. We were big supporters of each other. When Woods left for South Carolina, I told him I never wanted him to create a position for me there, but if ever an opportunity arose I would certainly be interested.

We had a similar conversation when he interviewed for jobs at the University of Missouri, East Carolina University and Wake Forest University. I never wanted anyone to be fired to make room for me. However, if the standard of care was not there, I certainly was interested in the job.

There was much turmoil and consternation at the University of South Carolina by the time Sparky arrived there as head coach. Joe Morrison, the head coach, died of a heart attack following the 1988 season, and the football program was attempting to survive a steroids scandal that had brought much bad publicity nationally to the university. Additionally, the university president had problems with finances that eventually forced him out of his position. There was ongoing litigation between the former athletic director and the university. The place was a mess.

So, when I called Sparky, he returned my call the same evening. He told me there was going to be a changing of the guard in the athletic trainer's position. Terry Lewis was going to be leaving as of June 30, 1990 and the team physician was going to be reassigned. He told me to sit tight before expressing any interest in the athletic trainer's position. Of course, I knew South Carolina officials would have to advertise the position. Sure enough, the following day Lewis received his news. When I finally called down to South Carolina I was led to Sterling Brown, the senior associate athletic director. Brown was the sports services contact for King Dixon, the athletic director. I submitted my formal application.

About one month passed before I was called for an interview, but it seemed like a calendar year. My initial interview for the job was held in Hickory, North Carolina, and Sterling Brown and Jim Price of the University of South Carolina athletic department flew in for the meeting. "JP" had worked with Coach Frank McGuire and was scheduled for retirement in May of 1990. The interview team flew on its private plane to meet with each candidate at the candidate's local airport. By flying a private plane, the university administrators were able to be very efficient with the interview process. I made the one-hour drive down the mountains from Boone. We had a cordial two-hour visit. I was impressed with what the University of South Carolina had to offer and with its overall operation as told to me by Brown and Price. Ten days later, Brownie called and requested that Barbara, my first wife, and I visit the Columbia campus. Again, I drove to Hickory where my wife and I boarded the University of South Carolina's athletic department airplane. When we arrived in Columbia, the pilot, Joe Baier, showed us all the city and campus landmarks from the air, including South Carolina's football practice field and Williams-Brice Stadium. I was excited as a thirty-two-year-old being considered for an athletic training position at an NCAA Division I-A school that was soon to compete in the prestigious Southeastern Conference. What an opportunity.

South Carolina needed to act quickly on several fronts since the athletic department also was without a primary care physician. The opening of spring practice was two weeks away, but I knew as I dined with South Carolina officials that night at Al's Upstairs restaurant overlooking the Congaree River in West Columbia that this was the job for me. We were housed during the interview process at the old Sheraton hotel, which at the time was owned by a big South Carolina booster, Bert Pooser. It would be the same hotel South Carolina football teams used for Friday night stays before Saturday home games, meaning I eventually spent more than 100 nights at that hotel. In our tour of the city, Sparky showed me the old Central Correctional Institution (CCI), which was in operation from 1912 to 1990. At the time of my visit, CCI was nearing its closing, but had been the home of soul singer James Brown. The tour was a great chance for us to reconnect and reconfirm our goals going forward.

The next day I visited with King Dixon, the athletic director, and was offered the job. King was the consummate athletic director for the university. He loved the state of South Carolina and more importantly, the University of South Carolina. He was a coveted alumni and football letterman; he was also a United States Marine. I felt if I did not do a first class job in my work, that he would not only fire me, but whip my tail. Truthfully, he was a great man to work for, but was just too connected to the university to effectively manage the day to day operations of the athletic department and all the associated functions that had to be dealt with, especially in those days. I flew out on the university's plane with Dixon. He was dropped off in Fayetteville, North Carolina for a speaking engagement and I was then returned to Hickory. I had a full day's work ahead of me, though it was the middle of the afternoon.

As I landed in Hickory, I called a meeting at Appalachian State with my athletic director. Later that day, I met with my staff and student athletic trainers and told them I was resigning, effective March 5. It was a difficult meeting for me as I really loved Appalachian State, my alma mater. But South Carolina afforded me a professional opportunity I could not turn down, one I believed may not come along again. Still, it was difficult to leave Appalachian State. We had just built a new facility for athletic training and weight training as an addition to Owens Field House, that I helped design. The facility had been approved for occupancy on January 15, and I had held off on moving in as I knew I would be leaving soon.

As I eventually learned, the underdog can succeed in about any profession, and I considered myself an underdog beginning with my work at Appalachian State and all the way through my career at South Carolina. What follows are a few examples of how I believed anyone could rise to the top.

Of course, there was no better underdog story in the history of sports—and one I can relate to—than Appalachian State's stunning upset of Michigan in football during the 2007 season. As any football fan can recall, Appalachian State entered the game played before more than one-hundred thousand fans in Ann Arbor, Michigan, as the two-time defending Football Championship Series national champions. Michigan was ranked number five nationally. A game that was expected to be a blowout for the Michigan Wolverines turned into a victory for the ages and illustrated for me just how far Appalachian State had advanced since my undergraduate days. The football team had difficulty winning games when I was a student there, but managed to win a couple of Southern Conference championships when I worked under coach Sparky Woods. Appalachian State eventually won three consecutive Football Championship Subdivision national titles and now is a perennial contender for national honors.

So, yes, underdogs can win.

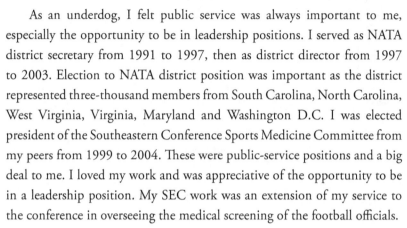

As an underdog, I felt public service was always important to me, especially the opportunity to be in leadership positions. I served as NATA district secretary from 1991 to 1997, then as district director from 1997 to 2003. Election to NATA district position was important as the district represented three-thousand members from South Carolina, North Carolina, West Virginia, Virginia, Maryland and Washington D.C. I was elected president of the Southeastern Conference Sports Medicine Committee from my peers from 1999 to 2004. These were public-service positions and a big deal to me. I loved my work and was appreciative of the opportunity to be in a leadership position. My SEC work was an extension of my service to the conference in overseeing the medical screening of the football officials.

My first meeting as District Secretary was the Mid-Atlantic Athletic Trainers' Association's meeting in Virginia Beach, Virginia in May, 1991. This was a favorite destination of many of the district's members. The meeting doubled as a family trip at the beautiful beaches and classic Cavalier Hotel. The meeting was a social haven for the attendees. The annual escapades of Warren Ariail and his partners Johnny Joseph and Tom Couch (legendary athletic trainer from Davidson College) were classics. They pulled the "snake in the bag" trick on poor Carlos, the Cavalier's doorman. Carlos had worked at the Cavalier for over five decades!

As much fun as we all had, the meeting was definitely a great educational venue. Robbie Lester (physician's assistant in Winston-Salem, NC and later Katie Walsh of East Carolina University) coordinated the educational portion of the meeting and always did a great job. They were two of the people behind the scenes that made this District Secretary and eventual District Director look good.

There were many classic characters in our organization. No one was smarter and more entertaining than the tandem of Dr. Bill Prentice and his side-kick, Skip Hunter. The pair had worked together at the University of North Carolina at Chapel Hill during their early career in the eighties. Bill remains at UNC today, while Skip owns a chain of physical therapy clinics across the southeast, and can often be found on his boat in the Charleston, South Carolina harbor.

From a business prospective, 1992 exemplified how my career was really developing. I formed a corporation that year. I organized and began to offer a summer camp at the University of South Carolina for athletic training students from high schools. That was about the time I was beginning to have public speaking opportunities. My first big trip was to Sydney, Australia. Not a bad start.

Another opportunity afforded to me was my consulting work with Donjoy. They have long recognized the impact athletic trainers offer physicians in sports medicine. They launched a tremendous business based on the leveraged contacts they have in sports. The influence and relationships of the athletic trainer and physicians has long been embraced by this company.

Michael McBrayer has been called the face of Donjoy. He has facilitated more contracts and relationships with physician practices and hospitals than any other single person in the company. Business practices have changed from Donjoy's early days as a privately held company to the days of the Wall Street acquisition, the success is impressive. While a privately held company in 1998, Michael asked for me to assist Donjoy in the expansion of their educational program for athletic trainers. It was Michael and the new athletic training and physical therapy coordinator Brian Moore's vision to expand their educational program to bring upward of fifty college athletic trainers to Southern California for a weekend of education. They sought my counsel to assist them in identifying the guests and coordinate the educational program. I agreed to take the challenge.

One of the first initiatives I was challenged with was the professional education of the athletic training community. Donjoy executives asked me to coordinate their annual conference for collegiate athletic trainers, which was held north of San Diego at their corporate headquarters near Carlsbad, California. This was not a bad job. We invited fifty of the nation's top collegiate athletic trainers and treated them to lectures from leading orthopedic surgeons and case studies presented by the participants. One of the forums we created during my early involvement was prophylactic knee bracing. We grew this program from under ten institutions in 1996 to over two-hundred fifty in 2011! My peers comment on how much they enjoy the education programs we provide every time I see them.

I continued this relationship for years and have expanded my role to working with Donjoy on a prophylactic knee bracing program, education of physicians and athletic trainers within its customer educational program, and finally advising Donjoy in the development of the Velocity ankle brace and an off-the-shelf elbow brace in 1998.

The little guy can overcome the odds.

Dr. Rod's
Treatment Plan

PROPHYLACTIC KNEE BRACING

FOR SOME COACHES AND athletes the term "knee brace" conjures the unpalatable image of Joe Namath and his big, bulky Lennox Hill brace from thirty years ago. However, the reality is very far from that. Knee bracing in sports has rapidly evolved over the past twenty-five years with braces becoming comfortable, highly functional and commonplace in many sports— not only to help athletes return after injuries, but to protect against certain injuries in the first place. The progress that has been achieved in bracing is important for high school coaches, trainers and athletes to carefully consider.

This improved efficacy of the knee brace, particularly on a prophylactic basis, is well documented by research and very evident in the wide usage of braces among college athletes and sports programs today. As demonstrated by the studies and other data discussed below, braces today are an important and valuable piece of equipment that should be evaluated as early as the high-school level athletics.

What We Find in Studies

It is important for physicians and athletic trainers to advise athletes appropriately relative to protective equipment. Recommendations for protection require understanding of biomechanics and anatomy. Prophylactic braces were initially designed to restrain abnormal knee motions, and the knee braces have now progressed to provide functional stability.

Physicians and athletic trainers commonly use prophylactic knee braces to protect the knee from impact forces. The principal factors that determine the impact response characteristics of a brace-knee composite are force distribution, energy absorption, and energy transmission. Material properties and the mechanical design of the brace are important factors in determining brace response to impact. Laboratory studies, using a surrogate knee model, concluded that preventive braces absorb fifteen to thirty percent of the energy of a direct blow. (Liu & Mirzayan, 1995)

Various authors have reported on the positive effect of prophylactic bracing on the incidence and severity of knee injuries (Albright et al., 1994; Hansen, Ward, & Diehl, 1985; Quillian, Simms, & S., 1987; Schriner, 1985; Sitler et al., 1990; Walters, 2000) while Grace et al.(Grace et al., 1988), and Teitz et al. (Teitz, Hermanson, Kronmal, & Diehr, 1987) reported bracing increased knee injuries. The increased incidence among players who wore braces was attributed to contact.(Teitz et al., 1987) Taft et al.(Taft, Hunter, & Funderburk, 1985) and Rovere and Bowen(Rovere & Bowen, 1986) reported knee bracing as effective on reducing the incidence of knee injury.

Patient Comfort

As an athletic trainer, I have always felt two places prophylactic braces cannot help: 1. Around the ankle or 2. In the locker. Needless to say, if the brace is not comfortable, doesn't fit, or just doesn't feel right, the athlete is not going to wear it. I think that is one of the beautiful parts of the new functional custom-fit knee braces. They provide superior protection against knee injury as thigh and tibial cuffs have snugger, firmer fits. Donjoy, the industry leader, has even changed the profile of the upper thigh cuff making it sleeker and conformed to the anatomical features of the thigh. The hinges are lower profile making the brace much sleeker than designs of the 1980s and 1990s. Braces covered athletes' knees more tightly and provided more protection for soft tissue.

In Vivo Research

More recent studies at the University of Vermont have been applied to functional knee bracing. Functional knee bracing was found to provide mechanical stress protection to remodeling graft following anterior cruciate ligament reconstruction surgery. The authors studied functional braces reduced ACL strain during open-chain activity (Beynnon et al., 1992) and found functional bracing had a significant strain protective effect on the anterior cruciate ligament in both weight bearing and non-weight bearing conditions (Beynnon et al., 1997).

Functional Brace Use

Functional knee braces provide restraining influence to control abnormal displacements of the knee and decrease anterior tibial translation without associated contraction of the musculature of the lower extremity. (Baker, VanHanswyk, Bogosian, Werner, & Murphy, 1987) With the ACL-deficient patient, brace use resulted in fewer episodes of giving way and utilization of the brace gave perception of stability in the knee. (Beard, Kyberd, Fergusson, & Dodd, 1993)

Unilateral vs. Bilateral Hinges

When deciding on style of brace to use, Liu reported brace designs incorporating bilateral hinges and rigid shells were more effective than unilaterally hinged designs in transmitting loads (Liu & Mirzayan, 1995).

In the 2000 edition of Biomechanics, I reported on the comparison of knee injuries from the 1997 University of South Carolina football season when players used traditional lateral braces, vs. the 1998 season when we made the shift to custom fit knee braces that are now common. While the scope of this study is limited, the results are nonetheless very revealing as the data illustrated a substantial drop in the number and severity of knee injuries incurred. The use of the newer custom fit braces resulted in a drastic reduction in the amount of time loss (performance) by athletes as well as a drop in the economic impact (medical expenses for knee injuries) for our football program.

I think physician and healthcare team members need to totally understand the concepts of prophylactic bracing when making recommendations to coaches, athletes and parents relative to this subject. Why else would these teams utilize this technology if it did not work? As I watch college football each year, the players at Florida, Ohio State, Oklahoma, Georgia, South Carolina, Florida State, Notre Dame—to name a few—have embraced prophylactic bracing principles, and effectively utilized this to protect their players' knees. Today's discussion of prophylactic bracing is completely different from the bracing concepts discussed in the 1980s. Those braces worn in sport were lateral braces and simply diffused the forces following lateral valgus blows to athletes' knees. Today, the braces are functional knee braces with double upright hinges and biomechanical design to vector force away from knee ligaments.

I have had several athletes bring their brace in to me following a practice or game and the brace is bent beyond belief, and may even be fractured! The design dissipates forces effectively and these players walked away from injuries with mild sprains. This scenario often is a heralding activity for the athlete and further substantiates brace usage. I must say, it is a sickening feeling when you examine an athlete and realize that their medial collateral ligament tear and possible anterior cruciate ligament tears which were received from a clipping injury, would have been minimized and probably prevented with prophylactic brace use as the force would have been dissipated laterally, and the double upright hinge would have also resisted the force medially.

Today, coaches, parents and athletes in high school sports are realizing that spending $350 on a standard knee brace, or even $600 for a custom brace, can be a wise investment in the effort to protect young athletes from significant knee injuries—injuries that not only can hamper a promising sports career, but also adversely affect a wide range of activities and lifestyle in later years. To do their part in supporting this trend, manufacturers are making it easier and more affordable for high school coaches and parents to outfit their athletes in prophylactic knee braces with programs such as Donjoy's "Join the Club" program.

The Future of Knee Bracing

The bracing industry is constantly seeking newer technologies to apply to the bracing needs. Just look at how materials which are introduced rapidly make their entrance into the industry. Further, as newer and more efficient hinges and brace composite materials evolve the product is significantly improved. Donjoy's new dampening hinge has been well received in the Sports Medicine community, and is now even being fabricated in a lower brace profile. Athletes seek sleek, clean designs that work. Remember the two places braces do not work: in the locker and around the ankle!

CHAPTER 4

PLAYING HURT

As long as I can remember, South Carolina's football team was sequestered at the Sheraton hotel in Columbia on Friday nights before Saturday home football games. So I spent a lot of nights at that hotel with the number probably reaching past one-hundred. I took my children, David and Ryan, along to the hotel many times. The boys would dine with the team and hang out with the players until it was time to go home with their mother and go to bed.

David, the elder of the two, loved hanging out with the players, and they were great to him as well as all the coaches' children. Head coach Brad Scott's sons, Jeff and John, had grown up on the South Carolina sideline. Today, Jeff still walks the sideline as the receivers' coach at Clemson, and his brother, John, is completing his medical training at Vanderbilt in cardiology.

One particular Friday night during the 1995 season, David was in elementary school and I began to panic because I had lost track of him. I could not find him anywhere in the lobby or restaurant area. About twenty minutes later I found him in the room of Duce Staley, one of South Carolina's star running backs. Duce was great around the kids and they, of course, were really fond of him.

We all grew to love Duce Staley during his days as a football player at South Carolina. He came out of Airport High School in West Columbia, South Carolina, as a wide receiver, and found his way to South Carolina as a running back via Itawamba (Mississippi) Junior College. Staley was a prince of a guy to the athletic training staff. We grew to admire him because of the way he played football and because of his desire to be on the field. His mother Tina was a very positive influence on Duce.

Late in Staley's senior season of 1996 he suffered a high ankle sprain in a game at Vanderbilt University in Nashville, Tennessee. This was long before the term "high ankle sprain" became part of the lexicon in describing injuries. But just like anterior cruciate ligament tears did not just appear on the scene beginning in the 1980s, high ankle sprains have been around for a long time. As Dr. Jimmy Andrews so eloquently states "you may not have seen the injury but it has seen you." That was a nice way of saying you have not seen the injury as you called it something else, or denied the patient was hurt!

Dr. Bob Peele evaluated Staley and identified the syndesmosis sprain. That particular injury can take a significant time to recover from, and Staley was sidelined the next three weeks of the season, which included games against Tennessee and Florida. He finally returned for the final game of the season—and the last of his college career before going to the NFL—against Clemson.

Staley's injury and his rehabilitation represented for me just how vulnerable student-athletes can be when they are injured. Their defense is down. They respond differently to adversity. They just do not feel good about themselves. The psyche of student-athletes when they are injured is altered. Athletic trainers are taught and skilled at getting the most out of their patients in these difficult and stressful situations. This often happens in public view in the most high-stressed arenas and on the biggest stages. For Duce, this happened during the season's most important games.

With Staley, our athletic trainers and team physicians first talked about working with a Columbia area orthotist, who made orthotics for our players. We asked him to develop an ankle-foot orthosis. This was designed to control Staley's foot. When your foot rolls over, or when you pronate, your big toe side rotates downward placing stress on the middle side of your ankle and foot. That rotation can cause a multitude of problems. By posting the foot with an orthotic, and developing a brace to address this concern, we had an effective solution. When Staley was out of that brace, he was unstable and just not functional. He could not walk, let alone perform as a student-athlete at a high level. With the brace in place, he felt much better and his functional stability was enhanced.

We continued to put Staley through rehabilitation with treatments and medication. You have to understand that Staley was a very dedicated player. He wanted to be back on the practice field and in the starting lineup on Saturdays. He bugged the fool out of me and the rest of the athletic training staff. Trust me, there was no problem getting him in for treatment. He was there every day asking, "What can I do? What can I do?"

We used a lot of topical applications in those days, a variety of treatments prescribed by physicians. The medication was applied topically, allowing it to go into the injury area transdermally. He loved the treatments because he was a curious sort and wanted to know why and how we were applying anything to him that might speed his recovery. If he felt something was special for him, he responded well.

At the time of Staley's rehabilitation, we had a pharmacist in nearby Camden, South Carolina who developed compounded medications suitable for transdermal treatment and iontophoresis. He developed an Epsom salt gel, as for years I had used Epsom salt soaks to help draw the swelling out of the injured tissue. In Duce's case, it worked well using electrical current from a low volt generator (iontophoresis) to effect change in his tissue. Between the gel, various other treatments and the brace, Staley was back on the practice field the week South Carolina played Clemson. In typical Staley fashion, he closed out his college career with a 133-yard rushing performance against his arch-rival. The entire athletic training staff was extremely proud of him because of the dedication he put into the rehabilitation of his ankle injury. I wish I had held onto that brace. Its value has certainly grown multiplicatively with time and you will see why shortly.

Staley had an outstanding NFL career with the Philadelphia Eagles and, on occasion, would send game-worn jerseys and Eagles gear to my boys. I cherished our relationship. I also enjoyed traveling to the Philadelphia area for the Eagles training camp. There, I would interact with the Eagles athletic training staff headed by Rick Burkholder. Rick had hired one of my former athletic training students, Scottie Patton. It was always great to see your students do well! As mentioned earlier, I would get ideas on things we could improve in our operations at South Carolina from what I saw at the Eagles training camp.

Dealing with swelling was an interesting challenge for the sports medicine staff. Edema is classified as swelling in tissue. This was common with contusions, strains, and general soft tissue injuries. The common treatment initially was ice, compression, and elevation, or I-C-E. Any student-athlete that has spent any amount of time in an athletic training room is familiar with I-C-E. The second common injury and associated challenge is the effusion, or collection of fluid within a joint. Effusion is commonplace with sprains of the joint. I-C-E is also the common treatment initially, but we have to eliminate the source of the swelling to effectively provide treatment.

As can be seen, the use of modalities in the athletic training room includes those which aggressively address effusion and edema. The sports medicine staff has to identify the origin of the problem and effectively develop a plan to treat the injury. I always have felt the most effective modality was exercise. We used modalities encompassing electricity, heat and cold, and sound to enhance or facilitate exercise.

Much of our treatment of syndesmosis injuries like that of Duce Staley was based on an article in *The Physician and Sportsmedicine* (Taylor & Bassett, 1993) magazine by Dr. Dean Taylor and Dr. Frank Bassett of Duke University. At the time, Bassett was Duke's team physician and Taylor was doing a fellowship in foot study at the school. The two collaborated on the cause of high ankle sprains. The article was of great interest to me because I was taught the foot was the source of problems in ankle injuries. The article addressed how pronation and/or supination of the foot produced sprains or injury to the syndesmosis (the joint between the tibia, or shin bone, and the fibula, the small bone on the outside of the lower leg). The syndesmosis is an articulation between the ends of the tibia and fibula occurring at the ankle joint. We had been thinking for years that the syndesmosis sprain was caused by hyper-dorsiflexion or hyperplantarflexion. Drs. Taylor and Bassett certainly challenged the multitudes, and effectively changed my thought pattern and treatment plan.

Knowing what had occurred in Staley's injury, I realized how important it was to consider the mechanics of pronation and supination of his foot and ankle. Even before Staley's injury, we had used orthotics with many of our foot and ankle problems. When I arrived at the University of South Carolina, Dr. Bob Peele already was prescribing a custom orthotic to any player with a foot or ankle injury.

Based on the Taylor and Bassett article and the science it provided, we expanded on the use of orthotics and further engaged the use of ankle-foot orthosis for treatment of high ankle sprains, or syndesmosis sprains. Staley was but one of the players receiving the treatment.

Stuart Ross and I discussed the concepts of a custom ankle-foot orthosis. We decided to form a partnership—along with Ross Broadwell—to develop custom-fit AFOs (ankle-foot orthosis) for sports participants. Our idea was to target colleges and professional teams. We probably sold fifty units a year, which meant we were not in this to make a lot of money. The brace cost about $400 per unit to produce and we were selling them at $500 apiece.

About four years later, in 2002, the partners were no longer interested in "chasing the dream," and I bought them out for their initial investment. Later that year, I approached Donjoy about making an off-the-shelf version of my orthosis, one that could be distributed to doctors and athletic training staffs. The idea was to make it available on site so it could be readily available for use when an injury occurred.

We met with the Donjoy team in July, 2002. Later that month, I received a disappointing letter from Rich Gildersleeve, chief technology officer for Donjoy, saying the orthosis was not a sound enough product and lacked potential. Later that fall, at a social event in San Diego, I happened to speak with Les Cross, the president and CEO of Donjoy. I told Cross how disappointed I was that Donjoy could not see the value of this brace. Cross discussed the brace with his staff and Donjoy reconsidered its earlier position.

The following June, 2003 at the annual NATA meeting and clinical symposium in St. Louis, Donjoy's development team took another look at the product. We had provided significant background of what the brace needed to do. The engineers did their homework, reviewed the proposed prototypes, interviewed athletic trainers as well as foot and ankle surgeons, about what they wanted in a brace. The team went to work at designing one that eventually would turn out to be a superior ankle brace that could be on the physician's office shelf for easy access and patient application as needed. It was fun to watch each level, each generation of the brace until it got closer and closer to being a finished product. Finally the "Velocity" was a reality.

BREG Orthopedics launched the Ultra ankle brace, a similar device six months prior to the release of the Velocity, but we felt our brace was the better product. Still, BREG was first to market, which often is most important in capturing the market. IBM did a tremendous job with plain paper copiers, but Xerox was the first to market it. Now, when you send somebody to make a copy, they are going to "Xerox" the copy rather than "IBM" it. Even though BREG was first to market, the Velocity from DonJoy quickly became the market leader as an off-the-shelf ankle-foot orthosis.

In March of 2004, at the American Academy of Orthopaedic Surgeons meeting in Washington, D.C., the Velocity was launched. I was there to talk to physicians about the brace. The launch was most successful.

About one year after the launch, Les Cross was quoted in his company's annual financial report that the brace was "the hottest new product in Donjoy's history." I was proud to be a part of it. It did well —$1 million in revenue the first year and now more than $3 million annually—because it was an exemplary product. The custom Fortis had become the off-the-shelf Velocity.

By the way, I still have Rich Gildersleeve's letter framed and prominently displayed in my office as a reminder not to give up when first turned down. Rich and I joke about this from time to time. It was not his initial decision, but the decision of the Donjoy team. I am glad Donjoy reconsidered the launch, as it has certainly been good for all.

The NFL is a tough proving ground for products. One reason is the high cost of advertising within the league. It is very difficult to have the NFL acknowledge a product for use on the field of play. Riddell helmets have a long standing relationship with the NFL, and there is no telling how much it has cost the company. The agreement is with the understanding that a percentage of NFL players will wear the helmet, and thus it is the "stock" item for use. Players have to request an alternative device for use if they prefer. The NFL is very protective of its brand, and any product that receives exposure by being used in a game generally has to be generic in appearance with no name or logo being revealed.

When Peyton Manning sustained an injury to his ankle during the 2006 season, he was seen in several games not only wearing the Velocity, but wearing it with no cover over the brace, therefore revealing its brand to the world. I guess the NFL policy on covering braces or products applies to all players, except Peyton Manning.

Athletes are never more vulnerable to the pressures of the games they play than when they fail drug tests. At no other time did I deal with student-athletes who were dejected, angry and depressed more than with the results of drug testing. It presented one of the most difficult challenges in my work. It certainly was not a skill taught during any of my professional training while obtaining undergraduate or graduate degrees.

Drug testing presented a chance for colleges and universities to assist a student-athlete. These scenarios are often student-athletes begging for help. The student-athlete's story in these events is often swept under the rug to allow a student-athlete's physical talents to be exploited at the expense of his personal development. Athletic departments and athletic directors must be transparent and have be objective in their plans.

We had so many things that were important to the care of student-athletes, but nothing was more important than drug testing. There was a chain of command at South Carolina regarding obtaining of specimens to the laboratory and the results to the medical director. The secured specimen was per protocol from the time the specimen was collected from the student-athlete until the results were reported to the institution. The most important part of drug testing is the integrity of the collection process. It was known throughout the department that drug testing was to be taken seriously. Upon receiving results from the medical director of the test, we reported all confirmed positive tests to the athletic director. We conducted fifteen-hundred tests per year at South Carolina to student-athletes in every sport. That is a significant number, maybe as many or more than every other athletic department in the country.

One reason drug testing was taken so seriously at South Carolina was because the football team became embroiled in a steroids scandal in the late 1980s, and our athletic director, Mike McGee, wanted no part of a repeat scandal. *Sports Illustrated* had an expose on the drug problem at South Carolina, and the scandal eventually cost many athletic department officials their jobs. During my early days there, there were still some residual effects of the scandal and the lawsuits that followed.

We knew, just like in every other athletic department across the country, that there were drug problems at South Carolina. Even though the percentage of student-athletes who were testing positive was likely much lower than the student body, the goal was still to alleviate all drug use. We later learned that by decreasing the time between notification and testing, we could decrease the student-athlete's ability to mask or ultimately beat the drug test.

Regardless of whether it is a drug test, an MRI or an X-Ray, any test is a picture in time, and it has to be taken as just that. Drug testing had tremendous sensitivity because there were serious ramifications, the least of which included suspensions from athletic activities and the strongest of which meant expulsion from school and loss of scholarships.

Interestingly enough, no student-athlete ever admits to drug use after testing positive. They would claim the athletic department was lying and trying to bring them down. Often, our staff would be attacked verbally by a student-athlete. It created strained relationships at times.

Even under such fire from the student-athletes, we maintained our philosophy—one strictly enforced and adhered to by McGee—that drug-testing was a means to modifying behavior. If we could modify behavior for four or five years of a person's life, then the testing was worthwhile as some degree of learning was taking place.

Unfortunately, not all schools adhere to that philosophy, and even South Carolina has sharply decreased its drug testing due to budget constraints since McGee's departure and the lack of administrative emphasis on drug testing. We had zero-tolerance testing, which said we tested at the lowest level possible. We tested at a lower level than the NCAA standards because we did not want student-athletes tampering or partaking in the use of marijuana or cocaine or any other street drugs.

Testing for the illegal use of recreational drugs is in the best interest of the student-athletes. Philosophically, I support drug testing to ensure a level playing field in competition. Likewise, it is important to provide the best possible care for an injured student-athlete.

My fear is the advent of managed care will restrict top-level care for student-athletes.

Let me use as an example the care of Luther Dixon, an offensive lineman at South Carolina from 1992 through 1995. Late in the 1993 season in a football game at Tennessee's Neyland Stadium, Dixon was clipped on a play in which he was hit on the outside of his leg and fractured his ankle. As fate would have it, Tennessee officials were scheduled to tear the artificial surface out of Neyland Stadium at the end of that season. It was one of the hardest turfs we played on. That dreary, rainy day made conditions even worse. The turf upgrade was three games too late for Dixon, whose ankle needed to be surgically repaired with internal fixation.

During Tennessee's 55-3 win, Dr. Bob Peele put Dixon's leg in a cast and administered medication so he was comfortable for the flight back to Columbia. As we were on the final approach to the Columbia airport, John Bradley of the university police department called to a dispatcher and requested an ambulance to be waiting at the airport. We immediately transported Dixon to Palmetto Health Baptist Hospital where he underwent surgery to repair the fracture. Dr. Peele knew Luther Dixon and his family would be much more comfortable with the quality nursing care, recovery, and supervision the Palmetto Health Baptist staff provided. It would be superior to the non-supervised care a couple of dormitory roommates could offer. This way, all parties—Luther, his parents, Dr. Peele and me—would get a better night's rest.

This was before managed care. Dixon needed to be taken care of in the hospital. He was monitored and kept comfortable. Today, all of what Dixon went through would have to happen at the university. Many of the players live in dorms or in off-campus apartments. You do not have the student health center with overnight services as they had in the past. It is very difficult to have a player hospitalized for observation. It is certainly not what our healthcare providers want to see done today. Too much medicine today is practiced by an MBA (Master in Business Administration) instead of MD (Doctorate in Medicine). To me, business decisions are being made for economics versus patient care.

As was true in the Dixon case, athletic trainers and physicians become attached to the student-athletes they treat and nurture to good health. It is a practice that pays dividends when student-athletes are injured, placed in a vulnerable position and need guidance from someone they trust and have formed a solid relationship with during their college career.

Andre Goodman was a defensive back at South Carolina from 1998-2001. He was an exceptional student-athlete coming out of Eastside High School in Greenville, South Carolina, where he was a track star with spectacular 10.5- and 22.4-second times in the 100- and 200-meter dashes. His legs were a big part of his game as a football player. After taking a redshirt season in 1997, Goodman became a starter the following season at South Carolina. But he went down in the second game of his career with a severe knee injury in a game against Georgia. He tore most of the major ligaments in his knee and the injury was feared to be career ending.

The injury was devastating to Goodman and his family. Following the surgery, the athletic training staff was by Goodman's side and developed a lasting relationship and trust with his family. Goodman was a quiet kid, but an extremely hard-working young man. He never complained about anything during his rehabilitation and went the extra yard at every turn. To see him run for the first time after the surgery was heartbreaking. We all knew it was going to be a long, arduous process for Goodman to get back to playing football at a high level. He struggled through the 1999 season as a reserve defensive back and only played in six games.

He continued to work hard at rehabilitating his knee and became a starter for the 2000 season. How fitting it was that Goodman returned an interception seventy yards for a touchdown in South Carolina's 21-10 victory over, you guessed it, Georgia, on the same Williams-Brice Stadium field he had been injured on two years earlier.

Goodman had another stellar season in 2001 and was a big part of South Carolina defeating Ohio State in back-to-back Outback Bowls. Prior to the NFL draft of 2002, Goodman ran a 4.36-second 40-yard dash for pro scouts, and no one was more thrilled than Dr. Peele and all of the athletic training staff at South Carolina. Goodman was a third-round pick of the Detroit Lions and has played eight seasons in the NFL with the Lions, Miami Dolphins and Denver Broncos.

Another feel-good story of the same ilk involved Ed Hrubiec, an offensive lineman from Berlin, Connecticut who played at South Carolina in 1993 and then from 1995 through 1997. He was an example of how you never know how a student-athlete and his family will respond when felled by an injury. During his official visit as a recruit to South Carolina, I got to know his parents and told them I would treat their son the way I would want someone to treat my two boys.

Hrubiec was injured during his freshman season in a practice session. The injury was serious. It was recommended that a screw be applied to his lower leg to restore the ankle articulation and allow the fractured bones to heal naturally. We called Hrubiec's parents and told them of the necessary surgery. I will never forget what his mother said. "Dr. Rod," she said. "You do whatever you would do for (your sons) David and Ryan." The fact she remembered our conversation impressed me.

My clinical approach to athletic medicine changed as I became a parent. I wanted to handle every case the way I would want people to treat my children. As I sat in staff meetings and worked alongside coaches, the toughest of men became the biggest pussycats when their children came to practice. Being a parent changes people, and this is a good thing. It was my policy to call student-athlete's parents to inform them of injuries or illness; especially if they were missing more than a couple of days of practice. I wanted to make sure the message the parents received was the correct information, and not skewed by a disenchanted child. I encouraged my staff to follow this activity.

Hrubiec was a big, strong kid who faced an entire year out of football as he worked hard to rehabilitate his ankle. He worked his way back and had an outstanding final three years as a starting lineman at South Carolina. During the summer before his senior season, he was working as he usually did. As was custom prior to the beginning of two-a-day practices, strength coach Dennis Tripp conducted conditioning tests. The players were challenged for this test, as some were away from team workouts in the summer, and it was mandatory that all be able to pass the test prior to practice.

Unfortunately, Hrubiec failed the test miserably, and came to the athletic training room where he was asked, "What's wrong? What's wrong?" Ed was accompanied by his ever-present teammate, Travis Whitfield. Both had trained all summer, and now Ed was facing these devastating consequences.

He snapped back, "I can't breathe!"

Turns out, Hrubiec had asthma problems. We referred him to our team physician who assessed him and prescribed proper medication to take care of the problem. Two days later, he passed the endurance test with flying colors. What a difference a day makes, especially when it includes medication taken as needed. Through the years, the staff at South Carolina developed a fondness for Hrubiec as well as a trusting relationship with his family. Now that I have entered the business world, I am often asked if I miss college sports. The relationships are what I miss the most. I do not miss what I left in 2007, but certainly I miss the student-athletes and staff members from the good old days.

Part of running an athletic training staff is instituting policies and adhering to athletic department rules and regulations.

Midway through my run as head athletic trainer at South Carolina we were beginning to have some pretty talented football players filter through Coach Holtz's program. These high-level players, late in their careers, seemed to have one eye on completing their college days and the other on professional football. Following their senior seasons, more and more players were turning to their agents for advice. These agents would call me with questions, concerns, etc. Sometimes these players—during their senior seasons—had some interesting questions to ask, mostly about how we were dealing with injuries.

Arturo Freeman was an extremely talented safety for the South Carolina football team who tore his anterior cruciate ligament during preseason practices in 1998. After having his knee examined by our team physicians, Freeman wanted a second opinion. Ultimately, he saw Dr. James Andrews in Birmingham, Alabama, and Andrews advised Freeman to have his knee surgically repaired. I do not want to insinuate that second opinions are not good, but that was the nature of the beast in those days. People in sports were talking about second opinions then. These student-athletes were angling for big signing bonuses and NFL contracts with loads of money attached. It was a sensitive situation and Freeman successfully recovered from the surgery and became a fifth-round pick of the Miami Dolphins. He played parts of five seasons in the NFL.

At the time, South Carolina did not have a formal second-opinion policy. The team physicians—especially orthopedists—sought support from the university in attempting to keep student-athletes in-house for advice and surgery. Private practice physicians needed a relationship with the university to absolve some of their liability relative to negligence (many states have limits of liability that state employees are accountable for). The physicians did not want to be saddled with all the day-to-day care of these high-profile student-athletes, then stand by and watch as the big surgeries were performed by well-known physicians elsewhere while being exposed with full liability for the patient care. As far back as 2001, there were many questions from doctors about getting a second-opinion policy. They questioned the ethics of their competition in town, and physicians from outside of town.

Sometimes, the most difficult decisions with student-athletes occur when dealing with those who have professional aspirations and potential. Arturo Freeman was one of those. He came to South Carolina as an all-state wide receiver from Orangeburg, South Carolina, where he also played defensive back. Freeman was extremely talented and became a starter in the defensive secondary from the start.

He maintained that starting position for the 1995, 1996, and 1997 seasons before tearing the ligaments in his right knee prior to the 1998 season. Arturo and his family requested a second opinion. This was granted, and after Dr. James Andrews examined Arturo, the request was made for him to perform surgery on the knee. Arturo sat out that entire season, but returned in good health for his senior season of 1999. This was to be his showcase season for NFL scouts, and few doubted he would play professional football. He certainly had all the necessary skills to play at that level.

During preseason camp, the team had a non-contact practice at Williams-Brice Stadium as it prepared for a scrimmage later that day. Coach Brad Lawing was in charge of the punt team and had Freeman on a dummy team during special teams play. Freeman was going through his practice routine when another player hit him squarely in the belly. Immediately, it was very uncomfortable for him and he removed himself from the walk-through practice. I asked the same question as the head coach, Brad Scott, and his staff—what was Arturo Freeman doing on the demonstration team for a walk-through practice? A team physician first examined Freeman on the field, then completed his examination in the physician's examination room under the west stands of Williams-Brice Stadium.

The physician was not comfortable with his findings and wanted to rule out a ruptured spleen before prescribing any medication for pain. He made the decision to transport Freeman to Palmetto Richland Hospital for a further look and tests. Once he arrived at the hospital, a CT scan was performed and it revealed our suspicion, a ruptured spleen. A ruptured spleen was one of the items on the "differential diagnosis" and certainly not the one I had hoped for. The spleen is a filtering organ in your body, but it's very vascular. Obviously, the tear in his spleen had clotted.

Dr. Peele arranged a consultation with a Columbia thoracic surgeon, Dr. Dalton Prickett. He assessed the injury and discussed his findings with the student-athlete and his family. The family decided to proceed with laproscopic removal of the spleen (the surgical technique to seek abdominal access of a patient via a portal in the umbilical cord). The procedure was tedious but successful.

This was an extremely emotional time for Freeman, and his psyche was fragile to say the least. It was our goal to keep him mentally stable, and we were positive with our reinforcement that he would return to the playing field. Freeman missed South Carolina's opening two games that season, but returned to impress NFL scouts and played in the Senior Bowl following the regular season. All was well that ended well when Freeman was selected by the Miami Dolphins in the fifth round of the 2000 NFL Draft and he played parts of six professional seasons with the Dolphins and the New England Patriots.

As with Freeman, we often talk about dealing with student-athletes at their lowest times. I reminded our physicians, when they are working with players, they have the ability to present a positive or negative story. A case in point is how physicians present pathology in a way that the patient can choose options. The ability of a doctor to have an unbiased presentation does not always occur.

Many injuries offer a conservative versus an aggressive treatment approach. A good example is how physicians deal with a lateral medial meniscus tear in the knee. Certain meniscal tears are not repairable and they must be removed. The lateral meniscus is a challenge to treat in this perspective. It has limited vascular tissue and the meniscus is hypermobile when compared to the medial meniscus. During arthroscopic evaluation, the orthopedic surgeon is able to visualize the tear, and those tears that are white on white (showing that the tear is in the non-healing or nonvascular region of the meniscus) are generally removed. Red on white tears, (those that are associated with the vascular part of the meniscus) will heal if surgically repaired. By repairing the meniscus, the integrity and stability of the knee is maintained, arthritis is decreased, and the patient has a better chance for long-term recovery. This information should always be relayed to the patient so they can better understand the treatment time involved.

This is a tough message to convey to coaches, as they often equate meniscus tears to three-week injuries, and do not want to hear about the six-month recovery often associated with a repaired meniscus. Further, we now move from missing a couple of games to possibly missing the entire season.

I recall attending the NFL team physician's "Football Injuries" course in San Francisco in January of 2003. The course was held in San Francisco and was conducted by the American Orthopaedic Society for Sports Medicine. Dr. John Bergfield of the Cleveland Browns made a significant point following a talk on meniscal tears. The question was asked regarding the decision-making process by the medical team. He stated many physicians lack the ability to make what is "the right call specific to this injury." I was talking with his athletic trainer, Mike Colello, about this particular problem, and Dr. Bergfield's eyes lit up with passion for the inability of physicians to do what is right.

As I flew back from San Francisco, I used the five-hour flight to reflect on my notes. The recurring theme was the ability or "lack of it" for physicians to stand up to coaches and do what was right, to make the right call, etc. This had never been a problem with Dr. Bob Peele. He did what was right. Little did I know the inability to make the right call would be a growing issue in Columbia and many cities going forward. The AOSSM had actually produced a session at the San Francisco meeting specific to objectivity and disclosure to the professional athletes, the agent, the family, and the team. As I reflect on the meeting, it certainly was a precursor of what was to come, especially today with the care of the concussed patient.

The sports medicine literature is replete with case studies of patients with aggressive treatment of repairable menisci. The decision may have been made so a student-athlete could return to play quickly and this decision often leads to damaging, long-term problems. If the decision to repair or remove is explained to the student-athlete, he almost always is going to select the short-term solution. That is the nature of the sports mentality. While returning to play is important, long-term healthcare stability and viability becomes much more important. Doctors must make decisions with patients' care in mind, not the impact their decision might have on the outcome of a game. Patients need to be adequately educated about their injuries and the potential impact, not only this season but for years to come.

Independent decisions or consultations outside of the team's professional staff are becoming more common. This is being embraced by many of professional sports organizations such as the NFL where concussions are evaluated by neurologists or primary care physicians with expansive concussion training outside of the organization with no ties to the team. That is a true independent opinion, not someone hired by the professional sports club.

Concussion management provides a platform for objectivity to be embraced so the medical team can apply findings to established best practices. Subjective assessment and screening are giving way to objective, quantifiable test procedures.

Injuries need to be assessed daily. The way my athletic training rooms ran, if a player could not practice he needed to be in my athletic training room at 6:30 a.m. the next day before his first class. Players knew this and they did not like it. When players came out of practice and were evaluated, they were scheduled to be in the athletic training room the next morning to make certain they were treated before they went to class. My point was that if a student-athlete could not practice, then he needed treatment. It was a good policy, one I followed throughout my career. Most all head coaches supported this policy. I wanted to see the student-athlete to get a valid, informed opinion to adequately represent his status to the coaching staff at our daily morning staff meeting.

It is very important to understand there is a constant challenge of the healthcare team to provide care at the highest standard while maintaining patient confidentiality. Each year, student-athletes must sign appropriate documents to allow the medical team to communicate medical information to coaches, administrators, and to the media. This was not an automatic release and one we took very seriously. There were very few student-athletes who did not want their protected medical information released, but if they so chose, it was certainly honored.

Likewise, the annual release of medical information to the NFL on graduating seniors was a tremendous challenge. Most institutions today release the information first to the student-athletes, who in turn release it to their agents or the NFL. Too many schools have been sued because of information released directly to the NFL or to the student-athlete's agent. Again, this release of protected health information is the right of the student-athlete.

Any time student-athletes do not get the outcome they want relative to draft status or contract, they can cite the case of Ohio State football player Joe Montgomery, who sued the university over information released. As has been reported by ESPN and multiple other news agencies, Montgomery—a running back at Ohio State from 1994-1998—filed a defamation complaint in January, 2010. He sued the school for "falsely reporting a medical condition," which he contends "prevented [him] from collecting adequate worker's compensation, disability and other benefits, and injured him in his NFL career," according to a press release from his attorney.

It was Montgomery's contention that documents sent from Ohio State to NFL teams via an NFL questionnaire on the medical and injury history of Montgomery in October, 1998, falsely reported that Montgomery had high blood pressure and hay fever. Montgomery contended he never was made aware of that report and that it was false. He also contended that eleven years later, in July, 2009, a physician doing a medical evaluation of him for the State of California division of workers' compensation cited that information when deciding that Montgomery's current medical problems were due "fifty percent" to pre-existing conditions before he entered the NFL.

Montgomery contended the 1998 medical evaluation, which was available to all NFL teams before the 1999 NFL Draft, probably hurt his draft status. Despite being a backup most of his Ohio State career, he was selected in the second round—the forty-ninth pick overall—by the New York Giants.

Cases such as this will lead to further "hands off" approaches of colleges and universities. The onus of discovery will be on the NFL clubs. NFL scouts have long sought the opinion of athletic trainers, equipment managers, assistant football coaches, and head coaches regarding their dealings with student-athletes. The investigative shadow is much greater with the projected first-round draft pick. The telephone calls are immense and the conversations being repeated by each professional club. By having a central repository of medical information and taking out the subjective interviews, this will go a long way in protecting the student-athlete.

Many schools are dealing with the release of information issue by copying the entire medical file of the student-athlete and releasing it directly to the student-athlete. It is then their responsibility to update the NFL or individual teams of the medical history and injury status. This process had been conducted by the institution's athletic trainers for years on behalf of the student-athletes after they signed a release of information. Times have certainly changed, and I would certainly agree with the trend of releasing the information to the student-athlete and letting them deal with the teams and agents.

I attempted to foster an atmosphere in the athletic training room that was not like a morgue, but at the same time not a place a student-athlete wanted to be. It was important, first and foremost, to treat them as human beings. Coaches' concern for student-athletes dealt with practicing and playing. I was much more concerned with them as people. I attempted to find out about a student-athlete's background. Many times, their home life helped explain any problems they worked through at college. I did not make excuses for student-athletes, but it was important to develop a relationship with them where they could trust conversations with the athletic training staff. I also told the student-athletes they could not get between me and the coach because I would side with the coach every time in these situations. The relationships I developed with student-athletes are something I still cherish to this day.

The banter among student-athletes in the athletic training room kept things light more often than not. One of my favorites was Cleveland Pinkney, a good-hearted kid and defensive tackle from nearby Sumter, South Carolina. Cleveland had not qualified for admission to the University of South Carolina following his graduation from Sumter High School. He attended junior college in Mississippi. Coach Wally Burnham often said in recruiting meetings that Cleveland recruited us as he badly wanted to be a University of South Carolina Gamecock. Everyone loved Cleveland.

Pinkney was sick once and had come to the athletic training room after doctors did not allow him to practice. He was vomiting and was prescribed medication to settle his stomach. He was given some composine suppositories, which knocked him out. As Cleveland had missed practice, he was required to see me the next morning. I arrived at 6:30 a.m., and Pinkney rolled in around 7:15. He was full of energy, fired up and joking with everyone. He obviously felt better. His vital signs were good.

I asked him if he had any problems.

He responded, "No, but those pills sure were slimy."

I guess the pharmacist did not provide detailed instructions for the prescription, or maybe he did like I do and "waived the consultation with pharmacist." In either case, Pinkney had not used the suppositories as directed on the instructions. As I said, Pinkney had a way of keeping things loose around the athletic training room.

Just as I got to know student-athletes like Pinkney, I grew to admire some as well, and none more than Phil Petty, the quarterback on South Carolina's two Outback Bowl champion teams of 2000 and 2001. You should understand that Coach Lou Holtz put tremendous pressure on his quarterback. Holtz rode the quarterback hard because he played the one position that was going to win or lose games for the coach. Petty handled it well, but Holtz was tough on him. Several times, Petty entered my office and declared he was ready to quit. He had a knee sprain once and another time a bad ankle sprain. He was extremely down when he was dealing with injuries, so I had to talk him out of quitting as did Skip Holtz, Lou's son and an assistant coach.

Petty was a tough kid, though, and he stuck it out every time. He proved to be a very efficient quarterback for Holtz and the Most Valuable Player in the Outback Bowl following the 2001 season. He represented everything that was good about college athletics as well as how athletic trainers are forced to deal with the emotions of the student-athletes during the most trying of times.

Those tough times further prepared Phil for the next chapter in his life, as it did his teammates. Few, if any of the old players, tell me "If I had it to do over again, I would not play football." Playing the games, enduring the wrath of coaches, lifting weights in the cold of winter, spring practice, summer conditioning, and all the other responsibilities make being part of the team something special, for the players as well as the athletic trainers.

I love to look around the southeast and see former student-athletes doing so well in coaching, teaching, business, or whatever. Athletics teaches us so much as it prepares us for life's challenges.

Dr. Rod's
Treatment Plan

CONCUSSIONS

SEVERE INJURIES TO THE head in football have been significantly reduced following the introduction of NOCSAE approved helmets. However, less-than-severe injuries continue to occur, and repeat events of these injuries can often lead to severe problems. Following any event producing altered awareness, unconsciousness, etc., the student-athlete or player should be immediately transferred to a medical facility for further treatment and evaluation. All coaches should have an Emergency Plan on hand to adequately deal with injuries prior to occurrence. Many sports agencies (NCAA, NFL, MLB, etc.) have mandated clear, concise concussion protocols be written and shared with all parties including the student-athletes/players, coaches, administrators, and medical personnel.

Of concern with head injuries, is that when a head injury has been diagnosed, players frequently downplay their symptoms so they can return to play quickly. It's important for players, parents, coaches, athletic trainers, officials and family physicians to know what causes a head injury or concussion to occur. It's also essential for everyone associated with sports to know how to tell if a player has suffered a concussion and how to manage the injury. This information is provided as a guide, and is not meant to replace good medical care in the form of team physicians and certified athletic trainers.

A direct or indirect blow to a player's head causes a concussion. A player sustaining a direct below is normally aware that something hit their head and is consequently assessed for a head injury. In comparison, an indirect blow occurs when a quickly moving player hits an immovable object like the field, a piece of equipment, or another player. This forces the player to stop or change direction suddenly, which makes their brain "crash" into their skull. A player who has suffered an indirect blow may not be aware that anything has happened to their head. The impact of both types of blows causes the player's brain to be injured because the rapid jarring of the head forces the brain to suddenly speed up or slow down. This disrupts how the brain works or processes information.

While both direct and indirect blows can make a player lose consciousness, you do not need to lose consciousness to suffer a concussion! Being dazed, having poor coordination or balance, losing memory, or ringing in your ears and headaches are some of the signs that indicate a concussion has occurred. No matter how minor the incident may appear, every head injury is a major health concern. This is especially true when a head injury occurs more than once.

Players:

- Make sure you have all equipment issued to you in good condition, it is fitted properly, and are taught features to look for with fit. Remember your mouthpiece, as this can help with reducing forces.
- Be prepared mentally and physically whenever you are practicing and playing. If you are tired or unfocused you are more at risk for injury.
- Be aware of your physical size and strength and use it appropriately. Work to maximize your level of conditioning.
- Always be alert during practice. Coaches should encourage you to stay on you feet, and under control taking responsibility for your actions.
- Be honest about signs and symptoms that may indicate you have suffered a head injury. Tell your parents, coach, athletic trainer and physician exactly how you are feeling.

Coaches:

- Enforce that players wear all mandatory safety equipment every time they practice or play. Coaches of young athletes must make sure their helmets and face-masks fit properly and are correctly fastened.

- Check practice facilities to make sure they are safe.
- Teach skills in a progression from simple to complex and make sure that practice activities are suitable for the age and experience, maturity and fitness of your players.
- Monitor your players during practices. Make sure they have good technique for blocking and tackling.
- Respect and implement all safety-related decisions made by the officials and medical personnel.
- Coaches should discipline players whose actions put themselves, or anyone else, at risk.
- Make sure your team has a written Emergency Plan. You must design the Emergency Plan if your team does not have an athletic trainer. Communicate the plan to your players and their parents.

Parents:

- Check that your child takes every piece of their equipment to practices and games. Then, make sure the required safety equipment is worn at all times and that it fits properly.
- Monitor the condition of your child's equipment.
- Support coaches' decisions that relate to safety. Be aware that coaches are responsible for making sure players obey the rules and wear all mandatory equipment.
- Help your child be prepared for practices and games.

- Monitor your child for signs and symptoms that could indicate that a head injury has occurred. Make sure your child receives follow-up care from a medical doctor.

CHAPTER 5

COACHES'
CONTRASTING STYLES

Perhaps as much as anyone in an athletic department, the head athletic trainer might as well be called a juggler. The position requires the person in charge of athletic training to wrestle with any number of jobs on a daily basis. Beyond that, the head athletic trainer must be a master psychologist with everyone from the athletic director, head coach in various sports, student-athletes and their parents.

It is not a job for the weak. You must be strong-willed and flexible at the same time. You must be a decision-maker as well as a listener. You must have sound business principles as well as solid parenting skills.

For me, it was paramount that I be able to work cooperatively within the athletic training world as well as the athletic department and the football coaching staff. Necessary skills included communication, knowing roles, understanding policies, dealing with internal politics and having outstanding time management.

All in all, a head athletic trainer must be extremely versatile within a college athletic department.

It is so important that everyone on a staff knows his or her role. Mike McGee, South Carolina's athletic director during the majority of my tenure, hounded doctors about their judgments. Head football coach Lou Holtz was the same way.

In the end, it came down to the fact that coaches coach, athletic trainers stay in the training room and handle things there, and doctors practice medicine. If it works any other way, we have conflicts and problems. It is important for all parties to respect one another, and it must be mutual respect.

Holtz was aggressive in making certain that his players practiced. His rule was that if a player did not practice on Wednesday, then he did not start the game on Saturday. If a player did not practice on Thursday, he did not wear a uniform or play on Saturday. Holtz firmly believed one had to practice to play. One thing no one could question with Coach Holtz was his intricacies. His mannerisms and habits from the University of Arkansas and Notre Dame were validated when Dean Weber and I discussed our dealings with Holtz. Dean worked with Holtz at the University of Arkansas. Dean had to deal with a young and wiry Lou Holtz. I would always share stories with physicians and athletic trainers who had worked with Holtz. In May of 2011, I was invited to speak at the Tennessee Athletic Trainers Society's Concussion Summit. Dr. Jim Moriarity, team physician at the University of Notre Dame was also an invited speaker. We shared our stories and experiences over a nice dinner in Nashville, Tennessee. We agreed as trying as Holtz was, the difficulties were well worth it.

My challenges with Holtz were especially apparent during South Carolina's preparation for the Outback Bowl following the 2000 season, one in which Holtz's team turned the 0-11 season of 1999 into a 7-4 record and bowl appearance. The team had several injuries during bowl practices, particularly among the offensive linemen. The 2001 Outback Bowl was special for coach Holtz. He had been on Woody Hayes' staff at Ohio State University. This was South Carolina's biggest bowl game in my tenure. Holtz was at his best.

Ohio State possessed an offensive line that had played pretty much intact most of the season. Our bunch of linemen was a different story. Melvin Paige started all eleven games of the regular season at right tackle,

Scott Browne started ten games at center, Travelle Wharton nine at left tackle, and C.J. Frye and Cedric Williams eight games each at the guard positions. Nevertheless, Holtz was not interested in how much playing time they had during the regular season. They were limited in practice during the two-a-days of bowl practice, and he wanted to leave any injured player home in Columbia when the team left for Tampa, Florida. He jumped my backside, preaching that playing time was based on practice time. It was his call on playing time based on his beliefs about practice time for a student-athlete.

When you talk about communication, it is important that physicians and athletic trainers do not take it upon themselves to say: "We're going to hold them out here so they are ready for Saturday." That is not wise because it is not part of our job description. Coaches coach, athletic trainers practice athletic training, and doctors practice medicine. Doctors do not need to make judgments about when a student-athlete can practice or not practice. They determine only if a student-athlete is cleared to practice or not. Doctors do not forecast the return of student-athletes to the playing field. That is the athletic trainer's responsibility. I certainly conferred and communicated with team physicians on such decisions.

With that said, there is a lot of talk around sports and discussions inside of staff meeting rooms around the concept of pain versus injury. It is widely accepted that players need to develop the ability to play with pain. At no time will players be totally exempt from pain. Injuries will have discomfort, and players that excel often have an innate ability to handle discomforts. On the other hand, injuries must be dealt with. The medical staff will recommend to the coaches and players when injuries preclude participation.

There are times when a player wants to play with an injury, and if the participation will further harm them, it is the responsibility of the medical staff to intervene. The coaching staff needs to be supportive of the medical staff. It should also be noted there are times when the player says they cannot participate, even if cleared medically by the medical staff. In times like this, I would have a conversation with the player and tell him "you are cleared medically, and if you don't think you can participate, I will inform your coach that you feel you cannot go." In this scenario, the player's request is acknowledged, and the coach will understand the player is making the determination he cannot participate.

Pitch counts are great in baseball because in athletics we have to make objective judgments. The same is true with practice time. You can either practice or not. It does not make sense to say a student-athlete can practice the first quarter, but cannot practice the next two. Or, he can only participate in certain parts of the game.

The medical team needs to make medical decisions, and have objective goals which are measurable and obtainable.

Having open lines of communication between the athletic department staff, the athletic trainer, team physicians and the coaching staff is so vital in college athletics. I witnessed that respect from the relationship between "Doc" Kanoy, Appalachian's athletic trainer, and Dr. Evan Ashby, Appalachian's team physician during my college days at Appalachian. The two were inseparable at work yet had very little in common away from the athletic training room.

My first full-time job at Lenoir-Rhyne College allowed me to forge a relationship with Dr. Benny Goodman. I was the school's first athletic trainer. As soon as he realized I did not want to be the team physician he supported me. That bumpy start to our relationship quickly smoothed over and I became an extension of him. Hickory, North Carolina was a mill town known for its furniture and textile industry. There was also a rich tradition in "small college" football, evidenced by Coach Clarence Stasavich's 1960 National Association of Intercollegiate Athletics (NAIA) national championship.

As I moved back to my alma mater in 1985, it was my time to work with Dr. Ashby. He proved to be just as supportive of me as he had been of "Doc" Kanoy. Dr. Ashby was the director of the student health center at Appalachian, yet he retained a keen interest in athletics. When a new student health center was designed, Dr. Ashby made certain student-athletes were taken care of. He also sought the input of athletic trainers when the school studied how to integrate with local specialty physicians. Dr. Ashby was the Watauga County medical examiner and a certified medical technician, so his knowledge of emergency medicine was useful in dealing with our student-athletes and athletic training staff.

When I left Appalachian State for the University of South Carolina interview process in 1990, Sparky Woods arranged for me to have dinner with him and his wife, Jean Ann. We were joined by Dr. Bob Peele and his wife, Nancy. Dr. Peele and I hit it off from the start. Our initial visit was actually held in Coach Sparky Woods' Williams-Brice Stadium office. Dr. Peele let me know from the beginning, he was very interested in continuing to work as team physician, and the university had no intention of making a change with his service.

He was the consummate team physician. He was an orthopedist, and had the overall health of the student-athlete in the center of his radar. He was very well connected in the Columbia, South Carolina community as well as the local hospital medical staffs. Dr. Peele always did what was right for the student-athlete. In deciding if a student-athlete needed either a surgical repair of a meniscus (knee cartilage) or removal of the same, he made the proper call, no matter how difficult. Dr. Peele was a big man in stature and imposing as a physician. Though many did not see it, he was a student-athlete advocate. Too many times physicians take the easy way out and succumb to the pressures from administration and/or coaches and make decisions in favor of the university, and not the student-athlete.

Dr. Peele had been the team physician providing orthopedic care since the 1980s when athletic trainer Terry Lewis came to South Carolina with Coach Joe Morrison. One of my favorite times with Dr. Peele was Friday nights before Saturday road games at South Carolina. One of my duties as athletic trainer was to plan team meals and make certain everything went off without a hitch. Then, he and I would head out for dinner. He was a restaurant connoisseur, and loved fine wines. Whether we were in New Orleans for the Southeastern Conference men's basketball tournament or San Diego for a Donjoy sports medicine client education program or Fayetteville, Arkansas to play the Razorbacks, he had the perfect restaurant picked out. He was this athletic trainer's best friend. He was one tough, strong, professional man.

Collegiate team physicians tend to run their course on campus. There are cases where a team physician has complete support and is embraced by coaching staffs and the athletic administration. Dr. Larry Bowman at Clemson University and Dr. Don Shelbourne at Purdue University are two good examples. Gaining that support from all parties begins and ends with good care. Dr. Bowman has been empowered and supported by Clemson since 1983. In turn, his recognition by the university is shown in the visiting team area—the Larry Bowman area—at Memorial Stadium at Clemson. His former players and physician associates donated funds for this recognition.

Dr. Shelbourne is one of the nation's leading anterior cruciate ligament reconstruction physicians. He has a very aggressive surgical and rehabilitation protocol. As a result, he has a quick return to play with his student-athletes.

The expectation for every team physician is to have one hundred percent recovery in every case. That is the expectation, regardless of the severity of an injury. We must constantly remind ourselves that there are incidents where injuries have poor outcomes. That can certainly be the case with high-profile student-athletes with multiple surgeries. So, the overall challenge is immense for team physicians. Colleges across the country maintain support for their doctors and encourage and stand behind these doctors. That support is both warranted and necessary. Physicians and athletic training staff members must have autonomy to make sound decisions. Unfortunately, sometimes the lack of autonomy and support will cost someone their job.

The value Dr. Peele brought will never be appreciated, but that is just the way it goes. Not saying it is right, but it is what it is. Dr. Peele established an excellent working relationship between the South Carolina athletic department and Columbia area hospitals. It was not that way when Mike McGee arrived as the South Carolina athletic director in 1993. One of McGee's initial orders to me was to get healthcare administered to student-athletes at the university's medical school hospital (Palmetto Richland Hospital). His belief, which I strongly supported, was that if care was good enough for the student-athletes it was good enough for the patients. In other words, we had to make certain South Carolina student-athletes had a hospital that could serve all their needs. While I understood that, I did not think Palmetto Richland Hospital was our best choice. It was the indigent care and trauma hospital in Columbia. If you were in an auto accident, that's where you wanted to be taken. With all the tension over getting second opinions and the perceived lack of support from the university's athletic administration, Dr. Peele decided to leave his role as director of sports medicine in the summer of 2002. This move hurt me personally as we had been friends since 1990.

Over time, conditions improved greatly at South Carolina and relations between coaches, athletic administration, athletic trainers and physicians ironed out. Today, South Carolina has a sound working relationship between physicians and the University of South Carolina medical school. No longer do team physicians need to operate a private practice while working with student-athletes. These physicians probably see twenty-five percent of the patient load on any given day that a private doctor would. That change was outstanding, and it began to show when orthopedic surgeons Jeff Guy and Angus McBryde came on board in the fall of 2002.

As I reflect on healthcare in colleges and universities, I do not think the public understands the difference between medical school physicians and private practice physicians. Medical schools have attending physician responsibilities and must mentor medical students, residents, and specialty fellows. The private practice physicians have the responsibility of revenue generation through surgical and clinical skills. The medical school physicians have the convenience of a teaching salary as a base, and are not as fiscally driven as the private practice physician. The private practice physicians see many more patients and often have superior skills as compared to the attending faculty physicians.

Doctors order tests to document clinical judgment. Many times, there are extra tests ordered to validate their findings. Doctors want to be objective and the tests validate this via visual evidence. That interpretation helps them form their opinion. Objective tests such as MRIs, X-Rays, CT Scans, any type of lab study, are a snapshot in time. They provide objective evidence. Sadly today, many tests are a response to patient requests.

Another reason many tests are ordered is to substantiate a medical opinion and avoid litigation. This creates a financial stress to our healthcare system and is just another reason we need to engage in tort reform nationally.

Unfortunately, a team physician working for an athletic department in a high-profile league such as the Southeastern Conference can last only so long. The job is grueling. Most physicians in the NFL or in big-time college athletics last about ten years. The jobs usually pay poorly. Dr. Peele's private practice, Midlands Orthopedics, gained much exposure through his work with the university, but I am not certain he received adequate support from his partners.

When Dr. Peele resigned as team physician following South Carolina's 2002 Outback Bowl victory, I was deeply saddened. I cherished our friendship. I could call on him any time of the day or night and he was there for me. If he was in surgery, he was accessible. If he was on vacation, he was accessible. I regret now how much I took of his personal time.

To this day, when I need orthopedic care or make a referral, Bob is the man I call.

Communication is a key trait of one's work and value. By the time I got to the University of South Carolina and was head athletic trainer in 1990, I had certainly gained a respect for communication. Never would I realize the impact failure to communicate can have on a team, a staff, or a university's fan base.

The South Carolina Gamecocks were preparing to play the Citadel Bulldogs. I was not overly excited about the game, as we had dominated The Citadel during our Southern Conference competitive days over the past five seasons I was working at Appalachian State.

The Citadel came to Columbia, South Carolina with a fine team and an excellent game plan. The Citadel ran the wishbone offense to perfection, and defeated the Gamecocks 38-35. Sparky Woods was livid post-game. He was even more distraught on Sunday, when I met with him to update the injury situation for the next game versus North Carolina State. I will never forget his conversation with me that day. He was so disappointed in the lack of communication his assistants had displayed as there was confusion on the defensive staff regarding player assignments and responsibilities. Specifically, there was confusion over who was taking the fullback, and who was taking the option back. Anyone who knows anything about football knows that this is one of the main points in defending an option team. Coach Woods could not believe such a basic principle of defending the option had not been realized by his coaches and the failure to make adjustments was the downfall of his team. The saddest part of it all, this was the beginning of the blame fans put on Sparky for hiring his staff from Appalachian. Decisions such as this make it difficult to defend their coaching. Sparky Woods would be constantly questioned by the silent majority of Gamecock nation for hiring his entire Appalachian staff.

Communication of injuries to coaches, student-athletes, their families, and to the media is an important part of being the head athletic trainer at any school. Coach Holtz was insistent on loyalty, and keeping family secrets in house. All coaches are paranoid about leaks, and Holtz was no exception. Assistant coaches would leak information to media about a recruit, an injury, or some administrative matter. I always thought it funny that these coaches actually thought they were getting the media to "take care of them" by feeding them information. I tended to believe the philosophy of George Steinbrenner, the late owner of the New York Yankees, who often said "information is power" and should be guarded accordingly.

It is important the public and the medical community understand sports medicine is nothing more than conventional medical practice applied to bridge the gap between the expectations and fears of the patient, student-athlete, coach, and treating physician. At no time should good medical ethics or good medical practice be abandoned for mere expedience and more importantly at no time should a student-athlete be returned to play before he or she is ready. Communication to all parties is key.

As was the tradition at South Carolina, I was the point person for medical information relative to communication. I would make an evaluation of injuries and consult with our physicians following their assessment. I always embraced the opinion of my assistants working alongside me with football. Phil Hedrick (1999-2002) and Bill Martin (2002-2006) were my right-hand persons, necessary ones with all my responsibilities of running the athletic training program. Prior to Hedrick's hiring, I had used a couple of graduate assistant athletic trainers.

When we hired Hedrick, South Carolina moved to the level of many of our peers in the Southeastern Conference. We finally had a full-time dedicated assistant athletic trainer for football. Many of our opponents had multiple full-time assistants working with football. Regarding my assistants, I took what they said as golden, and held them accountable. I wanted to know what was going on with each and every player, regardless of how trivial it may have been. It has now recommended NCAA Division I Football Bowl Series institutions (Glazier, 2009) hire three assistant athletic trainers on a full-time basis specifically for football.

We had a daily injury report prepared regardless of the time of year. This was a good process and provided a mechanism to communicate with our coaches, administration, and physicians on each and every injury. I needed to know, because if there was ever a question or problem, head coaches or athletic directors did not call Bill in the middle of the night or Phil on his cell phone. They called me. The athletic trainers were the point person communicators, and I needed all the information including all the details.

After each game, it was my policy to see the head coach, preferably prior to his post-game radio interview, to update him on the medical status of our players. This was a chance to update him on injuries sustained during the game. This was always updated in detail the next day following our mandatory check of all players.

A huge part of communication for a head athletic trainer involves the daily, nearly year-round dealings with the head football coach. Over the years I have observed how football coaches manage their staffs, deal with the athletic administration and with the media. I believe many of the principles coaches use carry over to athletic trainers.

Coaches deal differently with the media today. It used to be that coaches offered little insight into their players or their team. Cliches were the norm when coaches addressed the media: "We're taking one game at a time;" "You can throw the record books out the window;" "We're facing a great opponent."

With the explosion of televised events and the access to information through the Internet and social media, the public is more informed about the game. As a result, coaches need to be much more insightful in their comments and they need to decrease the use of media as a way to motivate their teams. We see much more delicate use of the English language in describing the player, the team, and the game.

Dealing with the media, teaching the game, and working the psyche of the players are all part of coaching today, and this contributes greatly to burnout in the profession. Coaches tend to over-identify their job. They don't have diversions, get very little exercise, have no outside interests, are control freaks, and refuse to delegate authority, all which leads to burnout.

Then you see coaches who open up and are not afraid to share with their staff. They tend to have greater success. As an athletic trainer, I always believed if I hired people who were smarter than me—and that certainly was not difficult to do—I could delegate to my staff and turn duties over to others. It empowers them, without me having to look over their shoulders. Further, by involving a staff in decision-making and policy development, the more likely the staff will collectively embrace the concept.

Unfortunately, I have found that most head football coaches are not great organizers. I recall Sparky Woods, when he was the head coach at Appalachian State, questioning me about my use of DayTimers. He never embraced the idea, but certainly asked a lot of questions about using one.

During the summer of 1995 I was traveling around the southeast visiting some of our players convalescing in their hometowns. One trip was to Germantown, Tennessee. While in the area, I dropped by Memphis State University (now the University of Memphis) and visited with my old friend, Coach Woods. He was in the staff room studying film and making notes in his Covey planner! I was impressed, as he too was embracing these great principles.

There are only twenty-four hours in a day, so being successful is not about time management. It is about event management. We need to manage events in our life as we are going forward.

It is so important that we balance work and home life. Chris Snoddy, who now works in Nashville, was one of my favorite athletic trainers. He was one of the most grounded people I was ever associated with in the business. I learned so much from him, including time management. He often said you cannot fight on multiple fronts. He reminded me the Germans lost World War I because they fought on too many fronts. As a professional association, if we are fighting multiple battles and multiple strategies, we are destined to fail because we are not united on any one front. We have to plan and we have to focus on the things that need to get done.

It is so important to plan. You do not only plan on a weekly basis. I try to plan annually; review quarterly; apply monthly; and set specific goals each week. My wife and I sit down and plot our business goals and family goals. Where do we want to be in twelve months? Where do we want to be financially? What are we going to do, and how are we going to do it? We then assess those goals quarterly. Then monthly, we make a prudent plan to meet those goals. I look at the goals weekly. Every day before I head out to work I set a plan for that day.

When we fail to plan, we are planning to fail.

The time demands in the NFL are difficult on coaches. I hear horror stories of NFL coaches sleeping in their offices, always in search of that one play to get them a leg up on their opponent. It is the same way in college coaching. I witnessed coaches with the same mentality, from Sparky Woods to Brad Scott to Lou Holtz, who had a cot adjacent to his office for convenience.

Steve Spurrier was different. He experienced tremendous success during his previous college stops at Duke and Florida. He won an Atlantic Coast Conference championship at Duke, then won six Southeastern Conference titles at Florida in addition to the 1996 national championship. Yet he did not believe in spending all day and night in the office, nor did he believe his assistant coaches should adhere to that philosophy.

During his first spring as South Carolina's head coach, instead of watching film all day like the defensive staff, Spurrier and his offensive coaches were playing golf multiple times each week. The defensive staff had the same opportunities, but their mentality and history was different. I am not saying either is better, just different.

Spurrier has been said to be hard on his quarterbacks. Prior to his arrival in Columbia, South Carolina, I vividly recall conversations with several different staffs addressing the way Spurrier handled his quarterbacks at Florida. The recent debacle with quarterback Stephen Garcia, who was dismissed during the Gamecocks' 2011 season, certainly accentuates and validates our discussions. The saddest point of Garcia's tenure was with all the reported incidents clouding this student-athlete, he never had any significant punishment at South Carolina until his talents were ultimately exhausted. If you recall, it was announced on October 11, 2011 that he was being benched due to his performance, and only ninety minutes later, it was announced he was actually released from the program! Coaches, regardless of their overall success, need to maintain their standards. I heard one time that "character is what we do when no one is watching."

Coaches are certainly different, each in their own special way. While Coach Spurrier is winning on the field, other coaches had their accomplishments. Coaching is a most difficult profession.

The Holtz era represented hard work and organization, tenets of his philosophy and teaching. As I travel in my work, I come into contact with people who worked with Holtz, and the theme is consistent regarding his mantra: Have a plan, and work your plan.

It is critical to remember that the principles, structure and foundation to a good team are applicable to our personal lives and in business. I found that out the hard way in March of 1989 when I was the head athletic trainer at Appalachian State, which had just changed head football coaches. Sparky Woods had matriculated to South Carolina and Jerry Moore took over.

Some wondered about Jerry Moore's prospects of success at Appalachian State. Moore began his coaching career at Corsicana High School in Texas and became assistant coach at Southern Methodist. After the 1972 season, he joined the Nebraska Cornhuskers as receivers coach, becoming offensive coordinator under Coach Tom Osborne in 1978. In 1979, Moore got his first head coaching job at North Texas. After two seasons, he was named head coach at Texas Tech and spent five seasons there (16–37–2). He transitioned to the golf course development business and after three years away from football, Moore joined Ken Hatfield's coaching staff at Arkansas for two seasons. Moore ultimately proved to be a sensational hire. He has won nearly two hundred games at Appalachian and includes eight Southern Conference championships and three consecutive Football Championship Subdivision national titles from 2005-2007.

New coaches often have a mission to change everything when they arrive on campus. Team activities, routines, even uniforms are changed to create a new environment. That makes perfect sense if the previous system was failing, which Appalachian State was not under Woods. It was quite obvious to all of us on the athletic training staff that Moore's staff was trying to discredit Coach Woods and his staff. My sense was that Moore was putting down the previous staff to build his own staff up.

To make this point, I reference a conversation from November 5, 1989. Moore was very negative toward me and the overall attitude of the support staff (athletic training, strength and conditioning, and athletic equipment) at Appalachian State during this meeting. It was a difficult conversation for me, but I remained professional because of my position as an assistant athletic director for sports medicine who oversaw the athletic training room, the weight room, and the equipment room. The nature of this conversation was injuries sustained by players during the season and a general dissatisfaction with the team's equipment. Remember, this is the time of year when many overuse injuries manifest themselves and new injuries tend to mount. Late in every football season, injuries often force key players to miss practice time and/or games.

As I sat in Moore's office, I sensed he viewed me as an outsider. He recognized that Sparky Woods and I had been very close. Moore also knew I was an Appalachian State alum and was very protective of the university. His staff blasted the previous staff in his initial team meeting saying: "You have to be able to get fourth downs in the fourth quarter and put games away." This was a direct dig at the previous team and staff, and it bothered me. I think the comments and attitudes bothered the players more than it did me indicated by the exodus of players from the program. (I should also note, it is normal for players to leave in the months following a new hire due to comfort with the previous staff or discomfort with the new coach.) He was exploiting one of the team's shortcomings and attacking the previous staff and players without giving any credit for the team's accomplishments. I recall one of Moore's assistant coaches saying the staff would not demand the team's respect, but earn it. Nothing was further from the truth. The players had a remarkable relationship with the previous staff, and now it was gone. The new staff was steeped in Texas football and very abrasive to Appalachian and its culture.

Jim Garner, Appalachian's athletic director also was from Texas, and he embraced this change. Jim was disappointed in Sparky Woods' departure to the University of South Carolina. However, Jim had to know deep down in his heart of hearts, this was a move Sparky had to make as there was no comparison to the program or possibilities when comparing Appalachian State to South Carolina. It could also have been said, if Jim Garner had the opportunity to move to a Division I school as the athletic director, he too would have made the move. It is just business.

Moore's new staff was attempting to bring a new mentality to Appalachian State and it had a great plan, but it still made for a very difficult transition period. Chip Sigmon, the director of strength and conditioning, and I met with Moore again to hear all his complaints about why we did things we did. Chip and I were good friends and lucky to have each other in those difficult days. I also reached out to associate athletic director Roachel Laney. He quickly referred me to Garner to gauge support from his end. Garner was supportive of both of us and reminded us that we ultimately worked for him. Chip already was looking to move, and I was quickly assessing my options.

In the coming days, there was the expected departure of players to other programs. This is not unusual with any coaching change. The feelings I had were felt by a lot of players. A few key players at Appalachian State—quarterback Bobby Fuller, offensive center Jay Killen, and defensive back Rocky Clay—followed their former coach to South Carolina, where fans questioned whether those players could make the transition from mid-level football to the "big time." In retrospect, the confrontations with Moore were part of the process as he established his team and his style of managing that team at Appalachian State.

Sigmon has certainly done well for himself since he left Boone. I was naive enough to think he and I would work together forever. Appalachian was our own little piece of heaven back in those days. Chip and his wife, Michelle, relocated to Charlotte, North Carolina, near his Kannapolis roots. He is a strength and conditioning specialist certified by the National Strength and Conditioning Association. When he moved to Charlotte, he became the strength and conditioning coach for the Charlotte Hornets of the NBA. He held that position for twelve years.

By March of 1990 I had the opportunity to reunite with Sparky Woods at South Carolina. I had a great affinity for him and we had become good friends. We had even roomed together previously while on Appalachian State road trips. Unfortunately, Sparky never turned the corner at South Carolina. His five teams from 1989 to 1993 won twenty-four games, lost twenty-eight and tied three. The highlights of his stay in Columbia were a couple of wins over the nationally ranked Georgia teams. Otherwise, it was difficult to argue his dismissal and the subsequent hiring of Brad Scott as head coach.

Odd as it sounds, *The State* newspaper certainly helped with the hiring of Scott. He was an offensive line coach and recruiting coordinator at Florida State prior to coming to South Carolina. Every Monday, *The State* ran a recruiting story, and it seemed like Scott was mentioned more for the recruiting of South Carolina's top high school players than the University of South Carolina's own coaches. While at Florida State, Scott led the recruiting charge and did a marvelous job mining South Carolina's best talent. Those players included Peter Boulware, a linebacker out of Columbia who became an All-American at Florida State and enjoyed a lengthy NFL career. In recruiting and signing some of South Carolina's finest players, Scott became very popular and a football coaching icon in the state.

When Brad was hired, I quickly realized I had never been around a coach who was so family-oriented. Brad's experience in the Florida State program and tradition was evident. His years of working under the watchful eye of Coach Bobby Bowden, who preached family and had tremendous Christian values, impressed the people around him.

Brad and Darryl Scott had two young children. Brad was in his mid-30s at the time he came to South Carolina. He was a very warm guy to be around. The first time I met Brad was at Williams-Brice Stadium. Athletic director Mike McGee was giving Brad and Mark Richt a tour of the football stadium facilities. Richt was the offensive coordinator at Florida State before later becoming the head coach at Georgia.

Brad immediately assembled a quality staff of assistant coaches. One of the knocks on Sparky Woods at South Carolina was that he did not have an NCAA Division I quality staff because he brought his entire staff from Appalachian State. That was a sensitive area to me because I also was an Appalachian descendant.

In keeping with the family atmosphere, each staff meeting began with a devotion conducted by a member of Scott's staff. The assignment rotated around the staff room and no one was required to participate—it was purely voluntary. His faith was an important part of his life, and he let others know it was important without pushing it on them. All the assistant coaches had the opportunity to present prayer and devotion before the meetings began. Some coaches worried about the devotion more than game preparation. I always liked it and thought it was great way to start a staff meeting.

Brad entertained a lot of recruits at his home and preferred to involve his staff, including the nine assistants, the strength coach, myself and the equipment manager. He really enjoyed hosting recruits at his home, which was remodeled specifically to be a head coach's house. South Carolina fan LaDane Owens, a custom home builder and remodeler did an incredible job of transforming Brad and Darryl's home to an entertainment and hosting mecca for prospective college football players. There was plenty of room for socializing and game playing.

Brad probably advanced the South Carolina program further than many of its fans are willing to recognize. His first team topped off a 6-5 regular season with a 24-21 victory over West Virginia in the Carquest Bowl. It marked the first bowl win in South Carolina's history.

However, he could not quite turn the corner and his record after five seasons stood at 23-32-1, including a 1-10 season in 1998 which resulted in him being fired from his job.

Lou Holtz replaced Brad Scott, and the hiring was a huge deal when announced. Holtz was an icon, having already won a national championship at Notre Dame and experienced success everywhere he had coached. He was very popular on television, a standup comedian and a personable man. He was handsomely compensated as a speaker and a highly coveted member of the Washington Speaker's Bureau.

Our fans were excited about the new coach. They were so true to their eternal optimism and were already planning for the next Christmas and bowl season. They forgot we had a lot of work to do and players to recruit to our down-trodden program. Mike McGee had attracted a high profile coach and we finished our first season with a 0-11 record, extending our losing streak to twenty-one games! The person the public did not see was the one who was intimidating to others: staff, players, and even the media. Because of that, his first season at South Carolina was miserable for everyone, aided by the fact that the football team did not win a single game that season.

The routine was pretty much the same. Every day in the staff room, someone would get their back side eaten apart by Holtz. The coaches banded together and helped each other with support. If he attacked someone else, you knew your day was coming. It seemed like everyone except equipment manager Chris Matlock was on the receiving end of Holtz's wrath. Holtz spared no one, and probably was hardest on his son, Skip.

Years after Lou departed, I received a high compliment from one of his players. He told me I was the only person who would stand up to Holtz. I recall one week we were attempting to find out if we were going to a movie on Friday night before a home game. Lou often would change plans at the last minute. So, if we had a bad week, we may not even know by Thursday if we were going to a movie on Friday. I would ask Skip, who then would defer to Clifford Snow, the director of football operations, and we would discuss a strategy to get the information. No one wanted to ask Lou about it because it would upset him. I had to know about the movie because I was the one who had to schedule and reschedule events. Usually, it ended up with me asking Lou and enduring one of his patented tirades.

Bowl preparation with Holtz was a trip to hell and back for players. It was tough, tough, tough two-a-days. We worked hard before we went to the bowl. When we got there, it was not party time and certainly no vacation reward for an outstanding season. We got ready and were polished. He prepared the team to win, and that is why South Carolina experienced such great bowl success under Holtz. He prepared his team and his staff well for bowl games and the result was back-to-back Outback Bowl wins over Ohio State.

Lou was temperamental and moody. You just did not know what to expect from him on any day. Early in the week, he was very difficult to be around. He would come in the staff room and just tear everything apart, challenge people, rip you up one side and down the other, then go back to his office and you would not see him again until practice. He would meet with the offense if he met with any part of the team. When he arrived on that practice field, it was his stage and it was where he performed. He mastered the art of tearing his team down early in the week of a game, telling them how bad, sorry and inept they were, and by game time, he would have them thinking they could beat the Green Bay Packers.

Holtz often talked about leadership and what made a leader. He said leadership was the ability to set goals accepted by a group and develop a plan. If you want to be a leader, you must develop followers, he said. You cannot make a person be a leader. It has to be inherent in what they are doing. He talked about being visionary, executing a plan, believing in goals and objectives in the organization and being able to meet those goals.

As a result, he had a tremendous ability to mold people and get teams working together. Holtz did an unbelievable job getting people on the same page, developing a plan and following his plan. He talked about those words: Trust, commitment and care. Are you someone I can trust? Are you committed to me, our team and our excellence? Do you care about your teammates? Do you care about our objectives?

He pushed these principles and he worked those words daily. There is a reason Holtz gets paid high sums of money by corporations to address their companies. The principles he taught his teams are the same principles that make both marriages and businesses successful. That's why he pushed so hard. He always said he wanted to make practices so difficult that players would better appreciate the games.

What a contrast again in coaching styles and personalities from the change of head coaches when Steve Spurrier replaced Holtz. The first time the team was introduced to Spurrier, he addressed the team with his vision and goals. Following the meeting, he stood at the door and shook every player's hand as they departed.

Steve was easy to work with as a head coach. He was not happy go lucky, but you could definitely say he was much more passive. Spurrier's famous quote was "we will practice and play with those that are out there." This was the truth. There was never any pressure from him to get players on the field, however the athletic training staff took great pride in trying to get all players ready to take the field within their limits.

Under Holtz, I dreaded giving him an injury report. Any injury made him believe I did not want to win and he would challenge me on that. Spurrier was so different from Holtz. He took the laid back approach and wanted to make sure players were ready to return to play.

Spurrier was hired in December and our winter workouts followed shortly. As we were preparing for our spring practice, we had a player from Sumter who had a stress fracture in his lower leg. We told the player if he continued to have problems, a bone scan would be needed. We received results from the bone scan on Sunday and the doctor told me to call the report to Spurrier. I called to say the player had a stress fracture and we were going to rest him for three weeks and re-evaluate his situation. This was seven or eight days before the start of spring practice. On the other end of the telephone line, Spurrier said, "I don't believe it. Florida is going to beat Kentucky." He was watching a basketball game and was fine with the report. He made it known he was going to coach only the kids who were available. This is so opposite from Holtz.

As I reflect on the coaches I dealt with, I think today's brand sets a better example for their players. Spurrier is perhaps the best example. He works out daily and stays in excellent shape. He eats proper foods and demands that his players do the same.

He tries to play mind games. Players see through the tactics. You don't change spots on a leopard. Coaches of the past only cared about winning. Not much else.

So, it is easy to see how an athletic trainer can develop a professional relationship with the head football coach, a relationship that develops into one of mutual respect and admiration. Face it, we get close to the coaches, closer in fact than the student-athletes or administrators.

Athletic trainers win and lose with the teams. They share in the jubilation of bowl victories as well as in the sorrow of lost jobs.

I recall one visit in Coach Holtz's stadium office on November 6, 2004. We had just defeated Arkansas in a key game, 35-32, a win that assured—we thought—South Carolina of playing a bowl game.

Nevertheless, following the Arkansas game rumors were flying about Coach Holtz's future and whether he was done at South Carolina. He was not one to talk about personal and especially personnel matters, however everyone on the football staff heard the rumors, and all the assistants were talking. It sometimes seemed like those of us on the staff knew the least. Little did I know that those people on the outside either knew something the rest of us did not, or the rumors were starting to come to fruition.

As I finished my post-game report to Holtz, he asked me to sit down. I did, though this was not the norm for our post-game visit. He lit his pipe, and commenced to tell me he was not sure what he was going to do, but he appreciated all I had done for him, his wife, and his players. He said he appreciated the way our medical staff took care of situations. This was so surreal, as Holtz is the toughest guy I have ever dealt with. But there is no one I ever performed for, or worked harder for, than him. He had that kind of influence on his staff and players. It is hard to explain. I guess you just had to be there.

Holtz said he was not sure what was going to happen in the coming days, but he would certainly be supportive of me and my work. As odd as this talk was, I certainly knew the end was in sight for him as South Carolina's head coach.

I left his office numb. As I walked down the hall, I opened the players' locker room door and headed through the lockers passing by the last of the players returning from the post-game press conference. The walk was much like the players take when they enter the field to the playing of "2001: A Space Odyssey" with all the artificial smoke serving like fog. While I was not pumped up like the players were in pre-game, I certainly felt I was walking in a fog.

I opened the door to the athletic training room, turned left and walked by the six treatment tables directly into my office. All the casting supplies and general shrapnel from the day's game were awaiting Dee Dee Harris and Sarah Myers for the post-game cleanup.

I packed my briefcase and exited through the locker room toward Gate 5. I decided to walk under the south end zone bleachers to the east side of the stadium where my lovely wife Susan parked with the football coaches' wives. Susan is the best entertainer in the world, but this day I was not in the mood for entertaining. We mingled with friends for a few minutes, gathered up the kids and headed home. Later that night I shared my post-game visit specifics with Susan, and she was as shocked as I was.

There are many ups and downs in the business of being a head athletic trainer, but that was a rock-bottom day for me.

I was a Coach Holtz fan. He was tough to deal with but delivered measurable results. When I visit my dentist (team dentist Joel Johnson) or go into a physician's office in town, Lou Holtz memorabilia still decorates the walls.

Like it or not, he is a part of Gamecock fans memories.

Dr. Rod's
Treatment Plan

DRUG TESTING

Drug testing has become a very common component of sports since 1985. Many administrators have approached drug testing as a deterrent to experimentation with drug use. The thought is that if behavior can successfully be modified for the four to five years a student is engaged in the program, that some form of learning takes place.

Once a program is written, it must be representative of the institution, school or league specific to participants. The program must be embraced philosophically by the leadership; and must be addressed from a legal perspective. Also important is the selection of a competent lab to provide both the screening of specimen and confirmation testing of positive screens.

Generally, substances selected for screening include substances identified by the Athletics Department or the NCAA as purporting to be performance enhancing or potentially harmful to the health, safety or well-being of student-athletes, or that are illegal under applicable federal or state law. Student-athletes are generally reminded they are responsible for the presence of any banned or illegal substance in their body, and are to refrain from areas of risk. The following substances are prohibited from use and are from the program I coordinated at the University of South Carolina:

1. Illegal drugs, including but not limited to, marijuana, phencyclidine, stimulants (e.g., amphetamines, ecstasy and cocaine), and hallucinogens (e.g., LSD).
2. Anabolic steroids (e.g., Anavar and Dianabol) and similar growth enhancing or performance enhancing substances.
3. Prescription or over-the-counter drugs not medically indicated.
4. Drugs banned by the NCAA.
5. Diuretics and "masking agents" designed to prevent the detection of drug and alcohol use, not otherwise medically indicated.
6. Alcohol.

The NCAA's list of banned drugs may change during the academic year. An updated list may be found on the NCAA web site (www.ncaa.org) and it is the responsibility of a student-athlete to make sure any substance they ingest be clean of any banned substance. Sport federations produce lists of nutritional supplements which are "clean." A student-athlete is accountable for any and all banned substances found in their body.

The costs for drug testing worldwide approach $30 million. The drug tests are designed to detect and deter abuse of performance-enhancing drugs by competitors. It has been feared that some athletes may initiate drug use due to the feeling they had to use the drug to "keep up." Most commonly, drug testing has been conducted by urinalysis.

Some athletes will try and beat the testing. When athletes know when a drug test will occur, they can prepare for it and thereby neutralize the effects of drug testing on the use of performance enhancing drugs and/or masking agents. The best way to maintain drug test integrity is to have as little lead time between the notification and actual collection process. Testing should be year-round so that administrative practices do not become cyclical and predictable relative to test procedures. One of the key components to successful drug testing programs is the spontaneity of tests.

Drug Testing Procedure

Relative to the drug testing procedure, the most important facet is the chain of custody and maintaining privacy of results. Once the athlete begins the collection process, it is imperative that the test administrator and collectors follow a rigidly written protocol and follow the process with no deviation. The specimen and athlete should be monitored from the start of the collection until the final packaging of the specimen and release to the transfer/shipping process of the lab.

It is imperative that a credible lab with federal registration and credentials be utilized for testing samples. During my tenure, we utilized the services of Aegis Labs in Nashville, Tennessee. The team at Aegis was very attentive to the athletic process. The toxicologists studied this process and further produced technology that allowed for "zero tolerance" testing. Their testing technology was much more specific than the federal standards which were embraced by the NCAA. For marijuana, the NCAA screens specimen for positivity at a level of 50 ng/mL and specimen are confirmed at 15 ng/mL. Aegis offers screening at a level of 20 ng/mL and confirmation at a level of 5 ng/mL. This lower or "zero tolerance" testing results in great positivity rates of specimen while the NCAA or federal levels are an alarming thirty-five percent of tests!

In summary, the testing process is very important and all protocols must be followed. The results should be analyzed and reviewed by a Medical Review Officer, specifically trained to interpret drug test results.

David Rodwell Walters II's first birthday, pictured with Dad. (June 29, 1958)

Rod Walters, athletic training student, Appalachian State University. (September, 1976)

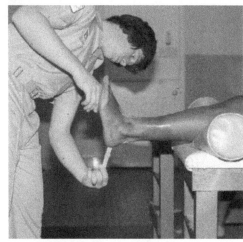

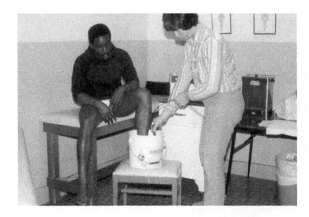

It was common for athletic training students to drop by the athletic training room to help out with treatments between classes during my undergraduate days at Appalachian State University. I am pictured giving Jarvis Moore some underwater ultrasound for a sprained ankle. (November, 1978)

The Appalachian State University athletic training room was a far stretch from the state-of-the art facilities the Mountaineers have today. This is a view of the treatment area as my classmates and I experienced it in the 1970s. Facility upgrades are one of the major differences one can see in college athletics today. The influx of money has certainly paid off.

My freshman year at Appalachian State University, I was the student athletic trainer assigned to the wrestling team. Alfred Ash was a wrestler from Gastonia, NC, and I was caring for a nosebleed sustained during a home match in January, 1976. (photo courtesy of Dr. Evan Ashby)

In 1977, Appalachian State traveled to Greenville, SC to play Furman University. Obviously something was happening in the stands, as my roommate John Keeton (83), our good friend, Andy Goins (43), and I observe.

Lenoir-Rhyne College was my first job. I had a staff of a couple of students. I loved Lenoir-Rhyne College and thought I would be there for the remainder of my career. I am helping a woozy Wade Barrett (61) from the field.

The talent pool of the Lenoir-Rhyne College student-athletes was not as high as Appalachian. One player was a tremendous talent. Glenn Ford transferred to Lenoir-Rhyne from the University of Tennessee. Glenn had played for Lenoir-Rhyne coach Henry VanSant at Greensboro Grimsley High School in Greensboro, NC. John Worley and I help him off the field.

I have said, an athletic trainer's best friend is his team physician. There is no bond in sports medicine that is more important than the relationship between the team physician and the athletic trainer. Dr. Benny Goodman (right) was the team physician for Lenoir-Rhyne College and certainly taught me so much in those formative years.

141

During my tenure as head athletic trainer at Appalachian State University, I traveled with both the football and men's basketball teams, as did many of my peers. This was a great basketball staff with head coach Kevin Cantwell (kneeling) and the ever-funny Gerry Vallancourt (hand to chin). Today, Gerry is the voice of the NBA New Orleans Hornets.

During my Appalachian days, Craig Denegar (left) and Dr. Evan Ashby (right) team up to help care for this official who definitely kept his eye on the ball! This was another Southern Conference win during the 1988 season for the Mountaineers against The Citadel.

My first football staff at the University of South Carolina. Front row: Anna Beatty, Laura Powell, Rod Walters, unidentified, and Beth Walters. Back row: TJ Jackson, Jeff Parsons, Scottie Patton, Bill Webb, and Jay Green.

University of South Carolina, Football Media Day, 1994.

This picture was taken prior to the Gamecocks defeat of the Kentucky Wildcats, September 24, 1994 in Lexington, KY. Pictured on the front row is son of Coach Brad Scott, John Scott; Second Row: Archie Manning and F.D. Mudd; Third Row: Graduate assistant Lee Gray, Erika Jackson and Stacy Baynum; and Back Row: Dr. Bob Peele, Rod Walters, Dr. Steve Youmans, and graduate assistant John Singerling.

We all have people who mean so much to us professionally. None meant more to me than these three who were my early teachers at the North Carolina Coaches Association's Student Trainer Clinics. I started attending these in the summer of 1972. Left to right: Phil Callicutt and Warren Ariail, who were early instructors, and clinic director, Al Proctor. Picture taken in 2006 at the North Carolina Athletic Trainers Association's Pioneer in Athletic Training recognition.

The facilities at South Carolina were impressive to me when I first started working there in 1990. I quickly realized the vast inadequacies we had. Most of our competition in the SEC was light-years ahead. With the recent renovation of the Williams-Brice Stadium facilities (2010), the Gamecocks are now competitive within the conference. But the sports facilities arms race never stops.

Kent Atkins was one of my first graduate assistants at South Carolina. He had been an athletic training student at Appalachian. Today he is the assistant athletic director at Lander University. Kent has worked at Lander since he graduated from South Carolina.

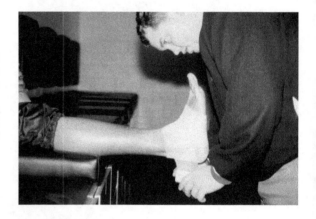

This picture depicts the injury to Andre Goodman's knee during a game at Williams-Brice Stadium in September, 1997. (TV still courtesy of South Carolina videographers)

144

This injury hurt me. Andre Goodman was blocked by a tight end from Georgia, and tore all the major ligaments in his knee. Following successful surgery, and a grueling rehabilitation, he returned to play, and enjoyed a career in the NFL ten years after his injury. (TV still courtesy of South Carolina videographers)

One of my proudest professional accomplishments has been the development of the Velocity. This off-the-shelf ankle-foot orthosis was my idea based on the care we provided Duce Staley for ankle injury in the fall of 1997.

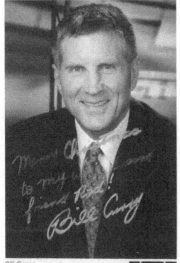

Bill Curry

ESPN

Years ago I started wearing dress shirts and ties on the sidelines. This was not the norm for athletic trainers, but I wanted to portray a professional image. Bill Curry was a commentator for ESPN, and called me his "best dressed athletic trainer."

1997 NATA Board of Directors. Front row: Carl Krein, Jim Gallaspee, President Kent Falb, Tony Marek, Rod Walters, and D.C. Colt. Back row: Sam Booth, Sandy Miller, Jim Whitesell, Pete Carlon, Steve Bair, Bill Lyons, and Sue Stanley-Greene. (Photo courtesy of NATA)

I had some great student-athletes to care for during my tenure at three different colleges and universities. None was any better person than Joey Unitas, the son of NFL Hall of Fame quarterback, Johnny Unitas. Joey was a great "team" player, and always appreciated by his teammates. Joey is receiving his standard hot pack and electrical muscle stimulation treatment prior to his required weight room workout during the 1998 season. (Photo courtesy of Keith McGraw, USC Media Relations)

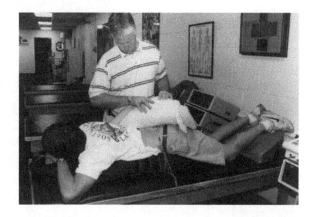

My work with the Southeastern Conference football officials was a labor of love. After our defeat of Mississippi State at Williams-Brice Stadium, a couple of the officials joined us for some post-game fellowship. Pictured from left to right: James Bing, David Walters, Susan Walters, Rod Walters, Ryan Walters, and Doug Linebarger. The football officials were very good to me, but they were great to my boys. Both David and Ryan took their turn at running timeouts to the game officials and established some neat relationships through the years.

146

Following clinical sessions, participants at the Donjoy Athletic Training and Sports Medicine meeting are treated to a sailing cruise in the the the San Diego harbor. On this trip in 2003, Susan and I shared a boat with Phil and April Hedrick (North Carolina State University), Denny and Linda Miller (Purdue University), Steve Cole (College of William and Mary), and Mike Ryan (Jacksonville Jaguars).

The Donjoy meeting provides what many of my peers grade as one of the best education meetings they attend each year. I have been privileged to work with Donjoy as the coordinator of the educational portion of the meeting since the late 1990s. Pictured above is the 2010 session held in Park City, UT. Tim Neal (Syracuse University), Scott McGonagle (Miami University), and Phil Hedrick (North Carolina State University) listen attentively to the lecture. Not a bad setting for good clinical education.

I have been coordinating the educational portion of the Donjoy Athletic Training and Sports Medicine meeting dating to 1998. Here, Alex Brown (classmate from Appalachian State University) mingles with Scott Anderson and others.

147

Picture Day 2001 Outback Bowl - Little did we know that we were about to upset Ohio State University the next day, January 2, 2001. One of my fond memories was some twenty-four hours after this shot, enjoying a celebratory cigar with Phil Hedrick and Jarod Grace. I wish we had pictures commemorating that event. Both of these guys have gone on to great careers as athletic trainers and family men.

I admired many of our players, and none more than Phil Petty, the quarterback on South Carolina's two Outback Bowl champion teams of 2000 and 2001. You should understand that Coach Holtz put tremendous pressure on his quarterback. Petty handled Holtz's pressure well.

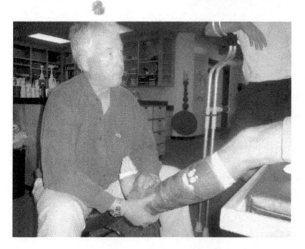

I got some first-hand training in splinting and casting during my work at South Carolina. This has provided great dividends today as I conduct seminars for 3M in orthopedic clinics, hospitals and athletic training rooms across the country. This was a fairly common scene in our athletic training room as we combined cold therapy with a non-weight bearing cast following an ankle sprain. Our goal was to rest this injury.

I love seeing former players. Corey Miller played at South Carolina in the early 1990s, and went on to a successful NFL career. Many of our former players would grace the sidelines on game days. Corey and I exchange greetings as I return to the field at halftime of a 2005 game.

One thing I loved about athletic training was the contact with the players. I guess it makes little sense that I sought to move more into administration, because as I did that, my contact with the student-athletes decreased significantly. As an administrator, I only dealt with problems—bills were not paid, injury not doing well, failed drug test. Here I am taping Darrell Shropshire at the taping station outside my office.

In 2001, the University of South Carolina participated in the Outback Bowl game versus Ohio State University. As the boys boarded the plane, they were given a tour of the cockpit. The events of 9/11 forever changed team travel as it had an impact on our country's security. I doubt this access would ever be available today.

149

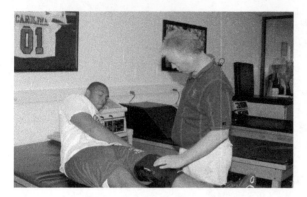

Athletic trainers deal with players when they are at their lowest point. Eric Stroman and I discuss his progress with his injured knee in the Williams-Brice Stadium athletic training room in 2004.

I am appreciative of honors and awards. It goes without saying, these are a testament to the fine personnel one works with. Some great staff members and friends join me to celebrate my NATA Hall of Fame (2005) induction in Indianapolis, IN. Picture from left to right are Phil Hedrick, Kent Atkins, Rod Walters, Brian Moore, John Singerling, and Greg Harmon.

Appalachian State was a special place for me. My mentor, Ron Kanoy is pictured here with me and classmate Mark White. This picture was taken during the North Carolina Pioneers in Athletic Training award recognition during Mark's tenure as president of the North Carolina Athletic Trainers Association in 2006.

Pictures become more and more important as we grow older. I hate to have my picture taken, but certainly enjoy seeing my beautiful wife, Susan.

Brian Moore, a good friend and senior executive with Donjoy, has been so supportive of my professional career. We are enjoying an outing at the Anaheim Angels baseball park as part of the 2007 NATA Meeting and Clinical Symposium.

In 2007 I delved full-time into the consulting business; I have always loved the business side of my work. One phase of my work has been conducting seminars on best practices in athletic training; leveraging the relationships I have developed over the years with vendors.

Susan had a special birthday in 2010, and I surprised her with a birthday party in Key West, FL. It was fun arranging travel around the kids' college classes for this special weekend. David, Bradley, and Ryan and I enjoy a cigar.

Some of the friends who joined us in Key West for Susan's special birthday party in February, 2010. Pictured here are Tera and Brian Moore, Greg and Erin Harmon, Susan, and me.

All our children attended the University of South Carolina, except Ryan. He was probably the biggest South Carolina fan in our house, but decided he wanted to study civil engineering at Clemson. (I must admit, writing those checks to that school up the road was not easy.) Susan and I hosted a dinner for Ryan on the eve of his graduation in May, 2011. I am pictured here with my long-time friend and Lenoir-Rhyne roommate Robert Barkley, the director of admissions at Clemson.

My oldest son David was married to Rebecca Seibert on March 6, 2010. They met on the football practice field. Rebecca was an athletic training student assigned to football. She was working with the running backs under Coach Madre Hill. David was the student manager assigned to Coach Hill, so the story starts there!

Seeing our kids graduate from college has been a tremendous honor (and relief) for Susan and me. We are very proud parents.

Ryan Michael Walters: Bachelor of Science in Civil Engineering, Clemson University, May 13, 2011.

David Rodwell Walters III: Bachelor of Arts in Journalism and Mass Communications, University of South Carolina, May 7, 2009.

Allison Erin Cogdill: Bachelor of Science in Fashion Merchandising, University of South Carolina, August 7, 2010.

The Walters Family Portrait, Christmas, 2011. (left to right Rebecca holding Grace, David and Fender. Second Row: Bradley, Susan, Max and Rod, and Ryan. Back Row: Allison. The theme for this picture was for everyone to sport their college affiliations. (Photo courtesy of David R. Walters III)

The David R. Walters family. Front row: Bradley Cogdill (step-son), Ryan Walters (son), and Sarah Walters (niece, daughter of Stuart and Beth). Row two: Garrett Kellerhals, Allison Cogdill (step-daughter) and Beth Walters (sister-in-law, wife of Stuart). Row three: David Walters (son), Rebecca (daughter-in-law and wife of David) and Grace Walters (grand daughter), Tommy Walters (nephew, son of Louis and Susan), Susan F. Walters (wife), Susan E. Walters (niece, daughter of Stuart and Beth). Back Row: Louis Walters (brother), Susan G. Walters (wife of Louis), David R. Walters (dad), Christine Walters (mom), Rod Walters and Stuart Walters (brother). (Photo courtesy of David R. Walters III)

154

CHAPTER 6

FANS, OR FANATICS?

T he fanaticism for college athletics amazes me. Many fans will give their last dollar to support their college teams, and it is the reason they give millions each year to support athletic programs. I saw this first hand during my days at South Carolina. Fans gave fervently to the Gamecock Club, the booster organization that raises money and provides financial backing for South Carolina athletics as other support groups do at most schools.

Fans numbering in the thousands upon thousands annually pay Gamecock Club dues, purchase season tickets, pay seat-licensing fees and parking fees just to show their loyalty to their teams. I was aware of this fanatical support for teams during my days at Lenoir-Rhyne and Appalachian State. While equally fervent at those smaller schools, the scale of fanaticism is just not the same as at NCAA Division I-A schools, especially in the Southeastern Conference.

South Carolina's first two football games of the 1990 season drew in excess of seventy thousand fans at Williams-Brice Stadium in Columbia. That was expected. Then the team went on the road to play against Virginia Tech in Blacksburg, Virginia. To my surprise, of the forty two thousand fans on hand that day, ten thousand made the drive north from Columbia. It was the same the following week at Georgia Tech in

Atlanta where, again, South Carolina fans made up nearly one-quarter of the forty six thousand fans at the game.

I still get goose bumps when the South Carolina football team enters the field at Williams-Brice Stadium in Columbia to the playing of "2001: A Space Odyssey." It is one of the better entrances in college football with players running through smoke, the song blasting over the public address system and usually more than eighty thousand fans cheering their team on. Today, the blaring of "Sandstorm" over the public address system electrifies South Carolina fans.

Whether it is fans or athletic trainers, I am always enamored by those involved in athletics. Most amazing to me are the one-hundred or so student-athletes who show up every fall practice on campuses across the country to try out for football as non-scholarship walk-ons. In most cases, these are ordinary students who just want to be part of the team. They receive no remuneration. They lift weights. They attend meetings. They put on pads in football and take hits, run wind sprints and sweat through the August and early September heat just like scholarship student-athletes. They too must maintain the same grade requirements of all team members. They miss evening meals because practices conclude after the cafeteria closes and are not eligible for the training table meals afforded scholarship student-athletes.

I often have wondered why students "walk-on" instead of enjoying the college life without all the extra work. My guess has been that these students want structure. They want to be told what to do with their time, and be directed about their schedule and activities. These same students often experience much better academic performances during the season versus semesters with increased free time. Since coaches and academic staff monitor class attendance, study hall participation, etc., it generally correlates to improved academic performance.

It breaks down this way for me when answering why students "walk on" to teams:

1. They want to be part of an athletic team.
2. They have a passion for the sport.

3.   They seek positive role models.

4.   They like the feeling of family associated with a team.

5.   They crave discipline.

It really is no different for athletic trainers. We get into the business because we want to be associated with athletics, just like our fans. We all want to be part of a team, part of a family.

I view athletic training as more than a job. It is a calling. That is why so many athletic trainers are so in love with their job, and why they pour so much of themselves into their work. This passion also can be costly, as they give so much time and love to helping others that they have little time for their own families.

In the early 1990s, Brad Scott and his staff attracted a kid from Tallahassee, Florida. Garrick Taylor was a very respectful student-athlete, and was always in the right place at the appropriate time. As good a person as Garrick was, he was not the fastest linebacker in his group. He was a kid you could not help but be drawn to. He had fine values, and obviously he had been raised the right way. In 1995, Garrick was a member of the special teams purely from his hard work. To his dismay, he sustained a knee injury requiring surgical reconstruction. Garrick's hard work was his trademark at South Carolina. He attacked rehabilitation just like he did his schoolwork—aggressively. Garrick was never on an academic casualty list. He never missed a breakfast check. When we made him an appointment for rehabilitation and treatment, if the scheduled time was 7:15 a.m., he would be there at 6:45. This was such a difficulty for our medical staff to comprehend. We were accustomed to student-athletes arriving one hour late for scheduled appointments. He was never a problem and always attentive to details.

I guess it is no surprise that Taylor's Pine Straw evolved from weekend sales of pickup trucks driving through neighborhoods in Lexington and Columbia, South Carolina delivering pine straw to residents, to a thriving lawn product business that offers clients varieties of mulch, stone, children's swings and outdoor fortresses, custom rock work, and custom fountains and water features. He has branched out to the low country of South Carolina with an office in Bluffton, South Carolina.

Garrick Taylor's values, that were taught at an early age are continuing to be honed as a Christian, a husband, a father, and least important as a businessman. His example is excellent for his former teammates to see.

When I think of the complete or ideal non-scholarship student-athlete, Garrick always comes to mind. Probably more important, when I reflect on the first-class student-athletes, I also think of Garrick. Few people around South Carolina athletics in the 1990s are surprised at what a success he has been in life.

Fanaticism can be positive. We see this with million-dollar compensation packages to coaches of high-profile sports in the NCAA's mega-conferences. Perhaps fanaticism begets compensation.

In the wake of corruption associated with Operation Lost Trust (Wikipedia, 2011) within South Carolina state government there were numerous changes in the way business was conducted in South Carolina by the time I arrived at the university in 1990. The transgressions of a few state legislators drastically changed compensation state employees could receive—even if legitimate compensation for credible and accountable work. One important change was that every state employee—from the governor to university's athletic trainer—could not receive compensation from any agency without it being evaluated and reported to his or her employer. This was a big deal in those days because coaches were compensated with outside shoe and apparel contracts. Equipment managers and head athletic trainers were compensated either financially or with an allotment of equipment from apparel companies.

Before the state ethics regulations, it was easy for athletic administrators to say "no" to the equipment manager while the head coaches of sports were approved. The head coach of a sport who was winning games and bringing national attention and money to the university, was a more difficult decision. Ah, the power of fanaticism.

Each year, all athletic department employees were required by the NCAA to submit documentation for outside compensation. These forms were administered by the school's compliance office on behalf of the NCAA. I submitted documentation for outside compensation in 2006 as required. These amounts were minimal compared to what coaches received for outside income, such as speaking engagements, endorsements, radio and television contracts, as well as shoe and clothing contracts. Much of the coaches' income was actually routed through non-university entities. My numbers were significant for me relative to my salary and were a source of income that allowed me to do some things for my family I would not normally do.

A couple of weeks after submitting my 2006 documents, I was visited at my home by Dr. Jeff Guy, an employee of the University of South Carolina who was assigned to the department of University Orthopedics. He worked directly with the athletic department in overseeing medical care for our four-hundred-fifty student-athletes. His visit was very strange. I could tell he was uncomfortable with the conversation, but he did state that Eric Hyman, South Carolina's athletic director, was shocked by the amount of my outside income. My documentation was complete and included consulting agreements established for writing for www.coachillustrated.com (the on-line website created in 2000 by the late Coach Joe Paterno) and consulting with Donjoy, as well as royalties for braces I had developed with Donjoy.

Most curious to me was why my personal finances were being shared with a team physician with no administrative or supervisory assignments over me. I reported directly to Charles Waddell, an associate athletic director. Charles played football and basketball at the University of North Carolina. He had previous positions as the athletic director at Fayetteville State University, an administrative position with the Carolina Panthers, and the Big Ten Conference. Little did I know that the ramifications of this visit with Jeff would enable me to quickly realize how college athletics was changing at South Carolina, and that maybe I needed to rethink my future. This was the beginning of my thought to move in a different direction professionally, from athletic training to consulting on a full-time basis. This is happening at many colleges across the country today.

For seventeen years at South Carolina, I was an integral cabinet member on Athletic Director Mike McGee's staff. I now felt that, because of my past, I was not a part of the new administration's plans. This is a common occurrence with changes in administration in college athletic departments as well as leadership positions in the business world. This athletic director was obviously getting his healthcare information differently than I was accustomed. I obviously felt undermined.

It had always been my goal to manage my department, as I always had, with all my efforts aimed at maintaining a high standard of care at minimal cost to the athletic department. Sporting events are exciting. I am a fan and especially enjoy watching college football. It amazes me how much money South Carolina fans spend annually on the sport. It has been said many times the number one sport at South Carolina— and at most schools in the southeast, for that matter—is football, the number two sport is spring football, and the number three sport is football recruiting. With Coach Ray Tanner's baseball team winning the national championship in 2010 and 2011, that might have altered the South Carolina athletic landscape some, but not much. With the departure of Eric Hyman, Tanner was chosen as athletic director where he would lead the athletic department.

I always have believed fans do not realize the power of television in college athletics. Billions of dollars are poured into college athletics from TV networks seeking the rights to broadcast games. In return, conferences and schools are getting unprecedented national exposure in football and basketball which is quickly trickling down to the non-revenue sports as well. The recent controversy over conference realignment has challenged college athletics on many fronts. College presidents hide behind "academic integrity" while they review their portfolios and what potential new members to their conference might bring to the table. The money in sports today is unbelievable.

Believe it or not, that exposure also worked with officials in the Southeastern Conference, Atlantic Coast Conference and others. Apparel and shoe companies, such as Nike and Adidas, sought exposure by providing officials in the top-level conferences with shoes and equipment with their logos affixed on material large enough for television cameras to see them.

During my tenure of directing and coordinating the healthcare of Southeastern Conference football officials, part of my goal was to obtain this type of support for the officials from Nike to provide them with good, quality footwear.

In 1993, I was working with Michael Dover, an ACC football official. Michael had sustained an injury and required off-season knee surgery. During his rehabilitation, he inquired about the assistance I had obtained for the SEC group regarding footwear contracts. After several calls to my Nike contacts, they were able to provide assistance to the ACC officials.

During Lou Holtz's tenure as head football coach at South Carolina, I moved the SEC guys from Nike to Adidas due to South Carolina's affiliation with the latter company. These shoe companies were more than happy to assist with this modest investment in exchange for the tremendous television exposure. This continues to be true with the mega-contracts the SEC and ACC recently have signed with CBS and ESPN.

The circle is complete in college athletics. It begins at the top with the fanatical interest in sports such as football and basketball, grows through endorsement contracts for coaches and continues with the national exposure gained through the proliferation of telecasts of just about every sporting event.

Everyone seems to benefit from fanaticism.

I have already shared some experiences about many of my former students and staff members. One of the sharpest guys I ever worked with was John Singerling, who came to me from Michigan State under the recommendation of Jeff Monroe. I had previously hired several of Jeff's students as Michigan State has one of the best undergraduate programs in the country. The school did an excellent job of professional preparation (certification) and also in making sure its graduates understood the duties of an athletic trainer, especially in Division I.

John did not take an easy route for his master's degree. We paid our graduate assistants a stipend, and covered their tuition. John and one of his Michigan State undergraduate classmates, Chip Wise, sought degrees in the school of public health, a very prestigious graduate program at South Carolina. They were not the last of graduate assistants to attend the University of South Carolina, as Michigan State University was a favorite source for candidates. One of John's curriculum requirements was the completion of an internship. I helped John land a position in the office of Chuck Beaman, then the president of Palmetto Baptist, the sister hospital of our medical school hospital.

John did a terrific job, and never left the Palmetto Health System— where today he is president. John is one of those who could say something to you and it would stick. During one casual conversation, we were talking about personnel. He reminded me "the number one reason people leave their place of employment is because they fail to respect who they work for." I remember that conversation as if it were yesterday. I love the things we learn from our students.

Chip Wise completed his work and married his college sweetheart. He initially worked with David Dodge of PHT Services, Ltd. providing a variety of risk management services to South Carolina's healthcare industry. Chip and his family reside in Scottsdale, Arizona and he has worked in the healthcare arena as Director of Business Development with Navigant Consulting since 2008.

Fans at the University of South Carolina are truly fanatical. The day was February 14, 2003, and like every red-blooded male on the northern hemisphere, I had planned a special evening for my sweetheart. Susan and I were joining several other couples and heading to the Kenny Chesney concert that evening. I planned to work out early. This being the week following national signing day, the football staff had a light schedule as we were preparing for spring football practice.

A little before noon, I made my way to the weight room at Williams-Brice Stadium. While on my treadmill, I noticed a young woman on the treadmill to my left. This was odd, as student-athletes are generally not in the weight room at this time of the day. I looked around after my forty-minute jog and noted a large number of strangers working out in the weight room. Quickly, I figured out that these were "invited guests" and not your normal run-of-the-mill people in the weight room. This facility was only for student-athletes, so these guys had to have some power.

I am not one to drop names, but I did have the chance to forge a friendship—at least for one night—with a celebrity. The pieces started to come together. I recognized Kenny Chesney. He and his band were getting their daily workout in South Carolina's weight room facility. I introduced myself and offered my assistance to him and his group during their stay. We exchanged pleasantries. I offered to bring a box of South Carolina athletic gear to him and his band, and told him we had a group of eight coming to his concert. In exchange for the gifts, Chesney offered to meet and greet my group on his bus, but I declined his offer.

Over dinner that evening, I brought the group up to speed on the workout routine for Chesney and his group. But the women in the group were livid that I turned down the offer to meet the band on the bus.

Nevertheless, we were excited about the concert, which was Chesney's *No Shoes, No Shirt, No Problems* tour. A young Keith Urban and the group Montgomery Gentry were the warm up bands.

Around 9 p.m., Chesney and his band took the stage wearing all the gear I had dropped by his bus earlier in the day. About halfway through the concert, Chesney sang an old Conway Twitty song, "I'd Love to Lay You Down," and he looked directly at our group, making eye contact with me and mouthing "thanks for the gear" while giving me a thumbs-up signal.

What a great evening with some great friends.

I have never really been an autograph person. I have never sought a lot of people to have my picture made with, obtain their autograph, or seek sports memorabilia. During my six years on NATA's Board of Directors, the ten board members were treated to backstage access following the annual keynote address by some sports or entertainment celebrities. Those pictures with Bryant Gumbel, John Smoltz, or Cal Ripken have never really excited me.

One missed photo opportunity really frustrates me, and it bothers me more than ever as I think back. My oldest son, David, was an eighth-grader at Lexington Middle School. His class was preparing for a field trip to Washington, D. C. His teachers, Coach Jason Williams and Sally Taylor, invited me to accompany the group to Washington as a chaperone. I already had plans to be in Washington on behalf of the Juvenile Diabetes Research Foundation. I had some additional responsibilities relative to my NATA Board of Director duties. I had a meeting scheduled with Senator Strom Thurmond of South Carolina, to seek his support of stem cell research on behalf of JDRF. I cannot begin to recall the amount of information and memorabilia that was in his office. He was the senior tenured senator at that time, and his office location and its size were much related to tenure. As I sat in his office, the reflections were amazing. He served our state since November 7, 1956 (the year prior to my birth)! When I was in the eighth grade, Wickie Smith required all the students in his Civics class to memorize each of the senators from all fifty states. This was one of his annual traditions. Yes, I remembered one Senator Strom Thurmond from South Carolina.

I will regret this missed photo opportunity for some time. Regardless of your political perspective, Strom Thurmond was a giant.

In 2004, during the Gamecocks' trip to Tuscaloosa, Alabama to face the Crimson Tide, I did seek an autograph. We played that evening on ESPN2, and prior to that game we had a visitor in the locker room to see Coach Holtz. This was nothing out of the ordinary, as traveling with Coach Holtz was like traveling with a rock star. You never knew who would be on the sideline. The list was endless: Tommy Lasorda dropping by the locker room before we took the field in 2001; Jerry Jones having his limousine pull up to our charter flight to greet Holtz during a trip to Little Rock, Arkansas to play the Razorbacks; Harvey Mackay, author of *Swimming with the Sharks*, was a frequent sideline guest; the list could go on. Further, you never knew if you'd have a sideline pass as he commanded quite a few for his fleet of guests. That night, I looked up to see Joe Namath.

Namath did stop by the taping area in the visiting locker room at Bryant-Denny Stadium. We exchanged pleasantries, and I had him autograph my sideline pass from that evening's game. Not sure why I asked Namath for his autograph, but it seemed like the thing to do at the time. He was always beloved by the Crimson Tide faithful, eighty-two thousand strong that night. They were saddened when the Gamecocks defeated the traditional SEC powerhouse 20-3, a big win for the Gamecocks in a down year for the Tide.

Meeting Namath reminded me of another storied event in 1995. It must have been the year of the quarterback. As was our tradition, we were practicing under the lights in Williams-Brice Stadium. Our student-athletes generally had laboratory sessions associated with classes on Mondays, so we would practice in the evening. The extra time was also a big favorite of the coaching staff as they prepared the week's game plan and never-ending film study and review. I would arrange to have dinner catered for all the players and staff. We served this at the stadium, to accommodate class schedules and maximize efficiency of pre-practice taping, position meetings, team meetings, and eventually practice.

Our team had gone through their stretching routine that evening, and I had wandered to the north end- zone to observe a couple of the offensive linemen trying to return following ankle injuries. Excitement was high that evening, as we were coming off a win. This practice, like most of our Monday night practices, was closed to the public. I noticed a couple of people enter the stadium via the player's entrance, adjacent to Gate 5. The man was slouched over, and the kid with him had a slender build, appeared to be around six feet tall. Remember, I am trying to observe this from the north end zone, roughly one-hundred-forty yards away.

As I meandered toward their location, it dawned on me this guy was no ordinary guest. The man was Johnny Unitas. Our football team realized who this guy was, as they were aware of football history. His son, Joey, was visiting South Carolina, and was interested in joining our team as a walk-on.

Joey liked what Brad Scott and his staff showed him, and Johnny Unitas obviously felt comfortable with the staff and team. He was comfortable enough to allow his son to come down from Baltimore, Maryland to attend South Carolina.

Joey was never a problem. He did not expect preferential treatment because of his last name. He did not have the athletic ability his dad possessed, but never complained. No chips on his shoulder, just a great kid.

Some fifteen years later, another student-athlete's parents gave me a copy of Johnny Unitas' biography. John Paul Gillis was a South Carolina football player, as had been his dad. John Paul's parents were very proud to have him playing for the Gamecocks. He encountered a low back injury requiring surgery. I was involved with his rehabilitation and care, and due to the nature of his injury he was placed on medical scholarship because of his inability to return to his pre-injury level of play. His mom and dad gave me the book as a token of their appreciation.

Television games were a big deal in the 1990s. Today's players would think it very odd not to have a conference game televised, but older fans know this just was not the case. In my early days at South Carolina, we enjoyed "entertaining" and "hosting" the television crews. To me, that was college football. Ron Franklin was such an icon. One specific weekend, he reported to our Columbia campus to watch the Thursday walk-through practice. Coach Brad Scott conducted Thursday practice with the team in shorts, T-shirts and football helmets.

Franklin and Gottfried walked around the practice field. They had their routine talk with me to obtain any information of interest relative to injured student-athletes. It was very evident that Franklin had a significant case of laryngitis. I inquired if there was anything our medical team could offer, and he gladly accepted an evaluation by our team physician. He was prescribed some medications. I also encouraged him to get into our steam room which he did.

Ron was very appreciative of the care from our healthcare team. I can truly say I always enjoyed visits with him.

As I reflect, there were many really neat game announcers and sideline reporters—some in the early stages and others in the later parts of their careers including Mike Golic, Jill Arrington, Bill Curry, Michelle Tafoya, and Erin Andrews.

The regular season of 2001 was drawing to a close. November references the time of year where coaches, players, staff, families and all those associated with college football teams get worn down. Again, this is the reason periodization is so important, as we cannot continue to repeat what we do on a daily basis without tearing down and just wearing out.

I received a call on November 7 from Coach Holtz. He was not feeling well, and wanted to see our team physician. I walked him over to his office, and he examined Coach, and ordered some medicine to address his symptoms and complaints. Coach was very tired and did not feel well. We all know how a cold can wear you down and make you feel.

The next morning, we did not have a staff meeting at the normal time. Holtz was not someone you just walked in to visit with, and you certainly did not try to see him when he felt bad. If he was sick, everyone had better watch out. I got a call from Holtz's secretary, Rita Ricard. Rita said he really was not feeling well, and asked if I would come check on him. I went by and had planned to have our team physician see him prior to his afternoon clinic in the Williams-Brice Stadium athletic training room.

That afternoon, I took Dr. Stoeckel up to Holtz's office in the Kay and Eddie Floyd building, in the north end zone of Williams-Brice Stadium. The Floyd building was sandwiched between the north end zone and the South Carolina State Fairgrounds. The walk was some two hundred yards from my office on the west side of the stadium. Obviously, the cold medicine Holtz had been prescribed had been taken at much larger doses than ordered, as he would reveal to the nation on ESPN's "College GameDay" in a couple of days. He was weak, his pulse was very rapid, he did not feel well or look good. The team physician turned to me and said he needed intravenous fluids, vital sign monitoring, and he needed it quickly.

I made a call to John Singerling at his Palmetto Baptist Hospital office and told him Doc's request. John told me to bring Holtz to the Palmetto Baptist Hospital, where Dr. Peele was finishing his surgical cases. They would take Holtz to the recovery room of the outpatient surgery wing, and monitor his vitals. Based on what they found, Doc had planned to give him intravenous fluids, as Holtz was very dehydrated. His initial plan was to provide the normal two liters of fluid. By the time the first bag was in to Holtz, we had a tough time convincing him to take the second. Holtz was one tough customer, and obviously he was feeling much better and giving any and everyone associated with the hospital a bag full of hell.

I was proud of how I had gotten this done without people outside the football family and the hospital staff knowing what had transpired. Holtz was a "rock star" in Columbia. He could not go anywhere without a following. I had gotten him assessed and treated.

We returned to campus, and slid him by the media without them even seeing him (they were waiting on his routine Thursday post-practice press conference). Lou had Skip Holtz conduct the conference, and all looked good.

On Saturday, the team was sequestered at the Sheraton hotel on Bush River Road in Columbia. We had our routine brunch at 10 a.m., and I settled down to watch ESPN's "College GameDay" as it was being broadcast from the state fairgrounds, adjacent to Williams-Brice Stadium. Holtz was its guest, and he was his usual great interview. The bigger the stage, the greater the performance by Holtz. I say that in sincerity, as he rose to the occasion with coaching, speaking, and challenges. As he was engaged in an interview with Chris Fowler, he was questioned about his recent cold. He quickly revealed how he had been taken to the hospital because of taking too many cold pills (pseudoephedrine) and causing palpitations!

Holtz was a challenge to work with. I have said many times he was the toughest person I ever worked with or for. I would not change one thing because he definitely got results. Those were some great years.

Dr. Rod's
Treatment Plan

NUTRITIONAL SUPPLEMENTS

TODAY IT SEEMS EVERYONE, in and around sports, is looking for an advantage. The nutritional/supplement market has certainly jumped on the bandwagon with the fitness craze. Each year nutritional supplements are marketed to consumers to improve performance, recovery time, and enhance muscle-building capabilities. Student-athletes in both high schools and colleges use nutritional supplements based on the irrelevant claims marketed by the nutritional companies. Very few, if any of these, have been proven effective with peer-reviewed research. These items are very expensive and may even cause harm to health and/or performance.

Scientist and medical researchers have produced evidence that high carbohydrate diets are associated with improved performance and enhance the ability of training. It is well reported that carbohydrates are the source of energy for metabolism. The carbohydrate content of diets should be roughly sixty to sixty-five percent of the total energy intake for active patients. The only reason the patient should ingest carbohydrate supplements would be in those cases where the athletes have problems consuming needed amounts of carbohydrates, i.e., the large volume of food they may need. Energy bars marketed for student-athletes can increase carbohydrate intake during intense training or provide a quick boost of energy. Protein supplements are popular with body builders and strength training student-athletes. It is a well-known fact that protein is used to repair and build muscle during strength training. However, most studies have shown that student-athletes ingest a sufficient amount without supplements. The recommended amount of protein in the diet should be twelve to fifteen percent of the total energy intake. Other commonly used supplements include vitamins and minerals. Most authorities agree that these do not enhance performance while training.

Regarding the NCAA, they prohibit purchase of any supplement which has greater than a thirty percent concentration of protein. Carbohydrate supplements are allowed, however, no protein supplements. Further, supplements can be used in or around the realm of nutritional supplements. The NCAA's limitations on protein supplements have drastically changed supplementations by institutions. From a point of experience, the percentage of substances found in nutritional substances is often different from what is reported. The industry has less control on nutritional substance manufacturers, especially when compared to the FDA's control over prescription medications.

Hopefully in the near future, more control will be achieved with supervision and monitoring of nutritional supplement manufacturers. Too often people try to take a short-cut to hard work. After all, how do you think a substance with no calories can give you energy? Think about it—it's not an energy source. It's a stimulant.

CHAPTER 7

FAITH, FAMILY, FOOTBALL

Objectivity and priorities are areas we have to pay close attention to in our processes. How many times have we seen the need to be objective and make a good evaluation of a process? Attention to our priorities changes as we move along life's highway. I learned from my parents the importance of our faith as the foundation of a family. While I did not always follow this in my career, I later realized how important it was to remember my foundation. The next tenets of that foundation are family followed by work. When these priorities fall out of order, our lives become out of focus and unbalanced. We need balance in our personal and professional lives.

The coaches and athletic administrators who had the most staying power were grounded in their faith, family, and work, in that order. They were generally most successful in their professions. Others might have won some of the time, but their success did not last. They either burned out or did not surround themselves with good solid staffs.

Everything we do, everything that happens in our lives, regardless of the perspective, regardless of the area, regardless of the content, has an influence on those around us. That is why it is so important to have priorities in proper order. Your priorities show exactly what is important in your life, whether it be your faith, your family or your work.

One of my goals in writing this book was to look at life principles and their relationship to business principles. In both of those areas it is important to have priorities. Here is how I have drawn up my priorities in life based upon teachings of many influential and spiritual people:

1. **Faith.** Who is your God? What do you believe in? Late in my career, when I visited with student-athletes, I talked about their faith. It is important to know who is going to be your God and how do you right yourself with your God. What's your faith, and how do you live that? It is not a one-day-a-week faith, but something we should practice every day. How we carry ourselves from day to day and what we are doing when people are not looking shows how well we represent that part of our life. If we fail in our faith, everything else goes awry.

2. **Family.** Our family must come before our jobs and career. If we have a belief structure embedded in the foundation of our faith, our family will be much stronger. Those who have a strong family life, almost without exception, perform better at work. Many young professionals live their entire lives through their work. They work, work, work, work, and they get to be thirty-two years old and they don't have a family or their family is destroyed. The function of family is a commitment. So many fail to make this commitment and consequently the family model is eroding today. We must commit to family. I have been fortunate to work around several coaches—Sparky Woods at Appalachian State and South Carolina, and Brad Scott at South Carolina—who had their priorities in order. Both encouraged families of assistant coaches and staff to be around the office and involved in our work. We also participated in many family activities when Lou Holtz was South Carolina's head coach. Holtz was a personal guy, and his faith was important to him. Student-athletes' ability to have that same relationship with God was important to him.

3. **Work.** Whenever we start putting our work in front of our faith or in front of our family, we are going to have problems.

Any time I have had strife or conflict in my life, it has been because my priorities were not in proper order. Of course, I could not have advanced in my profession without the guidance and influence of many people along the way. The same is true about my personal life.

How we view situations, how we respond to them and how we think, are all based on the influence of others. I thought it prudent to address those who have had the most influence on my life.

When Brad Scott was hired as head football coach at South Carolina, he brought Ken Smith with him from Florida State University. Ken has had an impact on the lives of many coaches and student-athletes through the years. He was the chaplain at Florida State from 1981-1988 and a pastor in Gainesville and Pompano Beach, Florida, prior to coming to South Carolina in 1994. He has also worked with student-athletes as director of player personnel at Mississippi State on Coach Jackie Sherrill's staff.

Ken joined Northside Baptist Church in Columbia, South Carolina, about the time I was going through a marriage separation and eventual divorce. I needed a new place to worship because it was a difficult time to take my children to the church we attended for worship as a family. About the time Ken joined us in Columbia, Ed Dudley, a former SEC football official, died. I had gotten to know and appreciate Ed during my work in the SEC. He was so loved and respected by his peers in officiating but even more by his family and the attendees of his Bible studies in Atlanta. I attended his funeral services at the Second Baptist Church in Atlanta. The services included some good old Baptist hymns that really touched me. I reached out to Ken and told him I needed to find a similar church in Columbia, and he introduced me to Northside Baptist.

Ken always steered me straight. I worshiped there with Steve Cloud as pastor and his fine staff. Susan and I were married by Steve in 1999. Steve has remained a friend through the years while shepherding me along my professional journey. Steve left Northside Baptist several years ago to develop a "coaching ministry" where he effectively coaches Christian businessmen and young pastors. He might have more of an impact on people through his ministry today than he did from his Sunday pulpit.

Brad Scott had great confidence in Ken. He conducted devotions in the South Carolina locker room during pre-game settings. Ken often talked about climbing the ladder to success in a person's profession. He emphasized how important it was to keep faith, family, and work in proper order on that climb. Ken constantly reminded our coaches and players, "as you climb that ladder of success, make sure it is not leaning against a burning building." He said to make certain you were not working for a person who has no values, poor values or compromised values. His message was to make certain you worked for those who reflect your work ethic and values. I share this message in my talks today, but probably not as effectively as Ken Smith.

I never worked with a chaplain who could reach student-athletes better than Ken. I have been around some influential people, but Ken was the one I connected with best. His influence on coaches and students was immeasurable. When Ken spoke, coaches listened. When he addressed the team, the players listened. When he attended practice, everyone from coaches to student-athletes to student managers to athletic training students gravitated toward him.

One of my favorite memories of Ken concerned his devotion in the locker room before a game at Louisiana State on October 1, 1994. LSU was not the team it is today, but it was still a perennial power. We were a young team under a new coach playing in a place called "Death Valley," which always is a hostile environment. Ken shared a story of a recent trip to Austria and how the local cattle would migrate from the lower elevations to higher elevations in search of vegetation. As the food source was exhausted at the higher elevations, the cattle would move back to the villages. This generally occurred later in the fall, and was a festive time. As the cattle came back, their horns were adorned with moss and briars from seeking out food in the woods. As only Ken could, he used the story to illustrate the "night the cows came home." Not only did he have a great Christian message to the squad that night in Baton Rouge, he also provided a great motto that later was printed on T-shirts to memorialize the occasion.

This was one of the many sermons by Ken that I could have listened to a hundred times. Ken talked about how we need more "character" and "fewer characters" these days. He constantly worked to provide a positive influence on student-athletes.

In addition to his weekly devotions to our team before kickoffs on game days, Ken held devotions prior to staff meetings when he was in town. Due to his popularity, Ken traveled a fair amount as an evangelist and was a popular speaker to teams around the country. He always arrived in time for his duties at South Carolina.

If I heard it once, I probably heard it a thousand times from Ken: Faith, Family, Football. He preached this to the coaches. Many times it fell on deaf ears. I am a slow learner, but I finally heard what he was saying. As I opened my ears, I heard how important this was for me, especially while dealing with a couple of life's tougher situations in my personal life. It remains one of the driving principles that have been so good for Susan and me as we share our lives together.

As a result, I believe if one is not happy in his or her faith and personal life, he or she has conflict at work. Further, if people have controversy and issues at home, they will be flustered and frustrated at work. People need stability and to get priorities in check to balance issues.

Service Opportunities That Have Influenced Me

Fellowship of Christian Athletes

I am passionate about the mission of the Fellowship of Christian Athletes. It is one of the last lines of witness Christians have in our schools. I got involved with FCA because I saw how many student-athletes in today's NCAA Division I programs come from broken homes, and having a model way of living was important to most of them. FCA provided a chance to have an influence on these kids.

A local FCA counselor, Andy Heen, reached out to me in 2004. I had met Andy through my board service with this great organization. Andy offered to lead a study with me on the book *Kings and Coaches*. This study was using Bible stories to apply to challenges people face working in athletics. This time with Andy allowed me to be exposed to a

Godly man. I appreciate the time Andy gave me, but more importantly the values he shared.

I recall one chapter in *Kings and Coaches*. It talked about the challenge to be a Christian called to coach, or a coach called to be a Christian. I have certainly seen the influence Christian coaches can have on student-athletes regardless of their sport. Further, we all are at various places on our walk and hopefully our walk with our faith. I cannot urge enough what an influence we as coaches and athletic trainers have on student-athletes. Every day, we are a positive or a negative influence. It is up to us to decide which it will be.

FCA also was a reminder to me to be the person I should be, not the one I wanted to be. I believed we could influence a young student-athlete's life every day. FCA gave me another platform to do what is right and set an example for others. With FCA there are no shades of gray. It is black and white. If I was in the training room telling dirty jokes and using inappropriate language, I was not setting a good example.

Susan and I enjoyed a marriage retreat sponsored by FCA early in our time together. Of course, Ken Smith was one of the retreat's best speakers. A variety of topics were covered from devotions to parenting to financial planning to time management. Callaway Gardens, Georgia was an awesome setting for a tremendous seminar.

My only regret with FCA is that I did not get involved in the program earlier in my career. I have certainly met some tremendous servants of God through FCA including Twig Gray. Twig directs the Midlands of South Carolina office and has had an impact on many young men and coaches with his support through the years. He directs a staff that is so strong. I met Twig early in my days at South Carolina, but did not really get involved until my time with Andy.

Little did I know or realize that coaches with the ability to turn their team over to a chaplain as Brad Scott did are too few. I think Brad realized how important priorities were not only to him, but his team. The chaplains I was exposed to at South Carolina did a tremendous service to the student-athletes. Adrian Despres, Jack Easterby, Ken Smith—what a talented team.

While I might not migrate to one, others may be very compelling to attract my attention. As I told a chaplain, "That's why there is more than one barber in town."

National Athletic Trainers' Association

The National Athletic Trainers' Association is the member organization for athletic trainers. By the nature of my work, NATA has been a big part of my life. I was introduced to the association by Ronnie Barnes and Alex Brown in 1973, but it was not until 1974 that I joined. As a high school student, athletic training was my love and I knew it was my career path. Following graduation in 1979, I sought certification to continue that path.

After eleven years of work, I was asked by the leadership of the Mid-Athletic Athletic Trainers Association to consider an office in our district association. MAATA is the group serving the states of Maryland, Virginia, West Virginia, North Carolina, South Carolina, and the District of Columbia. In 1991, I was elected district secretary-treasurer.

I evolved to the NATA board of directors in 1997. As MAATA's representative, I joined the other nine directors and President Kent Falb to forge NATA's pathways. The board of directors represented thirty-thousand-plus athletic trainers nationwide. While it was important to look after my district members' needs as well as the needs of my practice setting, it was equally important to remember I represented the entire membership. Sarah Teslik, the association's legal counsel reminded every board member prior to each board of directors' meeting of that challenge. Sarah was a vital part of the board's work, and provided the needed legal advice in directing an organization, engaging healthcare initiatives, and general best practices.

Along the way, I received the association's twenty-five- year award in 1999, was recognized with the Most Distinguished Athletic Trainer award in 2003, and was one of the youngest members to be inducted into the organization's Hall of Fame in 2005. All were humbling experiences. I share the humility of each Hall of Fame member each year—why me?

There were so many issues that came to the board's attention over the years. It would have been easy to overlook some issues, but I took it as a challenge to read all paperwork and review every issue thoroughly in order to make sound, informed judgments. The boards I participated on from 1997 to 2003 were attentive to details. The makeup of the boards was well representative of the issues we faced. The board was not afraid of conflict. It discussed issues with specifics. Regardless of the conflict that took place in the board room, there was total support when we left the room. Decisions in the board room were supported in the hallways of the meetings.

I will always be appreciative of my board activity. I met some people who still remain friends. None sticks out more than the friendships of Tony Marek and Sam Booth. We spent many years together in the board room. Sam was the representative from District IV, and sat to my right, as I represented District III (also referred to as the Mid-Atlantic Athletic Trainers' Association). We shared thoughts as sidebars, and sometimes were at each other's throat. When we walked out of the meeting, we had the utmost respect for one another. We remain friends today. Tony Marek also grew to be a great friend. He had a background in college athletics, so we had much in common. Today, Tony uses his excellent clinical skills to consult with the Professional Bull Riders Association.

The board had tremendous people, including future NATA Presidents Chuck Kimmel and Marje Albohm. We met face-to-face in December and May. Then we held extended meetings at the NATA's annual meeting and clinical symposium at sites around the country during the summer. We were kept in tune with issues via our monthly conference calls and the reams of paper mailed to us specific to association business matters. Many board members were accompanied at the annual meetings by their spouses. This provided spouses a chance to become better acquainted with one another and to better understand our duties. The boardroom spars with Tom Koto, D.C. Colt, Lyn Bott, Joe Iezzi, Kathleen Laquale, Andy Paulin, Tony Marek, Sandy Miller, Sue Stanley-Green, Chuck Kimmel, and, of course, Sam Booth were memorable. So, too, were the late-night discussions in the president's suite. As then, the board today has tremendous challenges and I recommend that it continue to never run from confrontation.

Each board member faced the challenge of serving with the NATA while continuing to meet the needs of their jobs. Because of the challenges I faced in dealing with coaches and administrators at South Carolina, I often was the last board member to arrive for meetings and the first to leave. There were many nights I took the last flight out while my peers enjoyed nice dinners on the town. I do not regret this because I was most concerned about making certain my duties were covered at home. What I take most from my board of directors experience was the depth of some valuable friendships. These people I may have never met, and now I cherish them so deeply.

Professional Influences

Warren Ariail

I met Warren Ariail in Greensboro, North Carolina during my inaugural North Carolina Coaches Association student trainer clinic in July of 1972. One has to understand the shadow this giant of an athletic trainer cast. He was a legend in this profession. He was a Marine veteran who landed on the island of Iwo Jima during World War II.

During a visit with Ariail in the spring of 2010, at the Brookview Healthcare Center in Gaffney, South Carolina, I had flashbacks to my early years and quickly remembered why this man meant so much to me. Though Ariail was eighty-six at the time, he was as sharp as that first day I faced him in my first student trainer clinic in Greensboro.

I had another visit to his residence in Gaffney in 2011. As I looked around his den and bedroom, Ariail's resume was displayed on the walls of his rooms with memorabilia and pictures from his days in the Marines, at Wofford, Iowa State, Indiana, Wake Forest, Gardner-Webb and in the CFL as well as with NFL teams in New Orleans and Houston. For his great service to the industry, Ariail was inducted into the NATA Hall of Fame in 1977. Outside of my immediate family, there is no one I was more proud to see at my 2005 Hall of Fame induction ceremony than Ariail.

For as tough a guy as Ariail was, he also had a charming side to him. I was working one summer in Greensboro as a counselor at the NCCA Student Trainer Clinic while on break from my athletic training job at Lenoir-Rhyne College. I was returning from dinner in the UNC-Greensboro cafeteria to one of the dormitories when a young man catapulted from the bushes along the sidewalk. Following behind him was the rippled sole of a Riddell coach's shoe. We quickly realized the young man was Ariail's son, Warren. Later that evening, we questioned Ariail about why he had booted his son out of the bushes. He explained that he had caught his son smoking a cigarette.

We learned that Ariail—tongue firmly planted in cheek—had no issue with his son smoking. Rather, he had issue with his son smoking a Kool, menthol cigarette. If his son was going to smoke, he should have been puffing on a Marlboro, like a man.

Later in my career, Ariail told me how thrilled he was that I had become the athletic trainer at South Carolina. It turns out Ariail was like most sports fans in the state of South Carolina who threw their allegiance behind either Clemson or South Carolina but not both. Ariail hated Clemson.

I overheard Ariail tell many stories over the years. One of my favorites was a conversation he had with my rival athletic trainer, Fred Hoover. The story goes back to the time Ariail first met Hoover some years ago.

Ariail said to Hoover, "I didn't realize you were a graduate of Florida State."

Hoover responded, "Yes, how did you know?"

Ariail quickly quipped, "I saw it on your class ring as you picked your nose."

Ariail always seemed to be one up on everyone.

Al Proctor

While Ariail was more of a character, Al Proctor was the politically correct administrator in North Carolina. Proctor was raised in Shelby, North Carolina and served as a student trainer at Wake Forest University under Ariail's tutelage. Upon graduation from Wake Forest, Proctor accepted a position as the athletic trainer at Greensboro (North Carolina) High School. During the summers, Proctor worked with the New York Yankees' esteemed athletic trainer Gene Monahan, at times in the minor leagues in St. Petersburg, Florida and at times in New York with the big-league club.

Proctor left his high school position in 1962 to take the head athletic trainer position at North Carolina State University. He worked alongside long-time N.C. State athletic trainer Herman Bunch and eventually earned his master's degree and doctorate. He left N.C. State in 1972 to join the North Carolina state department of public instruction before filling a new position in the state as the director of Sports Medicine Division.

I first met Proctor in the summer of 1972 when he directed the student trainer clinic, which was supported by the North Carolina Coaches' Association and conducted during its annual meeting. The people around this clinic had tremendous influence on me, most notably Phil Callicutt. In high school, Callicutt was a student athletic trainer for Proctor at Greensboro High; and Robbie Lester, a West Virginia University student athletic trainer for Callicutt. Callicutt and Lester worked with Proctor in the state's Sports Medicine Division. These athletic trainers were excellent teachers who knew how to convey their trade to teachers and coaches throughout North Carolina.

Soon after Proctor was hired at the North Carolina Department of Public Instruction, he worked closely with the state legislature. He supported legislation in the early 1980s that identified courses of instruction for high school athletic trainers and was the model for high school athletic trainers across the country. He quickly elevated the level of awareness for healthcare to high school and collegiate athletes in North Carolina. We all believed North Carolina was a leader in standards of care in those days. Much of our progress in athletic training can be traced to the early steps taken by Al Proctor, who left his imprint on me and other athletic trainers across the state of North Carolina and ultimately the country.

Len Maness

Len Maness was my high school football coach in Fayetteville, North Carolina. He earned great respect from his players and we always looked up to him. He was a father figure to so many of his players. He was a tough man to get close to, but we all revered him.

Maness believed in fundamental basketball as well and taught us the proper techniques for playing. He made a singular point: Master the basics and then move out from there. He often asked:

"Why shoot twenty-foot jump shots when you have not mastered the five-foot shot?"

In those days, players who needed rides home did not have to take the bus: He would drive them. Players who did not have a jacket, he provided one. Maness was not the most high profile or flamboyant coach, but he definitely was one of my favorites.

Ron "Doc" Kanoy

Kanoy was the athletic trainer at Appalachian State when I was an undergraduate student from 1975-1979. He was a man of few words, but a great mentor to us all. His mentor was Roger Thomas, who studied at Springfield (Massachusetts) College. Thomas was Appalachian State's first athletic trainer, and Kanoy emulated Thomas in learning the basics of athletic training.

Kanoy was old school, which led to him having some misgivings about athletic training. As coaches and administrators had more and more input and influence on decisions affecting athletic trainers, Kanoy became leery of the direction of athletic departments. You would never hear him complain, though, and he was wily enough to know how to work around problems.

He also was not big on the latest technology in the business, but it really did not matter. He mastered the basics to the point he could adapt as he went along and still rely on his vast knowledge. His leadership reminds me today that all is not taught in therapy and techniques, but more through ethics.

Fisher DeBerry

All you need to know about this former football coach is that he long ago established the Fisher DeBerry Foundation, which provides support for parenting development, mentoring programs, after-school activities and funding for academic scholarships.

Rather than preach his beliefs, DeBerry practiced them. He was the model leader of young men in every aspect of the game and life. He carried his beliefs from Appalachian State to Air Force, where he was the head football coach from 1984-2006, leading those teams to unprecedented success.

When Jim Brakefield resigned as head football coach at Appalachian State in 1979, he left many assistant coaches and their families in limbo, which happens with any coaching change. I met every day at noon for a jog along with DeBerry and assistant coaches Roachel Laney and Bob Ward. We ran on the beautiful, yet hilly, roads of Boone, North Carolina.

One particular day, DeBerry and I were jogging on Winkler's Creek Road when he informed me that he would not be in the office next week. He and Brakefield had been invited by Air Force Coach Ken Hatfield for a visit to the Air Force Academy in Colorado Springs, Colorado. Hatfield said he was seeking some insight into Appalachian State's use of the fullback in the wishbone offense.

A few days after DeBerry returned, Hatfield offered DeBerry the position of quarterbacks coach. One season later, DeBerry was promoted to offensive coordinator. Then, when Hatfield left Air Force for Arkansas following the 1983 season, DeBerry was promoted to head coach.

He left Air Force as its all-time most successful coach in 2006. His teams won three Western Athletic Conference championships and twice finished with top-ten national rankings. Air Force also dominated the Commander-in-Chief Trophy series with rivals Army and Navy under DeBerry by winning the trophy fourteen times and sharing another one in his twenty-three seasons.

Beyond that, DeBerry left an impression on every Air Force player he coached. He was that kind of person.

Greg Harmon

Through the years, I have had so much respect for athletic training students. They receive little, if any, compensation for their work, but still have a tremendous love for their subject area and work so hard to master their skills. I still get to see some of these athletic trainers in my travels across the country. While some have moved up the ladder to bigger and better jobs, others are still at their first job, doing an outstanding job caring for student-athletes and/or patient populations. Others have taken the skills learned in the athletic training room and applied them to their jobs outside the world of sports.

One particular student comes to mind. During the summer of 1992, I first met Greg Harmon as a student in my Walters Inc. Student Athletic Training Clinic at the University of South Carolina. Greg is twenty years my junior. He was a student athletic trainer at Thomas Heyward Academy in Ridgeland, South Carolina. Greg came from a family of avid South Carolina fans and was recommended to my clinic by Heyward Academy football Coach Claude Davis and Headmaster John D. Rogers, both of whom were Gamecocks' fans.

After that summer, Greg visited South Carolina during his senior year of high school (fall of 1993) with the intention of attending school and working as a student athletic trainer. I knew our staff would welcome him as a candidate for our program because of his work ethic. Greg had a lawn service in his hometown of Yemassee, South Carolina. I knew Greg was the kind of person, if you gave him a task, he would see it through. I knew this kid would be successful.

A couple of months later, in May of 1994, I was returning to Williams-Brice Stadium after my daily jog when I saw Greg and his parents climbing out of their car. It was a typical summer day in Columbia at ninety-eight degrees with ninety percent humidity. While standing there sweating profusely, I noticed Greg and his father lacked their normal congenial disposition. They dropped by to tell me they had visited East Tennessee State University regarding their athletic training program. Jerry Robertson, East Tennessee State's head athletic trainer, had offered Greg a significant package to be applied to his educational costs there.

The Harmons knew South Carolina had an athletic training curriculum, but lacked a scholarship program. The small stipends we offered were nothing compared to what Greg had been offered by East Tennessee State. All we could offer was in-state tuition versus ETSU's out-of-state tuition.

All I could offer the Harmons was that I would treat Greg like my son if he came to South Carolina. The message resonated with Steve Harmon and shortly thereafter a significant chapter in our friendship was forged.

Greg was not the top academic student in his freshman class, but no one outworked him. He wanted to do too much in the athletic training room, and I had to remind him to get his class work done first and enjoy being a student. I went to bat for Greg regarding his admission to the athletic training program and he did not let me down. He has brought significant pride to that program through the years. Classmates Andy Burris, Chris Britton, and Bo Shealy were characters. Those guys were great for me and certainly added to my gray hair while keeping me young.

Following graduation from South Carolina, Greg completed his master's degree at the University of Tennessee. A couple of years later, I was honored to read scripture at his wedding when he married Erin Thomas, his college sweetheart. Today, they reside in Columbia, South Carolina with their kids, Sarah and John.

In May of 2001, I recommended Greg for a sales position with ACO Med Supply, a company directed by my friend Stuart Ross. Stuart developed ACO Med into a major medical and surgical supply company in Charlotte, North Carolina. His primary line was Donjoy products, but has branched into other medical and surgical products. Due to my experience with Donjoy I was aware of the value of a good sales representative and realized what a void there was in South Carolina. Stuart was concerned over Greg's lack of experience in medical sales, but he hired Greg on my word. His work ethic outweighed his experience. Today Greg is one of Donjoy's top salesmen every year. Greg was promoted to regional sales manager in May of 2005 and then to chief sales officer in January of 2009.

Greg Harmon's work ethic from his high school days and his tenure in the athletic training program at South Carolina had significant carryover into his work in sales. He understands what commitment must be made for his business to succeed. This was something Greg's father had build as a foundation years ago. The athletic trainers bring their untiring drive they learned in the athletic training room (just like Greg did) and enjoy unparalleled successes in the business world.

Susan and I are honored to be the godparents of their first child, Sarah McTeer Harmon. I guess it all comes together in the end.

Chris Snoddy

We never know who is coming into our lives and how they will affect us. In athletics, this can be in the form of an associate, a supervisor, a coach, or even a student. Chris Snoddy was one such person. I was introduced to Chris by Len Griffin, a classmate of mine at Middle Tennessee State. Chris came to Appalachian State with interest in pursuing his Master of Arts degree. I had never hired a person with the experience Chris possessed. He was working at his alma mater, Lipscomb University in Nashville, Tennessee. He needed to obtain his certification as an athletic trainer because he failed to complete the requirements for certification as an undergraduate. Chris worked with me in 1986 and 1987.

Chris took charge the first day on the job. He was attentive to detail. If you told him to do something, it was done. There was no need to check on him. He handled tasks and loved the challenge.

One responsibility of mine at Appalachian State was to oversee the equipment room and to purchase equipment, particularly for the football team. In those days, Appalachian State did not have great shoe and apparel contracts. We had a "shoe agreement" with Pony: If we paid for their shoes, we could wear them. We actually might have gotten a free pair of shoes for every two pairs we purchased. The problem was our shoes were provided after companies fulfilled their agreements with the marquee programs. Our big competitors were Clemson and Iowa.

This particular year was a concern because it was our first year being associated with Pony. We had no inventory. Our product was scheduled to arrive by July 10, 1986. I was scheduled to be on vacation July 15-21. Chris was attuned to the issue and monitored it better that I could have. He kept me abreast of developments. We received our shoes, much too close to the start of practice for the comfort of Sparky Woods, our head coach.

As Chris came to work each day, he carried a large notebook and made notations in it often. I made jokes about it, and made light of his activities. You had to remember, I was the guy with the big job, and thought I knew everything. This was one of the first times where I realized how little I knew.

During the 1986 year, my administrative responsibilities dictated I deal with issues regarding coaches. Chris' insight was so valuable. Again, it was tough relinquishing control of my work to a graduate assistant, but Chris "got it." He introduced me to a great course: "Time Power: The Revolutionary Time Management System." It was a series of cassette tapes (yes, those little things you inserted into an audio player and listened to while in your car, or at home). The series was by Charles Hobbs, and he taught using a tool for calendar entry, centralization of schedules, journaling, and logging daily activities. The concepts of DayTimers have changed though the years, but the principles remain. Chris taught me to have only one calendar, to log activities, to schedule events, and to plan on a yearly basis. Chris and I developed a friendship that remains today.

I have learned more from Chris Snoddy than he ever received from me during his year at Appalachian State. He taught me there are only twenty-four hours in a day and we cannot manage time, but we can manage events. It is so important that we plan. We need to make our goals and plan with our organization, with our family, with whatever unit we are dealing with.

Personal influences

Mom and Dad

Any time I have had strife or conflict in my life, it has been because my priorities were not in proper order. I was most fortunate that my parents had their priorities in order and imparted their wisdom on their children.

I was reared in a Christian home in Fayetteville, North Carolina. No one influenced me more than my mother and father. We might not have had some of the luxuries growing up, but we never wanted for anything. Most important, we had happiness in our family.

We had great structure at home. For example, we knew Friday nights were family nights. For as long as I could remember growing up, we were required to have our Friday evening meal with family. Even when I got to dating age, I knew nothing precluded eating the family meal together on Friday night.

I admit to having a Beaver Cleaver upbringing. We attended church every Sunday. If we had a drug problem in our home it was that we were "drug" to church every weekend. When the church was open, we were there.

My parents helped create a very strong bond between myself and my two brothers, Stuart, who is two years younger than me, and Louis, who is ten years younger.

With both of my parents working during my preschool years, I often stayed with my grandfather, Leonard Curtis (L.C.) Dowd, during the days and forged a tremendous relationship with him. My grandfather was a dairy farmer, which was not a bad deal for me because I learned my work ethic while hanging out with him at his farm. Unfortunately, when I was twenty-five, Grandpa died of cancer.

My father, David, was a tough guy. He was not a touchy, feely kind of guy, not one to express affection, but there was never any doubt of his love for his family. He was the son of a Baptist minister who did missionary work around the state of North Carolina. His dad, Thomas E. Walters, was transferred from Rocky Mount to Gastonia to Fayetteville. Dad's family settled in Stedman, where he graduated from Stedman High School a year ahead of my mother in 1954. They were married in May of 1955 and settled into a home off Cedar Creek Road outside Fayetteville.

My first memory of Dad working as a salesman was at the Western Auto store on Gillespie Street in Fayetteville. He worked there until the mid-1960s when he went across the street to work for the General Electric store in Fayetteville. He continued his work there until 1980 when he and Mom embarked on a dream they had talked about for some time. They loved antiques and old furniture. They opened Antiques and Country Things where Dad sought out old furniture suitable for refinishing, and Mom added the furnishings. They had a great business that the economy downturn of 2008 has certainly affected. Regardless, "the shop" is still the source of country primitives in Fayetteville.

My mother, Erma Christine Dowd, was raised on a farm outside of Fayetteville. Mom had four brothers and two sisters, and they all worked on L.C. Dowd's dairy farm there on the Cedar Creek Road. I learned early that dairy farmers never get a day off as Holstein cows require special attention to relieve their udders twice a day, three hundred sixty-five days a year, no exceptions.

Maybe that is why my mother was rather atypical for women of her era. She worked while she was raising a family. Initially, she was a bookkeeper for Quality Parts until I was in elementary school, then for the 301 Truck Stop in Fayetteville.

During my elementary school years, we lived in a small, two-bedroom home. I recall cold winter mornings when we would dress for school in front of the oven, which was opened to draw heat. My mother was big on cleanliness and neatness. We might not have had the newest, brightest and fanciest, but everything was always clean, and it was always neat. I have an affinity today for clothes because of my mother. We owned a general store for a while during my childhood, and my mother ran it, in addition to her bookkeeping job.

When I finished the fourth grade, my parents moved our family into a quaint little Fayetteville neighborhood on Haymount Hill where we were afforded great schools. Upon graduation from Terry Sanford High School, I attended college, just like my two brothers behind me would do. The three of us never needed a student loan in college because our parents provided for us, both financially and personally in preparation for life.

It seems like all of my friends growing up were formed through our church, Snyder Memorial Baptist Church. Kay Baker, Selena Thompson, Paige Moore, Steve Byrd, Tony Byrd, Ellen Barbour, all these friends attended our church. We attended Sunday service in the morning, then returned in the early evening for youth choir practice, followed by youth programs. Afterward, we went out together for pizza.

We lived two blocks from our church, so we could walk there anytime. More importantly, we wanted to be there. My parents encouraged us to be there. We were very involved. We were very fond of our church and developing another family there through friendships, and that had a profound impact on me. I reflect today on my friends and our love of our church. It was a special place for worship and for so many friends to gather. Snyder Memorial Baptist Church is still a major part of Mom and Dad; as it is for my brother Stuart and his family. I appreciate what Snyder has done for them and has meant to me through all these years.

Susan Ferguson Walters

I saw how my parents were best friends to each other when I was growing up. Today, Susan is my best friend. She also is my confidante. While undergoing some difficult times in my life Susan was so loving and supportive to my children, which has been very important to me. She has done so many things for my sons, David and Ryan, dating to before we were married. She never has tried to be their mom, but always accepted her role and has been the most awesome step-mom.

When we look at the important things in life, we have to keep them in check at home, at work, and at play. Susan always has helped me do that. We share our Christian beliefs and the importance of that aspect of our life. She is the most important person in my family life. Our kids know how important they are to us.

Susan and I began dating in February, 1998 and enjoyed spending quality time together. I never tried to interfere with her relationship with her children, Allison and Bradley. Susan gave me all the freedom I needed with David and Ryan. The important thing was I loved this woman unconditionally. I am confident all four of our children saw this. It was important to me for our kids to see the respect I had for her.

On Valentines' Day 1998, Susan asked David and Ryan what they would like for dinner, as they were with me that weekend. I had a two-bedroom apartment that was very convenient for the boys to be with me. They were a high priority in my life, and I wanted to be with them at every opportunity. Ryan piped up that he wanted crab legs to eat. Susan took that info and plugged it into her catering database and further accessed the information she had acquired through the years from her mother's cooking skills.

The boys were playing in the yard at my apartment, and Susan and I were preparing dinner. We were enjoying a nice glass of wine. She called the boys to dinner and reminded them to "wash your hands." David was the first to the table, and noticed the folded, linen napkins mimicking a kings' crown. As Ryan sat at the table, he too was impressed with the napkins and the Valentine's Day dinner setup. They devoured the king crab legs. Susan is the consummate cook. (One look at me and you can see that.) As Ryan ate his dinner, he leaned over to me and said, "Dad, she's a keeper." The things she does for my kids, I hope I was half as impressive to her in support of her and her children.

Susan has enabled me to do so many things in life. Her support of what I do is phenomenal. A wife can either lift you up or bring you down. Susan's ability to support me and what I'm doing professionally is unmatched. I truly feel my success in the business world is greatly due to her support. Her social grace and beauty certainly help open doors for me.

When you have children and stepchildren, it is one heck of a challenge. Being a parent is the toughest thing we do, and there is no manual to show us how to do it. I now share this with my son, David, who became a father himself recently. He and his wife Rebecca gave birth to Grace Christine on June 9, 2011.

Charlie Ferguson

When Susan and I met in 1997, it was very evident she was close to her parents, especially her dad. Charlie Mack Ferguson and Martha Foxworth Ferguson had two daughters, Susan Marie and Cheryl. Both were born in Augusta, Georgia when Charlie was working at the Savannah River Site.

Charlie and I hit it off from the first day we met. Charlie was a huge South Carolina fan, and our friendship immediately gave him access to South Carolina athletics. It was nothing for him to be in the athletic training room watching my staff tape ankles and treat one hundred-five college football players as we prepared for practice. Charlie left us June 30, 2005, and I promised him I would take care of both his girls.

I have to tell one story about Charlie. In 1999, when South Carolina hired Lou Holtz, he brought a few traditions with him from his days at William and Mary, North Carolina State, Arkansas, Minnesota and Notre Dame. One of those was the "Victory Meal," on Tuesday evenings following Saturday wins. Holtz wanted a special meal, so I worked with Pat Moorer, our strength coach, and Clifford Snow, to meet the coach's expectations.

On one particular "Victory Meal" night, we decided to serve filet mignon and crab legs. Serving crab legs to one hundred-forty- plus people means we needed an adequate steamer on site. I talked to Charlie about this and he recommended we use Miss Betty's "Stadium Restaurant," which was located adjacent to Williams-Brice Stadium where we were serving the meal. Charlie arranged for a crew to cook the crab legs, and everything went off without a hitch. No one was prouder than Charlie. He was definitely in his element being around all the South Carolina players and coaches.

Dr. Rod's
Treatment Plan

HYDRATION AND PREVENTION
OF HEAT ILLNESS

HEAT ILLNESS IS A CONDITION of concern to those exercising in the extremes of weather, especially during the summer months. Heat is produced as a by-product of exercise. Thus, coaches and athletic trainers must be aware of the potential for heat-related illness in all environments and conditions—not just during the pre-season football practice. The evaporation of sweat is the primary way the body loses heat and regulates a safe body temperature. Thirst is not a good indicator of a person's fluid needs. By the time you're thirsty, you have already lost fluids and may be dehydrated. Coaches and athletic trainers must utilize strategies to monitor weight (fluid) loss and make sure dehydration is avoided, especially when athletes are exercising in warm weather.

Muscle energy produces heat from muscle contractions and metabolism. The main way to reduce body temperature is from sweating. When sweat evaporates from your body, heat is lost and so are body fluids. You need to replace those fluids to avoid dehydration and to maintain your performance. We monitor a player's weight by requiring weigh-in prior to and following each practice. Thus, our physicians and athletic trainers can monitor weight loss and make sure vital fluids are replaced prior to subsequent activity.

During exercise, heat is lost in four ways: radiation, evaporation, conduction, and convection. With radiation, heat radiates from the body to cooler objects. Conduction occurs as heat is transferred from the body by direct physical contact (i.e., skin immersed in cool water; person swimming in cool water). The transfer of heat by movement of cool currents of air or water over the body describes convective cooling. The conversion of sweat to water vapor and movement from the skin describes cooling via evaporation.

With athletes, we want to be aware of evaporation and radiation as effective cooling mechanisms. Radiation is generally effective in temperature less than 85° F. and evaporation effective in environments with less than seventy percent relative humidity. It is important that coaches and athletic trainers monitor the weather and make appropriate changes in practice schedules if temperatures approach such ranges. A good reference for a Heat Index Chart is the National Oceanic and Atmospheric Administration (www.gssi.com).

Guidelines I used during my Athletic Training Days

- Allow for acclimatization (adaptation) in hot seasons. Cut back on exercise intensity and duration in hot weather. Slowly build back to previous level over the next ten days.
- Drink up when it's hot. Once acclimatized, sweat losses will be higher, so fluid intake has to be greater. Monitor weights daily and encourage copious intake of electrolyte drinks.
- Don't be overly competitive under hot conditions. Try for a personal best on a cooler day. Monitor weather and adjust practice schedules and workouts accordingly.
- Don't just pour water over your head. It may feel great, but it won't help at all at restoring body fluids or lowering body temperature. Fluid has to go in the body. Again, monitor weight loss via weight charts and replace fluids.
- Carry electrolyte drinks with you if you know they will not be available at the exercise site. Bottle belts are great for this. Also carry money to buy something to drink.
- Select lightly flavored, sweetened beverages containing sodium. Sodium has been scientifically proven to encourage voluntary drinking and promote hydration. You can, and will, drink more Gatorade than water. Research and pilot studies are showing encouraging results in the utilization of sodium to facilitate fluid intake.

- Exercise in the morning or evening when the weather is coolest. Avoid the sun's rays to minimize the radiant heat load. However, if team practice sessions are held in the heat of the day, you need to condition your body to be acclimatized for the heat and humidity stresses of practice time.

- Wear light-colored, lightweight porous clothing. Do not change into a dry shirt at breaks or time-outs. Completely soaked shirts do better at cooling the body.

- Water is an essential fluid. However, it contains no electrolytes, carbohydrates or flavor benefits. As a result, athletes will not drink enough water to maintain fluid balance. Drinking too much water can also cause an athlete to become hyponatremic (dangerously low levels of sodium in the blood) which can impair an athlete's performance and prove perilous to health.

CHAPTER 8

THE COST OF CARE

My travels and visits with college administrators, healthcare professionals, athletic trainers and physicians have told me that the number one sports medicine challenge in college athletics today is the rising cost of healthcare. College administrators across the country are forced to deal with healthcare cost containment. We face increases in insured person's co-pay, decreased payments from the primary insurance relative to coverage of medical services, and overall decreased medical benefits. It all points to increased healthcare costs to consumers.

The challenge for college administrators continues to be finding ways to cover the remaining medical costs that primary insurance does not cover. This scenario is real, and one that I saw at all levels of college athletics, from my Division III days at Lenoir-Rhyne College to my Division I-AA days at Appalachian State University to my Division I days at the University of South Carolina. There is less coverage of out-of-pocket medical expenses and patient's co-pay by the institution in lower division athletics programs. The institution's ability to cover these rising costs will be greater in coming years.

Student-athletes with primary insurance listen to providers for direction and instructions on who to seek for medical care. The public does not understand or realize the service many institutions provide to student-athletes through coverage and the absolving of healthcare costs not covered by the student-athlete's primary or accident insurance plan.

Student-athletes in Division I would probably seek care wherever the student-athlete and /or institution so chooses. Those student-athletes with no insurance must be dealt with as well. No longer is it prudent to accept— as college administrators or departments—a simple percentage discount off medical charges. Insurance companies glean significant discounts for services, and it is prudent for athletic departments to obtain such discounts for student-athletes as well. Strategies must be engaged to stay on the cutting edge of providing services while obtaining discounts.

Finally, today's healthcare reform has few provisions for cost containment or the rising cost of healthcare to the insured. College administrators must deal with the portion of healthcare not covered by insurance. Based on the literature and recent trends, it seems prudent that out-of-pocket medical costs covered by college athletic departments could increase three-fold in the coming years. Yes, three-fold. An institution with out-of-pocket healthcare costs of $300,000 will approach $1 million in the next couple of years.

It is an alarming prospect for all college athletic departments. I have long said insurance companies do not build big buildings by paying claims. Athletic administrators must find ways to include student-athlete healthcare within covered benefits of primary insurance entities. That is the central challenge facing athletic administrators today.

One team's crisis is another's training ground. I remember driving across the University of South Carolina campus February 26, 2001, when the ESPN announcer broke the news that a Florida State student-athlete had died following an early morning team workout. I was aware of the intense workouts at Florida State because Coach Brad Scott and his staff had brought these same sessions to South Carolina and taught them to the Gamecock team.

I always attempted to analyze what had happened in these kinds of situations as a way of better preparing my staff in the prevention of such incidents. I constantly tried to review our processes and practices to make sure our standard of care was as high as it could be. Consider that as we discuss how we managed healthcare costs at South Carolina to the benefit of all, including the athletic department budget, we did this without sacrificing care.

Blake Mitchell was an emerging solid quarterback under the tutelage of Coach Steve Spurrier during Mitchell's redshirt sophomore season of 2005. Four weeks into the season, Mitchell suffered an ankle sprain in South Carolina's victory over Troy University. Almost immediately, our athletic training and medical staffs ushered Mitchell to the Williams-Brice Stadium training room where the team physician ordered X-Rays on his ankle. We considered the X-Rays a service we provided to student-athletes, so no bills were generated to recoup costs. Today, that might not be the case within many athletic departments, as they see this as not affordable.

We probably took five hundred X-Rays each semester during the orthopedic clinics held in the Williams-Brice Stadium athletic training room orthopedic clinic. The clinics were provided for all student-athletes on Tuesday, Wednesday, and Thursday evenings. The X-Ray facility also was staffed during home games and special NCAA events hosted by the university. The X-Ray services were performed by technicians hired by my office. We were careful to make sure they were current in their state regulatory services. My administrative assistant Sandra Schmale worked with me to hire the most qualified professional X-Ray technicians we could find. Further, the X-Ray facility was scrutinized by the university's safety office as well as the state agency overseeing the facility.

We referred Mitchell to Palmetto Richland Hospital in Columbia, South Carolina for special imaging studies to validate his injury. Because of the amount of services we sent the hospital's way, we had pre-arranged discounts for all of our student-athletes' care. The hospital also had "standing" reservations for our physicians to refer student-athletes for imaging studies. The slots were held to accommodate the student-athletes' class schedules and demands of college athletics. In this case, the claim for an MRI and doctor's services would have been approximately $3,000. Our discount brought the cost down to less than $700, of which about 80 percent was covered under the health plan of the student-athlete's family. The remaining balance of $140 was covered by South Carolina athletic department. This practice is very common among Division I institutions.

We managed healthcare costs so there were very little, if any, out-of-pocket expenses for the student-athlete or subsequently the athletic department. It was the result of much planning done by my staff and the university almost a decade earlier. Recounting how that came about is worthwhile.

The annual rate of inflation for the healthcare industry ranged from a high of 9.1 percent in 1990 to a low of 4.8 percent in 1994 (United States Bureau of Labor Statistics, 1990, 1991, 1992, 1993, 1994). Cost containment had to be addressed to prohibit out-of-control growth. Review of the 1990 medical budget at the University of South Carolina revealed insurance, out-of-pocket medical expenses, and contracts to physicians at $363,700 (2.18 percent) of our $16.7 million athletic department budget (University of South Carolina athletic department financial statements and schedules, June 30, 1989-May 31, 1990). Reviewing the average healthcare inflation rate of 7.2 percent from 1990-1994, we figured our costs would escalate to $464,184 (2.36 percent) of the $19.7 million 1995 budget. These projections identify the drastic need for measures to control spending without compromising care to our student-athletes. This foresight was vintage Mike McGee, our athletic director at the time.

In making our projections of subsequent years' medical costs, we considered injury trends, casual factors' impact on injury rates and treatment techniques. We collected injury data and reviewed this relative to national surveillance studies and reports. McGee welcomed well-planned and researched recommendations. His associate athletic director for finances at the time was Dan Radakovich. Dan's MBA background and perspective certainly helped understanding of what we presented. These cost containment strategies were welcomed as he understood the fiscal potential of healthcare expenditures. We also evaluated the services referred to "outside" practitioners. From our data, we concluded it to be more cost effective to treat student-athletes in-house rather than through off-campus referrals. This was a team process with me communicating with athletic administrators and our entire medical staff.

We linked our efforts at cost control with the university's medical school, private practice physicians, the university community, local emergency medical services, high schools and even local and regional businesses. It was all done with an eye on decreasing our costs while improving our equipment and standard of care.

The care an athletic department provides is specific to the level of athletic participation and funding by the department. An NCAA Division III school has next to no latitude in athletic referrals for healthcare. The staff at NCAA FCS schools such as Furman, Appalachian State, or The Citadel would have a little more latitude. None of those schools could match the latitude of a South Carolina or Clemson when it came to referrals for second opinions or specialty surgical needs. Athletic administrators face a diverse range of needs concerning budgets, programming and administrative philosophy. Each administrator must identify strategies to deal with shrinking budget dollars. As inflation increases, these amounts often are much greater than budget allocations. The available dollars to finance collegiate healthcare are drastically dwindling. It is important that we, as athletic administrators, understand what we are up against.

McGee was the athletic director for most of my tenure at South Carolina. He came across as gruff and could be difficult to deal with at times. But he was a smart businessman. He understood the financial numbers we had to deal with in the 1990s. He called me into his office at the time of our studies and projections and said, "At the rate we're going, if we're going to have healthcare, we're going to have to drop sports. We've got to do something."

Opportunities in which he was interested in being on the receiving end of a discussion were rare, so it was my intention that day to educate him on how we approached the medical coverage of intercollegiate athletic injuries. Like most of us who worked with Mike, I knew the time to make your point was not during initial discussions or presentations in a group setting. It was the follow-up where progress could be made. Mike did not like to be challenged, and you had to prepare your proposal for the appropriate time.

I explained how we combined the medical benefits from payments or benefits the student-athlete had with primary accident insurance with the discounts we obtained from our medical providers. Mike was interested in how we attempted to "self-insure" the above amount and purchase secondary, or excess, accident insurance with a higher deductible amount to cover us upward to catastrophic insurance.

Mike could certainly understand that the greater the amount of insurance coverage we had outside of what we either purchased or covered from budget dollars resulted in decreasing the financial liability of the department. His understanding of this got him on board with our recommendations. Radakovich was instrumental to Mike's understanding and acceptance.

College administrators everywhere must review the department's philosophy concerning medical benefits for injured student-athletes. Remember, it is perfectly legal for the institution to cover or care for every accident that occurs, regardless of the nature. This includes accidents and illnesses classified as NCAA permissible benefits. Institutions were limited to financing sport-related accidents until the early 2000s. It is cost-prohibitive for all care to be covered. Athletic departments generally file claims first with the patient's primary insurance company, then cover the unpaid balance through excess insurance coverage policies financed by the department. The decision of coverage should be made by senior administration and mirror the university's or department's mission statement and thus enforced department-wide for all student-athletes.

With a higher deductible for the excess accident policy, premium rates may be lower, but payments would not be initiated until a certain level is reached. For example, a premium for a $5,000 deductible plan might cost $100,000, while the same plan with a $1,000 deductible might cost more than $175,000. The school selecting the higher deductible is banking on its ability to manage the out-of-pocket expenses and pool savings related to the higher deductible and lowered premium costs. In those locales where few student-athletes have primary insurance, we want to review the number of annual claims, as well as dollars paid for out-of-pocket medical expenses, and determine the deductible amount. Regardless of the approach, out-of-pocket dollars and/or premiums probably will equate somewhere in the same range. With high deductibles, the department self-insures this initial amount and accepts a risk or gamble of savings.

For athletic departments, the ability to provide a high-profile group of student-athletes with a healthy medical record is exciting to hospitals and physicians. College athletics are high profile and many providers are willing to offer services in exchange for this affiliation. Further, from a risk perspective, the potential for significant loss is negligible.

Prior to scheduling the annual student-athlete pre-participation examination, our department at South Carolina obtained a copy of all primary accident insurance information from student-athletes. This was supported by McGee and was a key piece of our program's success. His support was unique, and is not found in many programs. This information was distributed to all healthcare providers in advance of the service. When an accident was incurred, all information was on record to readily file a claim. It was important to maintain a group of providers and to have all specialty referral groups within the network identified. Most primary insurance benefits pay at eighty to eighty-five percent of adjusted charges, and we usually obtained a significant discount from the network to cover our out-of-pocket liability. Such a plan was fairly common in the 1990s, but had to evolve to more aggressive adjudication of claims as lower reimbursement rates and discounts are being offered today by insurance companies. By having larger insurance pools, and being able to guarantee a certain number of cases or hospital stays annually, insurance companies can now demand greater discounts. Institutions are now trying to be included in such a pool arrangement, as significant discounts can be realized therein.

With our managed care plan at South Carolina, providers wrote off a percentage of any remaining balance, which was a significant savings to our department. Our basic excess accident insurance premium had a twenty percent co-payment. We guaranteed benefits for any student-athlete who had primary insurance coverage. We also obtained coverage for pre-existing injuries, or those medical conditions that occurred before the student-athlete enrolled at our institution.

Student-athletes seeking professional services outside their geographic area were difficult because it was not a normal referral pattern of the sports medicine staff. Special braces, MRIs, etc., often were covered by the institution and we had an avenue of coverage within our medical plan. By purchasing healthcare in bulk, and for association with our department, special pricing was obtained to utilize primary insurance and decrease or minimize the need to use departmental provisions.

Evaluation of efficiency and success of a healthcare delivery program included a prudent review of services and costs. We constantly reviewed the costs of providing healthcare for student-athletes. Such costs were inclusive of excess insurance premiums, out-of-pocket medical expenses, contracts for physicians, and a general medical pharmacy component. These specific areas were different from institution to institution, but a thorough evaluation of the program was necessary at each.

To quote one of my favorite sports commentators, Colin Cowherd, "fan is short for fanatic." Sports fans and the general public do not realize what a perk it is to be a Division I student-athlete. Athletic departments spend significant budget dollars annually to provide the best healthcare to student-athletes. This practice is going to be more difficult in the future with the challenges discussed.

Although the numbers in healthcare have changed—mostly skyrocketed—since 1989-1990, it still is worth looking in more detail at our expenses that year at South Carolina as an example of how it works.

Our medical costs for the fiscal year revealed excess insurance premium (zero-dollar deductible) at a cost of $88,400. Additionally, the athletic department paid a portion of a Student Health Center Sports Medicine Primary Care physician's salary. We utilized Primary Care physicians with specialty certification in sports medicine. Pharmacy costs were $24,700. Athletic training room medical supplies totaled $104,000. Our philosophy was that we could purchase items for our physicians to utilize and treat student-athletes, and provide more care at a decreased cost. The actual outlay for medical costs was $81,600. (It is important to remember healthcare costs rise due to uncontrollable variables such as inflation, which is based on national averages and trends).

To see how we increased our standard of care in services to student-athletes while reducing expenditures to the university, it is worth looking closely at our 1993-1994 numbers by way of comparing them to the 1990 numbers. (All numbers courtesy of USC Athletic Department Financial Statements and Schedules, 1989-1994.)

By 1995, as we reviewed our procedural changes and realized the significant savings we were afforded, the cost of healthcare had significantly decreased while our level of care had increased. We had united efforts with the University of South Carolina Medical School, specifically with the Family Practice group. The attending physicians and I supervised a Sports Medicine Clinic for resident physicians in sports medicine.

Athletic departments within a university often operate as a company. Decisions must be made relative to how much risk the department is willing to incur in the management of healthcare to student-athletes. Some institutions prefer to minimize risk and pay higher budget amounts due to the few number of contracts they have. Others prefer to negotiate coverage with local providers and pay all amounts out of pocket. As a result, they have excess accident insurance with extremely high deductibles ($25,000) while realizing significant savings with the excess accident insurance premium and negotiated or adjudicated claims of their student-athletes.

Most all NCAA Division I athletic departments use any available primary insurance of student-athletes, which mitigates out-of-pocket expenditures to the athletic department. Accident claims for intercollegiate injuries are filed with primary insurance plans. Those portions of the bill not recovered from primary insurance are filed with the excess insurance plan. These plans generally excluded general illnesses and medical conditions, as many institutions elect not to pay such claims.

We also must be cognizant of student-athletes who do not have personal health insurance and how we can meet their healthcare needs in a prudent financial manner. Many times a student-athlete comes to campus with an invalid or expired insurance card. This often is not discovered until a referral is made for care and you are informed that the patient has no primary insurance benefits on the plan. This may be due to the fact they are out of network, coverage has elapsed or a student has aged out of the plan. When this happens, one step to control expenses is to elect Consolidated Omnibus Budget Reconciliation Act (IRS, 2011) on that student-athlete, if such is available. COBRA is a continuation of coverage benefits enacted by the federal government in 1985. This act allows for continuation of coverage on a group medical plan should coverage be lost due to a qualifying event. By electing COBRA, a large claim can be taken and the costs picked up under primary coverage rather than having all the costs go toward secondary insurance. There are specific rules and time frames when this can be done, but the bottom line is that anyone can elect COBRA. The cost of electing COBRA on a large claim and paying for the premiums for the duration of the injury will be far less expensive than paying for the entire injury and having the claim go against your loss runs. Schools should investigate the availability of COBRA for those situations where the insured person loses coverage.

The second part of this example is that the student-athlete's insurance benefits card was never active, so any injury that occurs will result in the school paying more than it had planned to pay. If a school requires coverage for a student-athlete to compete in sports, health insurance cards need to be verified from the outset and checked regularly. There are companies that can do the checking for the school. The minimal cost up front for this step can save a school thousands of dollars on the back end. Learning after the fact is the worst way to find out this information. Bad news never gets better with time, so find out early.

It is important that healthcare spending decisions and practices by any institution be representative of the athletic or institutional administration. At Lenoir-Rhyne, it was an institutional decision. At South Carolina, the athletic administration made the call. The NCAA Manual has structure for allowing benefits to student-athletes. Any and all medical services are eligible for payment per NCAA bylaw 16.4 (NCAA, 2010a). Identified medical expense benefits incidental to a student's participation in intercollegiate athletics that may be financed by the institution are:

a. Athletics medical insurance; Death and dismemberment insurance for travel connected with intercollegiate athletics competition and practice;

b. Drug-rehabilitation expenses;

c. Counseling expenses related to the treatment of eating disorders;

d. Special individual expenses resulting from a permanent disability that precludes further athletics participation. The illness or injury producing the disability must involve a former student-athlete or have occurred while the student-athlete was enrolled at the institution, or while the prospective student-athlete was on an official paid visit to the institution's campus. An institution or outside agency, or both, may raise money through donations, benefits or like activities to assist the student-athlete or a prospective student-athlete. All funds secured shall be controlled by the institution, and the money shall be used exclusively to meet these expenses;

e. Glasses, contact lenses or protective eyewear (e.g., goggles) for student-athletes who require visual correction in order to participate in intercollegiate athletics;

f. Medical examinations at any time for enrolled student-athletes;

g. Expenses for medical treatment (including transportation and other related costs) incurred by a student-athlete as a result of an athletically related injury. Such expenses may include the cost of traveling to the location of medical treatment or the provision of actual and necessary living expenses for the student-athlete to be treated at a site on or off the campus during the summer months while the student-athlete is not actually attending classes. Medical documentation shall be available to support the necessity of the treatment at the location in question;

h. Surgical expenses to a student-athlete (including a partial qualifier or a non-qualifier) who is injured during the academic year while participating in voluntary physical activities that will prepare the student-athlete for competition;

i. Medication and physical therapy utilized by a student-athlete during the academic year to enable the individual to participate in intercollegiate athletics, regardless of whether the injury or illness is the result of intercollegiate competition or practice;

j. Medication and physical therapy utilized by a student-athlete (even if the student-athlete is not a full-time student) during the academic year to enable the individual to participate in intercollegiate athletics, only if the student-athlete resides on campus (or in the local community of the institution) and appropriate medical documentation is available to establish that the student-athlete is unable to attend the institution as a full-time student as a result of the student-athlete's injury or illness; and

k. Preseason dental examinations conducted in conjunction with a regular preseason physical examination (NCAA, 2010a).

As mentioned, any and all medical services are eligible for payment if such service is connected to participation. While the institution is eligible to cover any such cost, it is not required. The prudent step would be to develop a policy and communicate it to all student-athletes, coaches, administrators, and parents.

Specific to my work at South Carolina in 2007, I realized things were changing, and not necessarily for the best. One particular incident made me aware of that. We were paying eighty percent of an $18,000 surgical bill at Palmetto Richland Hospital when the same surgical charge was $3,500 at Columbia area outpatient surgery centers. For an athletic director (Eric Hyman) who preached cost containment, I simply could not sell this savings to his new staff. It was the goal of the university to continue to provide services at the Palmetto Richland Hospital where the physicians were located versus outpatient centers where significant savings could be realized. This is a prime example of college athletics today—there is access to more money than ever at the higher-profile conferences of the Big Ten, Southeastern, Pac 12, Big 12, and Atlantic Coast. With the influx of monies, prudent business decisions are not being made. Athletic directors are playing with house money. I fear this will be their downfall.

Healthcare and healthcare costs are driving many Americans bonkers. The above scenario is a prime example. Why is there a medical bill, and then an adjustment to the bill? Why do we not have one single bill? Further, why are people with no insurance charged more than those engaged in an insurance plan? This is a tremendous challenge today for our government. When McGee was the athletic director, he was constantly seeking feedback from me so he better understood the athletic training environment as well as the community where we lived. He recognized that learning was not all about going to meetings and continuing education. Many times, continuing education is all about having interaction in our daily activities with experts outside the athletic department.

McGee was gracious in allowing me to experience a wide variety of activities. I did some speaking in Australia. I was involved with the National Athletic Trainers' Association, served as director of the Mid-Atlantic Athletic Trainers' Association, president of the Southeastern Conference Sports Medicine Committee, and as a member of the board of directors for the Fellowship of Christian Athletes.

First and foremost were my daily activities and responsibilities with the university. Then came the outside activities that proved to be great educational tools and learning experiences over the years. Unfortunately, with a change in administration at South Carolina, I was seen as an obstacle and as someone who was loyal only to McGee. I might have felt singled out except that nearly every member of McGee's administration departed South Carolina within months of Hyman's arrival as athletic director.

Toward the end of my South Carolina days, several issues concerned me. Foremost was the minimal input I was providing relative to the cost containment and medical spending for our student-athletes. Also, there was the issue of sharing my personal information with a team physician who I was not comfortable with and who I believed was undermining my efforts at cost containment for our department. This validated for me that there is nothing more political than healthcare, especially on a college campus.

Athletic trainers generally are there to be seen yet not heard. I had challenged the system along the way, was considered entrepreneurial, developed products and engaged in contractual relationships outside the university. Now I was being chastised and questioned for such activities. There were no issues with my performance, so it appeared it just came down to an athletic trainer making too much outside income, had too much influence in his area, and an administration that wanted no input in his area.

Millions and millions of dollars are pouring into college athletic programs. Athletic administrators show support for programs by where they put their resources. Everyone from administrators to athletic trainers to team physicians must do a better job of showing outcomes and showing value to their institutions so these programs are embraced, enhanced and supported.

In the future, institutions must continue to be aware of network requirements relative to benefits. We must make sure not to lose benefits for insured student-athletes as some insurance providers refuse coverage for injuries to student-athletes. It is difficult for student-athletes to return home to receive physician care during the academic school year. For a continuum of care, athletic departments often prefer the physician who supervises day-to-day care be involved with surgery when indicated, not some network-assigned physician and certainly not a surgeon who does not understand sports medicine.

We must continue to be aware of the demands of those involved in physically active environments. As a member of the sports medicine team, there is a sense of urgency with evaluations in caring for injuries. Special testing such as MRIs, cardiovascular screenings and other special radiographic studies often is needed to make timely diagnoses. Such special studies aid providers in making diagnoses and for planning care. Further, prior to returning to activity, student-athletes often need special braces to protect them from the stresses of injury or re-injury. These services and devices often are excluded from insurance benefits and must be paid for by the athletic department or by the patient. Costs historically borne by the insurance industry, whether through primary care or excess, may in the future be passed back to the institution.

NCAA Division I athletic programs are facing cutbacks. Division I-AA and levels below are facing similar cutbacks in all areas, and those institutions generally have fewer dollars to play with. As a result, at those levels, general medical conditions and non-accident claims are being left up to the student-athlete for his or her plan to cover, thus placing the responsibility of insurance coverage on their parents. Insured student-athletes are required to go where providers direct them, leaving little latitude for claims.

Any in-depth review of program efficiency would involve a ratio between what services are received and what is actually paid for by the institution.

The ratio is based on what is spent departmentally versus professional services received by student-athletes. According to arrangements and philosophies developed, the ratio might be skewed accordingly. Merely calculate healthcare costs and factor in the actual benefits obtained by the department. The lower the ratio, the more benefits are being received at a lower outlay by the department. This would be seen as efficient use of primary insurance and write-off agreements with providers.

Athletic administrators strive to provide maximum care at a cost the institution can afford. Administrators today must minimize liability from a care, coverage, and financial perspective. The NCAA requires an annual statement from each institution addressing healthcare coverage and coverage of benefits up to the catastrophic insurance coverage provided by the NCAA.

This requirement, like so many the NCAA imposes, is in direct response to negligence by member institutions. Significant discussions are taking place daily around company water coolers specific to healthcare reform and the impact it will have on all Americans, rich and poor, insured and uninsured. As an athletic trainer, and more specifically as an athletic administrator, I dealt with the administration of healthcare benefits for student-athletes on a variety of athletic budgets from the lower divisions to the highest division. At all levels, the NCAA now allows member institutions to cover any and all medical benefits/medical services to student-athletes.

While Congress has not created the latest healthcare reform laws to deal specifically with student-athletes, athletic administrators will have to monitor closely the new regulations. The challenge will be to see what health services are not covered by either primary accident insurance (purchased by the institution) or managed care programs negotiated by the institutions.

This is a difficult subject to discuss. Some would see laying out significant amounts of dollars for healthcare as appropriate care by the athletic department. Another institution could have a very efficient and effective healthcare delivery system that requires a greatly reduced percentage of outlay of financial resources while providing an equitable level of care. *We must be objective of the quality of care provided.*

The ability to be objective is an expectation of college administrators. Parents and guardians expect a standard of care to be provided to their children; and the athletic administrator needs to guarantee this is provided. Further, the ability to cover these costs is a challenge, but it is an implied expectation.

Dr. Rod's
Treatment Plan

PROTECTIVE EQUIPMENT

PROTECTIVE EQUIPMENT IS OPENLY viewed as an avenue to prevent injuries. The Sports Medicine team collectively feels these areas can help minimize both the incidence and exposure of athletic injuries. The following discussion will highlight several areas of the body. It is important for physicians and athletic trainers to advise athletes appropriately about protective equipment. Recommendations for protection require understanding of biomechanics and anatomy.

It is the collective belief of coaches, physicians and athletic trainers that all should take special care to see that the players' equipment is properly fitted, particularly the helmet, to minimize the chance of injury.

Ankle

The foot and ankle are among the most commonly injured body parts of recreational and competitive sports participants. An estimated twenty-five-thousand ankle sprains occur daily in the United States (Lassiter, Malone, & Garrett, 1989; Safran, Benedetti, Bartolozzi, & Mandelbaum, 1999; Safran, Zachazewski, Benedetti, Bartolozzi, & Mandelbaum, 1999). From 1997-2004, the ankle was the second most common sports injury reported in the National Collegiate Athletic Association's Injury Surveillance System for football with a range of thirteen to fourteen percent of all injuries (NCAA, 2005). The greatest predisposition for ankle injury is the history of at least one ankle sprain (Smith & Reischl, 1986).

Perception of instability is identified as functional instability and is often associated with recurrent ankle sprains due to proprioceptive and neuromuscular deficits following incomplete rehabilitation (Tropp, 2002; Verbrugge, 1996). Ankle sprains rank high in incidence, especially among physically active persons. Around twenty to fifty percent of the lateral ankle sprain patients have chronic ankle dysfunction (Freeman, Dean, & Hanham, 1965; Smith & Reischl, 1986).

Does taping of ankles actually help prevent injuries? Many college and professional athletic trainers believe taping can help prevent injuries to the ankle. The majority of the time, people tape for one of two reasons. The first is using common white, non-elastic tape to prevent excesses of motion. The second method used a more elastic tape and actually feels tight when applied and stimulates nerves in and around the ankle.

It should be noted many coaches and athletic trainers embrace the use of braces for ankle protection. The braces employ protective aspects utilized when taping. One major difference is that braces can be reused, and that any amateur athlete can use one even if he or she does not have an athletic trainer. Many schools see this as a major area of savings relative to their budgets.

Shoulder

Protection of the shoulder has certainly evolved over the years. "Shoulder pads" comprise equipment which provides protection with fitted front and back panels combined with cantilevers over top of each shoulder to protect the AC joint. The basic principles of shoulder pad design include the channeling of forces away from anatomical structures, which disperses forces over a large area. Mechanically, the force reduction by mechanical structures helps decrease potential injuries.

Mouth Guards/Concussion

No controlled experimental study has confirmed or refuted the idea that a properly-fitted mouth guard reduces the likelihood of sustaining a concussive injury. But evidence is mounting that the device could play a significant role in this critical area of player safety.

The four types of guards most commonly used are: a. stock over-the-counter, not mouth formed; b. boil and bite, well worn, mouth formed; c. cut-off, no posterior tooth coverage; and d. custom fabricated over a model of the upper dental arch (Barth, Freeman, & Winters, 2000). No advantage has been found from wearing a custom made mouth guard over a boil-and-bite mouth guard to reduce the risk of cerebral concussion in football players (Wisniewski, Guskiewicz, Trope, & Sigurdsson, 2004). The increasingly popular custom-fit mouth guards produce a posterior separation of three to four mm between the mandible and maxilla (jaws). This thickness converts to time and distance, over which acceleration occurs if a blow is delivered to the mandibular complex (Winters, 2001).

CHAPTER 9

MOUNTAINS AND MOUNTAINTOPS

Athletic trainers are no different than most other professionals in every walk of life. We experience the highs and lows of our profession, just as doctors and construction workers and receptionists deal with the ebbs and flows of their jobs. What might separate our profession from others is how closely we are tied to athletics, and the competition involved seems to make the highs even higher and the lows even lower.

There is nothing quite as exhilarating for an athletic trainer than being part of a winning team effort, whatever the sport and whatever the level of competition. By contrast, the depths of despair often go along with heartbreak defeats on the playing fields. Rarely is there an in-between feeling.

In discussing the highs and lows of my experiences in athletic training, I must begin with the highest of highs. There was no more exciting and invigorating experience in my career than South Carolina's back-to-back Outback Bowl victories over mighty Ohio State following the 2000 and 2001 football seasons.

To fully understand just how South Carolina reached previously unattained heights in college football with those wins, you have to know a little bit about the program's history. If there was a stamp on the South Carolina football program over the years it was one of mediocrity. As late as the 2011 season, the program was still flirting with an all-time record of the same number of wins as losses. Along the way South Carolina produced a couple of top-ten caliber teams and won a league championship in 1969 when it was a member of the Atlantic Coast Conference.

Despite South Carolina's smattering of success in football it could never get over the hump when it came to bowl games. Gamecock teams played in eight bowl games from the 1946 Gator Bowl to the 1988 Liberty Bowl and not one time returned home to Columbia with a winning trophy.

Then came the January 1995 Carquest Bowl, my first postseason experience with a South Carolina football team. This bowl game was played before the proliferation of bowl games deemed many of them meaningless. Believe me, the South Carolina team that played in that Carquest Bowl saw the game as a big deal. It had won six games and lost five during the regular season and deserved to be playing in the postseason against a darned good West Virginia team that had a similar 7-5 record. It was an intriguing matchup of teams not affiliated with conferences.

The excitement began with our acceptance party in downtown Columbia. Bill Dukes was a South Carolina alum, fervent fan, and most successful businessman. He had restored a historic Columbia train station into a restaurant to be opened under the name "Blue Marlin," with low-country cuisine. It was the perfect atmosphere to accept the bowl invitation and celebrate Coach Brad Scott's first-year accomplishments.

Attending and working a bowl game was an all-new experience for me. As soon as we accepted the bowl bid, a group of administrators was sent on the university's private plane to the Ft. Lauderdale, Florida area on a fact-finding mission. John Moore, an associate athletic director, Jim Shealy, an athletic equipment manager, a couple of ticket office staff members and I were among those in the travel party sent to map out the week we would spend in Fort Lauderdale prior to the game. We selected the Marriott Marquis on the waterway in Fort Lauderdale. I recall walking out by the swimming pool on that early December day seeing the inter-coastal waterway where the boat of financial mogul Charles Forbes was docked. It was green—like money—and was the first boat I had ever seen with a helicopter landing pad on top. Our trip to south Florida was going to be fun.

There were several perks to being part of the bowl experience, and the one that stood out the most for the players was a bowl ring. It was a nice gift, and reward, for a season full of hard work and success. The staff/coaches' rings and wives' pendants were ten-karat gold, while the players received the traditional Josten Lustrium rings. The upgrade for staff is fairly common with many institutions. As Coach Steve Spurrier came on the scene, we quickly learned he does not reward bowl games with rings. He reserves rings for championships only. He has certainly been successful, so no one questioned his judgment. He did award his 2011 Capital One Bowl championship team with rings to commemorate the significance of the season.

Another perk for me at the Carquest Bowl was the use of a suite at Joe Robbie Stadium. This was provided to me by our bowl host, an executive at First Union Bank. My parents came down for the game, so I knew I could put the suite to good use. I also invited Nancy Peele, the wife of our team physician, Dr. Bob Peele, and their four children.

There were only fifty-one thousand fans at the game, but that did not dampen the spirit of South Carolina fans who were so starved for a bowl victory. Quarterback Steve Taneyhill earned Most Valuable Player honors by completing twenty-six of thirty-six passes for two hundred twenty-seven yards and Brandon Bennett ran for one hundred yards as South Carolina held on for a 24-21 victory. The win was big enough for South Carolina Governor Carroll Campbell to join the celebration in the locker room afterward. Those who were not in south Florida to celebrate the monumental achievement were at the Columbia airport to extend the excitement upon our return the following day. An estimated five thousand fans greeted the team at the airport.

Unfortunately, that was the peak of Coach Brad Scott's years at South Carolina. The next three seasons, Scott's teams had records of 6-5, 5-6 and 1-10, including ten consecutive losses to conclude the 1998 season and Scott's career at South Carolina. The high of that Carquest Bowl victory was quickly forgotten when Scott was fired and Lou Holtz was ushered in only to see his first team lose all eleven games of the 1999 season. So, South

Carolina had the nation's longest active losing streak, one that reached twenty-one games and sunk the program to new lows. It is amazing how quickly the highs can become the lows.

I recount all this to set the stage for one of the most remarkable turnarounds in college football history, and to give you an idea of just how much winning back-to-back Outback Bowls meant to South Carolina, its fans, the city of Columbia and, yes, the team's athletic trainers and physicians.

The 2000 football season began with a victory over New Mexico State to snap the long losing streak, and students celebrated by tearing down the Williams-Brice Stadium goal posts and parading them across campus. A week later, South Carolina stunned number nine-ranked Georgia, 21-10, then disposed of lightly-regarded Eastern Michigan, 41-6.

Then came one of my fondest memories as a member of the South Carolina staff, when legendary Coach Jackie Sherrill brought his twenty-fifth- ranked Mississippi State team to Columbia for a televised game in front of a homecoming crowd. Down by a field goal with the final seconds ticking down, the Gamecocks were driving toward the south end zone. The crowd of eighty-thousand was in a frenzy until quarterback Phil Petty went down with an ankle injury. My assistant, Phil Hedrick, and I rushed to assess his injury. Our worst nightmare played out. Petty would not be able to play.

Coach Lou Holtz called on reserve quarterback Eric Kimrey, who was the son of a successful Columbia-area high school football coach. Eric was the prototypical walk-on quarterback who studied film and tendencies of opponents like no other player on the team. He eventually leveraged his college studies to success as a high school coach with five consecutive South Carolina Independent School Association championships.

Eric and Coach Skip Holtz were having a conversation regarding play selection when Lou Holtz entered the huddle. I will never forget the two questions Holtz had for Kimrey.

"What is your favorite play?" Holtz asked.

"Fade route," Kimrey answered.

"Who's your favorite receiver?"

"Kelly," Kimrey replied.

"Run the play." He quickly turned away and resumed his patented pacing of the sidelines.

The quarterback jogged to the field. Center Larrell Johnson snapped the ball to Kimrey, who launched the fade pass. Jermale Kelly gathered it into his hands in the corner of the end zone to thunderous cheers and South Carolina remained unbeaten with a 23-19 victory.

By the end of the regular season, South Carolina had won seven of eleven games and earned an invitation to play nineteenth-ranked Ohio State in the Outback Bowl.

Holtz prepared his teams for bowl games as if they were playing in the Super Bowl. He worked his team very hard in practices before they headed to Tampa, Florida the week before the Outback Bowl. Holtz was a slave driver with everyone. He drove everyone nuts during bowl preparation with his rough, relentless, and grueling practices. He was tough on the players, the assistant coaches and the medical staff. He wanted his players available for practice and really took it out on those who missed practice because of an ailment or injury. The public cannot imagine how demanding Holtz was of his players and staff.

Following the intense practice sessions on campus, Holtz dismissed the team for four to five days to be with their families for Christmas. Those who lived near the bowl site were allowed to meet us in Tampa. All others returned to Columbia and traveled Christmas afternoon via chartered airline to Tampa. We were housed at the downtown Hyatt hotel in Tampa and there were family events scheduled throughout the week. Gawking South Carolina fans experiencing their first big-time bowl game were everywhere we went.

As the week wore on, Holtz scaled back on his practices and made it a more enjoyable experience for all without losing sight of the fact this was a very important game for South Carolina and its fans. He and his football staff had planned activities to maximize the student-athlete's experience in Tampa. Events included visiting an art gallery, attending a National Hockey League game, and going to Busch Gardens. Many of the activities were supported by Jim McVay and the Outback Bowl committee, and some of them were supported by Holtz. People never heard about the things he did for student-athletes off the field. He was tough, but he was good to the players.

The final day of practices Holtz staged a tag football game among the coaches, which was just one of the many traditions he brought along from his coaching career. The game was generally held at the final walk-through and was usually in the stadium we would be playing in the next day. The players loved it, and nearly every one of them had his picture taken with the head coach. Holtz was a tough-love kind of coach, but he knew how to motivate a team and the players really rallied around him.

Ohio State, a longtime power from the Big Ten Conference, was the favorite to win the game in 2001. It meant a great deal to Holtz because he grew up in Ohio and had worked on the staff of legendary Coach Woody Hayes.

Ryan Brewer was an undersized running back who was pretty much overlooked by Ohio State coming out of Troy, Ohio. He was the kind of hard-nosed player Holtz loved and he was happy to bring Brewer south to play football. Brewer had the game of his life in that Outback Bowl, earning MVP honors with one hundred and nine yards rushing, ninety-two yards receiving and three touchdowns. South Carolina rolled to a 24-7 win. No one enjoyed the victory more than Holtz and Brewer.

A year later, we were back in Tampa and as fate would have it, playing Ohio State again in the Outback Bowl. This time, South Carolina carried an 8-3 record and No. Fourteen national ranking. Ohio State was the twenty-second ranked team in the country. South Carolina bolted to a 28-0 lead. By the end of the third quarter we watched helplessly as Ohio State rallied to tie the game. As time expired, a forty-two yard field goal by Daniel Weaver was the difference for the Gamecocks.

The players loved bowl games as they were another opportunity to showcase their talents. Coaches loved bowl games as they were another chance to develop the team, and especially the younger players. The administration loved the bowl games as they were a chance to show-off the university's product, and hit up big boosters for donations. One of the perks of the bowl games, at least from the student-athlete perspective was how much they would receive in bowl gifts, travel allowance, and per diem meal money and incidental expense allowance in accordance with NCAA guidelines. As student-athletes are required to stay at the university for practices after classes have finished, the university was able to provide travel money for them to either travel home and to the bowl site, or home and back to the university for the team's charter flight to the bowl venue. Again, the NCAA was very clear in what provisions could be provided.

There was some flexibility on meal provisions, though the NCAA oversaw this to make sure abuse did not take place. Institutions had to stay within university or state guidelines. Some staffs elected to provide the student-athletes with all their meals via per diem while some preferred to have one team meal per day and the balance provided in per diem. Either way, we generally would not give a lump sum amount, but gave the travel allowance prior to departure from campus, and three installments of the per diem was provided progressively through the bowl week to make sure the poor managers of money did not run out of funds.

While you certainly savor the moment and all the fan excitement that surrounds the wins, it really is not until years later that you fully appreciate such occasions. Until South Carolina won the SEC Eastern Division championship in 2010 and the eleven-win campaign with Capital One Bowl victory over Nebraska in 2012, the Outback Bowl wins represented the greatest moments in program history. For me, they represented the highest of highs in my athletic training career. These were great team accomplishments with successes at the end of good seasons, and thus significant events I love to reflect upon.

Before those good times at South Carolina, we experienced some down times. Nothing was worse or more trying than the 1992 season under Coach Sparky Woods. I had worked with Woods at Appalachian State and again at South Carolina. We developed a tight friendship and shared a common respect for each other's work. So, it was particularly difficult for me to watch him suffer through the start of the 1992 season when his team lost five consecutive games.

You could not help but sense the team and program was getting away from Woods when the players threatened to boycott practice the week

South Carolina was preparing to play fifteenth-ranked Mississippi State. The players also voted to ask for the removal of Woods as head coach. Neither act came to fruition, but the players' actions probably signaled the beginning of the end for Woods at South Carolina.

When you form the kind of bond I had with Woods, I hurt along with him.

Amazingly enough, South Carolina defeated Mississippi State, and then extended the winning streak to four games with victories over Vanderbilt, Tennessee and Louisiana Tech. A season-ending win over Clemson followed by a season-opening victory over fourteenth-ranked Georgia in the 1993 season seemed to save Woods' job. But it was false hope. The team never stabilized and finished with a 4-7 record. A new athletic director, Mike McGee, was hired that year and that profession does not take kindly to coaches who are not successful on the football field. Woods knew that, and on one October night outside Palmetto Baptist Hospital he told me he would likely be fired. Woods was at the hospital visiting a player who was recovering from surgery.

In your career as an athletic trainer, you can only hope the experience of a head-coach firing only comes along once. Unfortunately, Woods' firing was not the last I would experience. I had to endure the same kind of pain when Brad Scott was fired five years later, following the 1998 season at South Carolina. His firing was one of the low points of my career because Scott was so easy to work with. We were close in age and shared many of the same values. He always was understanding of my role in the athletic department and was supportive of our medical staff.

Scott developed a solid reputation in his eleven seasons as an assistant coach at Florida State. He was the offensive coordinator when Florida State won the national championship and quarterback Charlie Ward captured the Heisman Trophy in 1993. He parlayed that success into his first head-coaching gig at a time when schools around the country were plucking assistants off Bobby Bowden's Florida State staff. The thirty-nine year-old Scott seemed the perfect fit at South Carolina, a young assistant with the energy and moxie to tackle a difficult assignment.

Scott's first season as head coach was South Carolina's third competing in the SEC. While he brought in strong recruiting classes, Scott had difficulty filling out depth charts with SEC-caliber players, a problem South Carolina still faces today. (Spurrier has done a superb job in the recent years with signing of South Carolina high school superlative student-athletes along with a group of classmates of the same quality.) It did not help matters that Florida and Tennessee were fielding powerhouse teams during that period with Florida winning a national championship in 1996 and Tennessee in 1998. Yet Scott broke out of the gate fast, leading South Carolina to a 6-5 record in 1994 and the previously mentioned Carquest Bowl victory. Scott's record in bowl games at Florida State was 10-0-1, so the Carquest Bowl win seemed like just another step in building his program.

The bowl win and a victory over twenty-second ranked Clemson two years later were the high points of Scott's five seasons at South Carolina. His teams' won-loss records were 7-5, 4-6-1, 6-5, 5-6 and 1-10. There just were not enough wins to keep Scott on board, and he was fired. Soon after, Scott hooked on as an assistant coach at Clemson. Sadly, South Carolina fans have never forgiven Scott for taking a job at their rival school. He often is a punching bag for jokes in Internet chat rooms, a sad testament to those who cannot look past their petty differences to see a good man.

October 24, 1998. Nashville, Tennessee. It was a partly cloudy day with a slight breeze out of the north from downtown Nashville, but the temperature was a balmy 70 degrees. We always enjoyed trips to Nashville, as Vanderbilt provided the one team my Gamecocks could generally dominate. That was true until 1998. The Commodores devastated us that day with a victory, their first of the season while we lost our sixth straight conference game. The proverbial wheels were starting to run off our bus. It was not a pretty sight. The one good thought was that fewer than thirty-thousand fans were reported in attendance for the 6 p.m. kickoff at Vanderbilt Stadium. The numbers were probably padded, as their fans just don't support the team.

On the flight home, I was checking on a couple of players who were injured during the game. I quickly recalled a trip home a few years earlier when our running back, Duce Staley had severely injured his ankle. As I came to the coaches and staff section, I noted offensive coordinator Chuck

Reedy was reading Lou Holtz's book *Winning Every Day*. I commented to him on his read and he quipped "I'm reading about your next coach!"

I was confused, as I had heard little about this. It certainly seems those in the staff room do not hear all the noise and discussion in the community. Little did I know how much was going on, and little did I realize how much things were beginning to change.

Next in the coaching line at South Carolina was Lou Holtz. I was in Dallas, Texas for a NATA board of directors meeting when Holtz was introduced as the new coach in December, 1998. It was an exciting time for the athletic department to bring in a big-name coach, someone who brought the football program instant credibility.

From the outset I recognized how straight-forward and detail-oriented Holtz was as a coach and administrator. He was a no-nonsense person. There was no small talk in meetings with him. You did not go see him in his office unless you had something that needed to be addressed. In meetings, you needed to be prepared for anything. I can remember carrying armloads of files into these meetings. This, of course, was before the age of wireless communication. If a question was fired at you from the head of the staff room conference table, you knew you had to have an appropriate answer.

Throughout 1999 and 2000 I suffered from elbow problems. Turns out I had two full-blown cases of chronic tennis elbow, or specifically degeneration of the extensor carpi radialis brevis. I had surgery on my right elbow in 1999, and the same pain and problems returned in 2000 in the left elbow. When I underwent a second surgery on the other elbow, my surgeon joked that the problems were the result of carrying all those files into meetings with Holtz.

Holtz's five seasons at South Carolina went much like those of Scott. After a 0-11 start, Holtz led the team to back-to-back Outback Bowl wins, but then faltered to 5-7 and 6-5 records his final two seasons. Unlike his predecessors I had worked with, Holtz decided to resign from coaching.

By the time we departed for our game at Clemson on November 19, 2004, news reports had broken that Holtz would resign at the conclusion of the season and Steve Spurrier would be South Carolina's next head coach. My sons, David and Ryan, made the road trip and rode in an escort provided by representatives from the South Carolina Highway Patrol. After getting the team checked into our team headquarters at the Greenville Hilton, I continued a tradition of fine dining across the street at Stax's Peppermill Omega & Grill.

When we returned to the hotel, I checked in with my assistant athletic trainer, Bill Martin. There were no issues with the team, but there was much excitement as the team prepared to meet its in-state rival. I never cared much for Clemson, and was not aware that my feelings toward that program would one day be tempered when Ryan decided to study civil engineering at our state's agriculture and technology institution.

That same night the Detroit Pistons and Indiana Pacers engaged in an ugly brawl that spilled into the stands. The pregame meal conversation the following morning centered on that incident and how sad it was for professional sports. The South Carolina-Clemson game was always big. At the end of the 1996 season I started a personal tradition of writing a note to each senior and placed it in his locker prior to the Clemson game. My notes made a point with each player reflecting on their career at South Carolina. I reminded them the best way to end it was with a win over Clemson. I told them, "This is the game the fans will remember you for." I am afraid the game always has meant more to Clemson than South Carolina because the Tigers have dominated the series. During my seventeen seasons of on-field work at South Carolina, we beat Clemson only five times.

Little did I know that this would be the final game I worked on the field. I had proposed to our administration for some time that I move out of patient care and into administration to oversee the entire healthcare of student-athletes. Be careful what you ask for. I did not realize how important patient care was to me. It is the only area in which I interacted with student-athletes. In administration, you only deal with problems. This was much tougher than I ever anticipated. As friends in the athletic training community from around the country call me as they contemplate moving to a larger institution or moving into full-time administration, I urge them to move for the right reasons. Bigger is not always better. You probably have more control on work and professional autonomy at a smaller institution. I certainly lost my autonomy as I transitioned from Lenoir-Rhyne College to Appalachian State University and finally to the University of South Carolina. I have heard athletic trainers say to be appreciated, you should work in high school as the appreciation for what is done as an athletic trainer is lessened as you go from high schools to colleges and eventually professional sports.

Pre-game warm ups that evening were pretty much like any other game on a cool, fall evening. I met with Danny Poole and his Clemson athletic training staff prior to the game. Our physicians visited with their doctors, and we all reviewed medical policies and how injured student-athletes would be taken care of relative to acute injuries. Things seemed fairly routine.

Holtz gave another of his rousing pre-game talks. This was his passion, and I will never see anyone in sports prepare a team like he did. As much as he often tore his teams down early in the week, he had his team thinking they could compete with NFL teams at this point.

Our team was ready to get out of the dismal visiting locker room at Clemson's Memorial Stadium. I despised that locker room. It was, without a doubt, the worst I ever endured. It made the small confines of Vanderbilt's Commodore Stadium look like the Taj Mahal! It did not help matters that we dressed too many players, and all the non-travel players were allowed to come to the game by charter buses we provided. This was the non-dress team's reward for a season of practice. The extra players were always in the way. It was a difficult place to work. With the excitement of the game, the awful locker room conditions and the tension of the season, it seemed everyone was at odds. Senior administrators with their "all-access passes" were everywhere, as they all wanted to see what Holtz's next step would be.

As the teams took the field, Clemson entered the stadium with its traditional run down the hill. There was player interaction, by both teams as the Clemson Tigers ran down the hill at Memorial Stadium and our players were there to greet them, or taunt them as the Clemson fans say. We thought the SEC officials did a poor job of maintaining control. South Carolina coaches had long believed we had better officiated games in this rivalry game in Columbia using ACC officials (It is common for teams to dictate the visiting team in non-conference games be allowed to have the visitor's officials assigned to the game.)

I was always partial to SEC officials due to my work with them.

The NBA fight was a portent of things to come that Saturday at Clemson. With five minutes and eighteen seconds remaining in the game, fights spread over the field. Wild punches were thrown. Helmets were thrown. Players were kicked on the ground. It was ugly. Highway patrolmen and campus police were called from their sideline posts to break up the fights, which lasted for six long minutes.

That might be one of the few times in my career I was scared. We did not know if that entire stadium might break out in fights. Thankfully, no fans got onto the field and no players went into the stands. My two sons happened to be on the sideline that day. As soon as the fighting began I instructed them to sit down on the bench and not to move. My sons usually enjoyed being on a college football sideline, but this was one day I wish they had been seated in the stands. Susan commented about how frightened she was as she watched from her seat in the athletic department's staff section.

The fight overshadowed Holtz's final game as a head coach, a 29-7 loss to Clemson. Afterward, Holtz said he would be remembered "along with Woody Hayes for having a fight at the Clemson game." Hayes' illustrious coaching career at Ohio State ended when he slugged a Clemson player near the sideline late in the 1978 Gator Bowl.

A national audience watched footage of the South Carolina-Clemson fight over and over again during the next few days and it created an unnecessary black eye for both universities. It was a black eye for the state of South Carolina and a black eye for college football. It was embarrassing to all, a shameful display of unsportsmanlike behavior and thuggery.

Presidents at both universities met with their athletic department staffs on Sunday and talked with representatives from their respective conferences. By Monday morning both schools had decided to punish the teams by not allowing them to participate in postseason bowl games.

Later that day, Holtz met with his team and gave it the bad news that there would be no bowl games this season. Immediately following the meeting, several players revolted and looted the locker room. It was a sure sign that the program had gotten away from Holtz. The players were out of control and criminal charges eventually were brought against the offenders.

This was the pathetic and sad end to Lou Holtz's long and storied career as a college football coach. No coach should ever leave under those circumstances. Holtz deserved better.

I was luckier in the way I left the University of South Carolina athletic department. It was my decision and I got to leave on my own terms in February, 2007.

It became apparent I was no longer the go-to person for healthcare the way it was when Mike McGee was our athletic director. When you worked for McGee you were responsible for your area. I saw very quickly when the new administration came in—whether it was because I had been there a long time or because the new athletic director wanted his own person—that questions of my department were not being asked of me.

Fortunately, I had plenty to fall back on professionally. I decided to pursue my consulting business on a full-time basis. I really believed I could grow that business as it was providing significant opportunities in 2007. I am grateful it has continued to grow since that time.

I talked to my attorney and we drafted a letter of resignation to the administration. Then I met with my staff and told them how appreciative I was of the opportunity the university and athletic department had given me. It was time for new leadership, and I recognized an opportunity to grow my own business.

When I left the athletic training business I recognized I would never again experience the great satisfaction of being around student-athletes. I cherished the joy that came with nurturing them to good health. I never realized how much I would miss those consultations about injuries, intervention on personal problems, or those conversations with student-athletes' parents about injuries and other matters.

I have since missed the fellowship I had with our physicians and the meetings with SEC athletic trainers. I am a people person, and I enjoy relationships. As much as I miss these relationships, I realize I disliked what I was doing when I left the athletic training room and made a move into administration. In the latter role, it seemed like all I dealt with were problems: positive drug tests, unpaid medical bills, coaches upset about how a staff member handled an event, or administrators looking to pass blame along for budget shortfalls. The problems went on and on and ultimately I missed working directly with the student-athletes.

There was never a day I did not enjoy being an athletic trainer. That was true until February, 2007.

I was taught from a young age, that everyone is different. As my fraternal grandfather Walters is quoted as saying, "everyone has good in them - just sometimes you have to look extra hard to find it." Taking his comment a step further, I have certainly noticed that not all people are the same. As I reflect to my first year at Appalachian State University in the freshman dormitory, each and every one of the forty or so guys on the ninth floor of Eggers dormitory were different.

Based on aptitude and accomplishments, I have long felt that people or professions are divided into thirds. The smartest third of the people, whether they are plumbers, surgeons or teachers, make the best researchers. The middle third makes the best practitioners, and the bottom third makes the most money! Think about it - it is so true.

Dr. Rod's
Treatment Plan

LIGHTNING PLANS

EVERY YEAR, ABOUT TWO hundred people are killed and more than seven hundred people injured by lightning accidents. This is more than floods, hurricanes, and tornadoes combined. Due to the outdoor nature of many sports and recreational activities, it has become a standard practice to establish a procedure to follow in the event lightning is in proximity to the activity. The National Athletic Trainers' Association established a procedure which has been embraced by practitioners worldwide. Further, the protocol includes best practices and procedures which should be followed.

It is important to establish a chain of command that identifies who is to make the call to remove individuals from the field. For sport activities (recreational or organized sports), name a designated weather watcher. It is important to have a means of monitoring local weather forecasts and warnings. The plan should include a designated safe shelter for each venue.

The hallmark factor when dealing with lightning is to know the relative position of the lighting to the location of the activity, coupled with the required time it takes to safely vacate the practice/competition area. The greater the distance the safe shelter is from the practice/competition area, the greater the amount of time which should be allowed. Thus, for safe shelter in close proximity, the field must be vacated later than when the safe shelter is approximately six miles away; while safe shelters which are not close should be sought when lightning is within fifteen miles.

To calculate the proximity of lightning to the specific area, we use flash—to—bang count to determine when to go to safety. A five second count equates to one mile of distance. Avoid the highest point in an open field. Do not take shelter under trees, flagpoles, or light poles. Assume the lightning safe position (crouched) for those exposed in weather. Once activities have been suspended, wait at least thirty minutes following last sound of thunder or lightning flash prior to resuming activity to make sure lightning has cleared the area.

The injury and damage to the human body caused by lightning is due to the transfer of large amounts of electrical charge flowing from cloud to ground. Some portion of this moving electric current can pass through, over, or around a victim, causing the injury pattern. This large flow of electrical current damages the human body through the sudden release of electrical, thermal, and mechanical energy, and the injuries suffered from a lightning strike may involve tissue damage from one or all of these mechanisms. Almost three quarters of the people who survive a lightning strike will suffer life-long severe complications and disabilities.

Lightning-caused injuries fall into categories which depend on the actual path the electrical current of the lightning strike takes as it flows through or over the victim on its way to ground. The most common mechanisms are:

Electrical Injury

Typically, over forty percent of lightning strike victims experience heart dysfunction in the form of temporary heart stoppage and longer-lasting arrhythmia. The age and pre-injury health of the victim are important in gauging the damage caused by the lightning strike. A person with serious heart problems prior to a lightning strike is much more likely to experience serious and life-threatening heart problems from the strike itself.

Thermal injury

A lightning strike may reach a temperature of twenty thousand degrees or more, and this rapid heat release is the source of thermal injuries. Because a lightning strike is a short duration event (typically less than a tenth of a second), the thermal energy usually remains at the outer skin level and results in burns and other surface injury.

Mechanical injury

The lightning strike produces a shock wave in the air as it is suddenly heated and cooled. The strength of the shock wave is dependent on the amount of current in the strike. Larger strikes produce more energy release and therefore stronger shock waves. These types of blunt trauma injuries are the same as for any form of explosion and can range from broken bones to more severe trauma injuries involving the nervous system.

In summary, have a plan for dealing with lightning events. As we have said so many times, prevention and planning is so important.

CHAPTER 10

THE EVER-CHANGING CHALLENGES OF COLLEGE ATHLETICS

The climate of college athletics has certainly changed since my 1979 graduation from Appalachian State University. The average fan cannot fathom how much money is involved in professional and college athletics. I saw revenues generated from affiliation with the Southeastern Conference increase from paltry amounts in 1992 to tens of millions of dollars by 2010.

Inherent with increased revenues are an abundance of problems that have infiltrated athletic departments and have made management of sports so much more challenging. In this chapter we will look at athletic administration thought patterns and some underlying challenges of administrators from policies and procedures, drug testing, and screening for potential life-threatening conditions.

Let me begin this discussion with a story that illustrates the chain of command within an athletic department. This story exemplifies the challenges of athletic trainers in their attempts to maintain a high standard of care and institutional integrity, oftentimes while dealing with high-profile people.

Drug testing is a necessary evil in athletics today, an important procedure that helps level the field of athletics at both the professional and amateur level. Lots of administrative matters must be addressed prior to engaging any drug-testing program. The program must be outlined and embraced by the institution from a program and philosophical point.

Specific to test administration, dates of testing and times for tests would be selected based on student-athlete availability. Testing dates would be set so scheduling of collection teams could be organized. Test dates also would be arranged to accommodate team practice and game schedules. To minimize the chance of altering urine samples, student-athletes would be notified a maximum of four hours before impending tests. The goal would be to take student-athletes directly from the practice site to the test-collection center.

Updated rosters of the drug-tested teams would then be exported with an identification number—not a social security number—and a sport name to an outside agency to select subjects for drug testing. We instructed this agency to draw names randomly on ten to fifteen percent of the roster, according to the number of people we wanted to test at that time. The agency would provide the random selections back to the university and we would identify who was to be tested.

To show the sensitivity of drug testing, let me share a call I received from a client. To protect those involved, let's not reveal the institution, gender or sport in this incident. The institution embraced a one-time self-referral program. This was a mechanism of help for a student-athlete who acknowledged a substance-abuse problem. The student-athlete was required to notify the institution's administrator of drug testing of any intent to "self-refer." Consistent with most "self-referral" programs, the student-athlete had to request "self-referral" prior to being notified of selection for drug testing. Thus, it was not an avenue for avoiding bad behavior with a "get out of jail free card." Once the student-athlete exercised this option, he or she entered counseling with weekly testing to follow and monitor behavior. Such a program allowed student-athletes to seek help on the front end with the hope of avoiding substance abuse on the back end. Those who did not notify the director of testing of their intent of entering the self-referral program were tested.

This particular drug-testing session happened to have two no-shows among the twenty-five who were screened via observed-urine collection. The administrator of drug testing immediately notified the athletic administration of the no-shows, as was the department's policy. Subsequently, the athletic administration called the administrator of drug testing to say the student-athletes had contacted their coaches and had opted for a self-referral. Any program must have a strong written structure, and it did. The administrator of drug testing reviewed the procedural guidelines and believed the student-athletes had skirted procedure by failing to notify him of a self-referral at the outset. This was an example of student-athletes circumventing the process and trying to cover a wrong.

The athletic administration admitted both student-athletes into the self-referral program, against the advice and understanding of the director of testing. Throughout the process, the administrator of drug testing documented everything, including his refusal to allow a late self-referral as permitted by the athletic administration.

A few weeks later, the same two student-athletes were on the manifest to be tested because they were not tested earlier, and their tests came back positive. Another student-athlete who was a friend of the other two student-athletes also had a positive test. His result was a second positive. He tested positive initially when his buddies were given a pass by the coaches' request to the athletic administration.

The program did not suspend anyone for a first-time positive test, only for a second-time positive test. A second positive test mandated a suspension for ten percent of the student-athlete's regular season. When the parents of the student-athlete who tested positive a second time got involved, they blew a gasket. They were aware the other two student-athletes avoided the first testing. In other words, the two student-athletes got off, and their son was facing a suspension.

This created quite a firestorm, attorneys got involved. The student-athlete contacted the university, and the university's legal counsel contacted the administrator of drug testing. The administrator of drug testing checked his copious notes and reported what had happened, creating a rift between the senior administration and the administrator of drug testing.

The director of testing was in a no-win situation. Because his supervisors did not support his actions, he was now at odds and labeled a trouble-maker. My recommendations to those in college athletics:

1. Have a contract that outlines your responsibilities and who you report to.
2. Make certain your program has a whistle-blower option to allow for transparent activities.
3. All actions should be transparent because student-athletes can see through non-transparent programs and activities.

As the leader of an organization or company, you must have information, and the information must be valid. The president of the company cannot bite the head off of an associate who reports bad news. The president must be informed and apprised of any and all information that may be in circulation. Failure to be informed forces you to run a company in a vacuum, and this is a bad business practice.

As I reflect on my career, I was more convinced than ever that a chain of command exists for a reason. You have policies. You have procedures and they must be followed. When that does not happen, problems are certain to follow. Any time you deviate from policies, you open yourself for interpretation of the rules and, ultimately, backlash from student-athletes.

The importance of chain of command was evident during my first days on the job at Lenoir-Rhyne College in Hickory, North Carolina. We had an athletic department. We had a physical education department. There was a supervisor of physical education and athletics to coordinate those two areas. In the athletic department, there were about twenty employees. We did not really have various areas of the athletic department as I later experienced at South Carolina. If I needed something in the athletic department at Lenoir-Rhyne, I went to the athletic director. If I needed something in physical education, I went to the director of physical education. If there was something bigger, ultimately, I might have to go to the dean's office.

In this chain of command, it is vitally important to have the respect of your supervisor. Dr. Keith Oaks was the supervisor of physical education and athletics at Lenoir-Rhyne. I thought the world of Keith and had tremendous respect for him. From a football standpoint, Hanley Painter was the athletic director. Dr. Jane Jenkins was the chair of the physical education department and an advocate for her staff members. She supported me to be a good teacher, and made certain I had all the materials to succeed.

Athletic trainers have primarily received their education in physical education. In my college preparation, you earned a teaching degree and were hired as a teacher for vacancies in public education. You also would work as an athletic trainer. It was similar to coaches who were school teachers while receiving a supplement for their coaching duties. A coach might have a teaching salary of $30,000 to $40,000, then receive $3,000 to $10,000 as a supplement to coach. I wanted to pursue a career in athletic training. My goal was to obtain a master's degree while I was at Appalachian State. Following graduation, I was hired at Lenoir-Rhyne to teach physical education and athletic training classes to undergraduate students while providing healthcare to university student-athletes.

My first-year salary at Lenoir-Rhyne was $12,000 for a ten-month contract, and I negotiated an additional $1,200 for another month's work in the summer. My salary was not of huge importance because I loved my job and figured I would work at Lenoir-Rhyne forever. After three years, I was promoted from an instructor (athletic training duties also were assigned with release time from physical education) to assistant professor. The academic progression in college and university systems was instructor to assistant professor to associate professor to professor. Just like in any agency, advancing to certain levels offered increased stability, improved salary, etc. Everyone aspires to increase their status on campus and in business.

Lenoir-Rhyne's interim president at the time, Albert Allran, told me the administration liked what I was doing with our athletic training program from an educational and a healthcare standpoint. We were attracting students, and the parents of the student-athletes were pleased with the care they were receiving. There was a family atmosphere of caring and sharing between physical education and athletics. The departments worked together efficiently, something I would not see again on a college campus where I worked.

With proper support and a solid chain of command that was adhered to at Lenoir-Rhyne, I was fortunate to build my foundation and acquire my basic philosophy for healthcare. The best healthcare is good education, and when we are practicing good healthcare this equates to good teaching opportunities for our students.

We all have occurrences in our lives that have taught us valuable lessons. One of the goals of this book was to share some of my "life's lessons," and how they not only had an impact but how they molded me as a person.

There is a saying about the pendulum swinging, and we go from a status of conservatism to liberal and back. The pendulum swings on many issues in life. So many times a child that has been scolded is often the picture of the perfect child for the coming days. Then the newly learned behavior begins to dwindle to his or her old habits.

I saw this happen in college athletics. In March of 1984, the TKE fraternity at Lenoir-Rhyne College had an off-campus party with its sister sorority. This was not an unusual occurrence with the college groups, as alcohol was not allowed on campus, especially for those under the legal age of consumption.

Around 2 a.m., I received a phone call from one of my athletic training students, a member of the sorority at the party with the TKEs. There were some local attendees from the Hickory, North Carolina area, and this often spelled trouble. The story goes that one of the more popular TKEs was John David Moose, captain of Lenoir-Rhyne's football team. The honor student was the son of John David Moose Sr., who also had played football at Lenoir-Rhyne on its 1960 national championship team. Young David had made a comment about a local visitor—a non-student—and the young woman's boyfriend took issue with David. Shortly thereafter, the two were entangled in a fight, and David was left with multiple stab wounds to his upper torso and neck.

He was rushed to the hospital and taken immediately to surgery. I made a call to his family to notify them of the event, and members started the drive from their beach house to Hickory. Shortly thereafter, we were informed John David Moose did not survive the surgery.

I learned some valuable lessons that night. The first was a list of key phone contacts. Today, we have our emergency action plans. In 1984, I had nothing. I knew my athletic director's (Dr. Keith Ochs) home phone number, but I did not know the information for the college chaplain (Dr. Larry Yoder), the college president (Albert Allran), or Coach John Perry's home phone number. You can bet your bottom dollar that from that night on I had these numbers available at all times. Remember, we did not have cell phones in those days.

However, the bigger issue was now meeting the Moose family when it arrived at Frye Regional Medical Center in Hickory. The family's estimated time of arrival was 6 a.m., and we planned accordingly. Our assembled group of athletic department and college administrators stayed together, and supported one another. There was a gathering of TKE fraternity brothers, and other students that needed our support.

Around 6:15 a.m., the Moose family arrived. As John David embraced our group he said, "I'll never forget you guys for being here tonight—thank you."

A couple of years later, fewer memories were present of John David Moose's tragic death. The sensitivity to the situation was eroding, and more activities were allowed. In a few more years, it was business as usual. Only those still in the athletic department remembered—students transition every four years, and that is a short swing of the pendulum.

Fast-forward to my years on the NATA's Board of Directors. As board members, we enjoyed three year terms, with a second term if re-elected. Thus, every six years the potential for a new board existed. Likewise, issues were often addressed every six years, as the memory of activities was short. Today, the terms have been minimized to two, two-year terms, and the memory is even shorter.

244 | TAPE, I-C-E, & SOUND ADVICE

An athletic trainer might have the best view of the ever-changing challenges in college athletics these days. They are many and they are complex. It takes strong leadership to deal with the multitude of problems and continually attempt to find solutions.

When NATA was formally organized in 1950, the norm was to have athletic trainers working with the football and track teams, they were not nearly as common with other sports. Ducky Drake, the famous athletic trainer who worked with the great UCLA basketball teams under Coach John Wooden from 1942-1972, doubled as the school's track and field coach from 1947-1964. Obviously, the role of the athletic trainer was much different then. Word has it that Drake was somewhat of an advisor to Wooden. His athletic training duties were secondary.

When I was hired at South Carolina in 1990, the goal of the athletic administration was to centralize athletic training from a budgetary and equity point of view. No longer did they want a couple of staff persons with football, one with men's basketball, and one with women's sports while also coordinating their athletic training curriculum. Instead, they wanted a comprehensive program with staffing and equity applied across all sports.

Compare that to today. For the 2010 football season, South Carolina listed on its medical staff a medical director, three team physicians, a director of wellness, a team chiropractor, a team dentist, a head football athletic trainer, an assistant football athletic trainer and a sports dietitian. The South Carolina staff also included a sports medicine director, an associate athletic trainer, seven athletic trainers and an administrative assistant. The strength and conditioning staff included a conditioning director for all sports, a conditioning director for football and six strength and conditioning coaches. We have moved from centralized staffs caring for all student-athletes to team staffs caring for only those particular student-athletes. The centralized concepts were implemented for efficiency in staffing and costs containment. With the micromanaging coaches of today, there is a move back to decentralized staffs caring only for their student-athletes. Sometimes bigger is not better; nor is bigger progressive.

We have come a long, long way, but I am concerned that we still have a long way to go.

Staffing is a significant concern. The application of equitable care is a concern with all the attention on concussion management, screening for sickle cell trait and Marfan syndrome, and the overall incidence of sudden death from unknown heart conditions.

The NATA's recommendations and guidelines for appropriate medical coverage of intercollegiate athletics offer college and university healthcare providers a system by which they can evaluate their current level of coverage for student-athletes. (NATA, 2011) These recommendations have been created for the safety of student-athletes. To that end, certified athletic trainers in this setting must have a thorough understanding of the recommendations before implementing the system.

The document addresses appropriate medical coverage involving more than basic emergency care during sports participation. It includes provisions of many aspects of healthcare for student-athletes. Appropriate medical coverage also includes activities conducted daily by athletic trainers:

- Determination of student-athletes' readiness to participate, in conjunction with the team physician (i.e., pre-participation evaluation and post-injury/illness return).
- Risk management and injury prevention.
- Recognition, evaluation and immediate treatment of athletic injuries/illnesses.
- Rehabilitation and reconditioning of athletic injuries.
- Psychosocial intervention and referral.
- Nutritional aspects of injuries/illnesses.
- Healthcare administration.
- Professional development to maintain and improve.

These guidelines are great. They must be applied and used in real-life applications with good reasoning. When I visit with an institution and review this document, and the information suggests the staffing level of the institution is two positions down, we present a proposal to justify increased staffing and raising the standard of care.

University of Central Florida freshman student-athlete Eric Plancher died in March, 2008. There was some question about whether adequate staffing was provided to Central Florida student-athletes. Plancher was another in a line of student-athletes who have died from conditioning-related activities in Division I football. The offseason workout was determined to have triggered his sickle cell trait. The case received a great deal of attention.

Following Plancher's death, the University of Central Florida commissioned a high-profile investigator, Michael Glazier, to review the Knights' football athletic training practices, policies, etc. The report compiled by Glazier (Glazier, 2009), a former NCAA investigator and attorney based in Kansas City, Missouri recommended that Central Florida improve communication between its athletic training staff and athletic department administrators, consider adding a fourth certified athletic trainer exclusively devoted to football, and enhance its nutrition education and support for players. The report addressed staffing at Central Florida, and referenced like institutions in Division I.

Sadly, I am not certain larger staffs equate to a higher quality of athletic training. What we have today at many institutions is coverage with minimal or little healthcare being provided. Why else would student-athletes with sickle cell trait be expiring in cases where the healthcare team knows the student-athlete is positive? There is a duty to educate the student-athlete, coach, strength coach, and to communicate all this to the student-athlete's parents or guardians.

One underlying principle athletic trainers must deal with today is the concept of "care" versus "coverage." Care involves a hands-on, comprehensive service including the prevention, care, and rehabilitation of athletic injuries. Care is what we have tried to provide for years. However, today administrators are more interested in having coverage as this is much less expensive and requires less institutional commitment. Healthcare providers need to fight for care, and administrators with any prudent understanding will embrace and support care over coverage. The problem is, healthcare is not glitzy like shiny uniforms or JumboTron scoreboards or expansive facilities.

Healthcare costs are often greater at smaller institutions as they are not able to manage care and costs associated with injuries. The state of North Carolina pooled its requests for insurance proposals several years ago to try to lessen the premium with the increased exposure and spreading the exposure over so many more student-athletes (one premium for all sixteen state public member institutions). The problem is the larger schools have larger staffs to provide intervention and care and thus lower the rate of injury and subsequent healthcare costs. Smaller institutions are not afforded such a healthcare staff, and often have much higher losses and thus affect the rates for the group.

During the 2011 NATA meeting and clinical symposium in New Orleans, I met with Andy Massey, the head athletic trainer at Tulane University, and he gave me some valuable insight.

"As athletic trainers, we are held accountable for care, but are not given position, power, or authority within the framework of the athletic department to manage that accountability," Andy said.

He was correct, and I see it as a growing problem in college athletics. Part of the problem is that, regardless of the level of play, athletic trainers working in college athletics are responsible for all activities related to the nontraditional sports season. As student-athletes are on campus more of the summer, there is an issue with providing healthcare.

The 2010 NCAA Manual, Bylaw 17 addresses regulatory activities specific to playing seasons. The following items are specific for football and referenced from pages 266-267:

- An institution shall designate nine consecutive weeks between the conclusion of the academic year and its reporting date for preseason practice as its summer conditioning period. During this nine-week period, institutions shall designate one week as student-athlete discretionary time. (Adopted: 4/14/03 effective 5/1/03, Revised: 1/16/10)
- During the remaining eight weeks of the summer conditioning period, student-athletes may be involved in voluntary weight training and conditioning activities pursuant to Bylaw 17.1.6.2.1 and prospective student-athletes may be involved in voluntary weight training and conditioning activities pursuant to Bylaw

13.11.3.8. Such activities are limited to eight hours per week. (Adopted: 4/24/03 effective 5/1/03, Revised: 1/14/08)

- All remaining days between the conclusion of the academic year and the institution's reporting date for preseason practice that are not part of the institution's designated summer conditioning period and not already designated as student-athlete discretionary time shall be considered student-athlete discretionary time. (Adopted: 1/16/10) (NCAA, 2010a)

These rules are specific to football, and certainly address what activities can be engaged and what is prevented. The challenge for the athletic training staff is that these rules are written for EACH sport. Even with dedicated off-seasons, some sport is always practicing and therefore there is no down time for the athletic training staff.

So, we must provide healthcare to all student-athletes as an institutional responsibility. Such coverage minimizes the liability and areas of exposure for negligence specific to accidents or illness. The option exists for athletic trainers to provide coverage in place of care, and with nonsupport or minimal application of funds, the goal of care quickly becomes coverage.

The College Athletic Trainers' Society (CATS, 2011) was formed in 1992 by a group of college athletic trainers sensing that its profession was growing rapidly. The CATS was headed by Don Lowe, and the first meeting took place in Denver during the 1992 NATA convention. The CATS organization has worked to address the immediate concerns faced by the college athletic trainer.

Scott Anderson is a past-president of the CATS. He sounded the alarm in college athletics in January, 2011 with his comment to senior writer Dennis Dodd on CBSSports.com.

"The way we're training college football players in this day and age is putting them at risk," Anderson said. "Twenty-one dead football players and we're still today training them the same way as we did dating back to at least January, February of 2000."

Any death is a concern, so the number of non-practice field deaths should alarm everyone. Many of these deaths have been sickle-cell trait related.

The first known case of sickle-cell trait causing a death at the NCAA level was discovered at Colorado in 1974. More recently, Florida State player Devaughn Darling died in 2001 during "mat drills."(Wikipedia, 2002) His family settled with Florida State for $2 million. There remains disagreement about Darling's cause of death, but both Devaughn and surviving brother Devard, who transferred from Florida State to Washington State after the death, were found to have the sickle-cell trait. Also, there was Dale Lloyd II, who died a day after he collapsed during a conditioning workout in 2006 at Rice University. Lloyd's family requested in its suit settlement with Rice that the NCAA mandate member institutions to test for the sickle-cell condition.

As I visit with institutions and athletic trainers, the number of sickle-cell trait positive deaths concerns me. There are identified steps to be taken for these cases and excellent education and information is provided by the NATA, the American Medical Society for Sports Medicine, the American Orthopaedic Society for Sports Medicine, as well as other groups. The NCAA also includes information, but I prefer to obtain my medical information from medical organizations, not a membership or sanctioning organization.

The education of the healthcare team and coaches over the recent years has certainly grown. My fear and constant concern is with all the testing and education that is being mandated by the NCAA and other organizations— we still are having deaths to student-athletes known to be Sickle Cell Trait positive! The bottom line is we are not adhering to the guidelines which have been established.

Somewhere, somehow, something is wrong.

Today, athletic trainers are healthcare providers. The problem is they cannot obtain employment in high schools and at smaller colleges based primarily on healthcare. They have to be hired in a dual-credentialed, or a dual-duty situation as healthcare providers and teachers.

In 1997, the athletic training profession changed its educational criteria for athletic trainers. Many of my peers had not attended NATA-approved or recognized curriculum institutions such as Appalachian State. Many served as apprentices under certified athletic trainers. This was a major route of education for many athletic trainers in the 1970s and 1980s. The curriculum institutions had a set program, and graduates would then be eligible to take the Board of Certification's examination, much like attorneys, accountants or physicians. In 2003, the standards changed again, requiring all students to major in an athletic-training program or its equivalent.

That all sounds good, but there are problems with this model. A person can now graduate from college with five years of education in athletic training, and not find a job because he or she is unable to teach. In South Carolina, for instance, one can get a critical-needs position and in about six months can take courses to get special approval for teaching classes. So, the student spends five years in college to earn a $3,000 supplement as an athletic trainer, then earns a teaching equivalency in six months to earn the $20,000 to $30,000 teaching salary.

It makes little sense.

There always has been an evolution that we take the best athletic trainers, say, at Lenoir-Rhyne, and move them to bigger schools. When I started at Lenoir-Rhyne my goal was to be at a bigger, better school. When Sparky Woods left Appalachian State to be the head football coach at South Carolina, I asked him to look out for me. I never wanted him to create a position for me, though. I never wanted a coach to fire someone to make room for me. When I eventually followed Sparky to South Carolina it was under the best of circumstances.

The way school teachers get raises is to climb the education ladder. Some become principals. Yet nowhere does it say that teachers are prepared to be a principal. Consequently, principals get raises by moving on to administration, and, likewise, they often are not prepared for that higher position. The Peter Principal occurs in athletic training as well. As I moved up at South Carolina, I had more administrative responsibilities including—but not limited to—the managing and evaluating of personnel, the managing of a budget, the overseeing of drug testing and the administering of healthcare contracts with providers. I was not trained for these tasks.

In 1993, I had the opportunity to attend Mike McGee's Sports Management Institute, which was hosted on four college campuses. When McGee was fired as head football coach at Duke following the 1978 season, he invested his severance pay to complete his doctorate degree work at North Carolina. His dissertation centered on professional preparation for athletic administrators. From his dissertation, McGee further formalized his concepts and, with the support of the UNC faculty, developed an institute for executive training of athletic administrators.

McGee eventually became the athletic director at Cincinnati, Southern California, and South Carolina. He recognized a need to teach athletic administration skills and organized management training courses in North Carolina and Michigan. In the winters, the seminars would be at either South Carolina or Southern California. My rotation was North Carolina and Southern California, and I learned a tremendous amount about management and administration.

It is important to have well-trained and educated people in supervisory roles so they can oversee their staff and provide effective communication. We must have checks and balances within our departments to make certain we have good outcomes. In the past, administrators ruled with a dictatorial iron fist. Today, athletic administrators are better schooled in management techniques and much more understanding of what makes effective teamwork within a department.

There is a difference in the way McGee dealt with his staff as athletic director at South Carolina and the way Eric Hyman, his successor, deals with his staff. Two different people. Two different styles. With McGee, you knew where you stood. He was blunt and straightforward. He also was a top-down manager. Hyman seems to be more of a manager who seeks input from below before making decisions.

Every administrator or athletic trainer must develop his or her own management style. Whatever the style, it is important that administrators today have ample communication throughout their department. These departments seem to be growing in size by the day, so it is paramount to delegate authority to a staff and make certain communication lines are open from the football program to the soccer program to the administration.

NBA player LeBron James serves as a good—OK, bad—example of how things can go wrong without good advice and communication. James announced his free-agent move from Cleveland to Miami during an interview on national TV. He angered fans in Cleveland with his decision. He also turned a nation of NBA fans against him with the announcement on TV. You have to believe James got some very poor advice. The perception was that he is so insulated he does not get feedback from those outside his bubble. Likewise, athletic administrators or bank executives sometimes can hear only what is mentioned within senior management and do not understand what is going on within their departments.

Within the South Carolina athletic department we had many subdivisions. The department had upward of three hundred employees, compared to maybe one hundred at Appalachian State and twenty at Lenoir-Rhyne. At NCAA Division I-A schools, you now have a business office, compliance office, support services in academics, athletic training, strength and conditioning, marketing, promotions and media relations. All of these factions are headed by one person, the athletic director.

Athletic administration now also has several associates and assistants. Further, Hyman has utilized the title of "director" for many of the department or area administrators. While McGee succeeded in many areas—one was better at bringing big-name coaches to the school—he tended to surround himself with associates who told him only what he wanted to hear rather than what he needed to know. It was similar to the LeBron James case. James' posse obviously told him what he wanted to hear and not what he needed to know. That can create a dicey situation when we have a lack of transparency, where people do not communicate well with their department as supervisor and don't encourage information coming forward.

McGee was a frugal administrator. He would not spend money, which served him well in balancing budgets and making his athletic department prosper. Unfortunately, when he was at South Carolina, the Southeastern Conference was in the midst of a facilities arms race. Because of his ways, McGee failed to keep South Carolina up with the Joneses of the SEC. Finally, years after McGee departed, South Carolina is building quality facilities. It was a credit to Hyman, who benefited from the annual lucrative SEC payouts to member schools as well as an unpopular seat-license tax

(Yearly Equitable Seating—YES) for football patrons at Williams-Brice Stadium that he instituted.

McGee's management style certainly served South Carolina well and had many benefits that far outweighed the shortcomings. However, that top-down management style can ultimately lead to a supervisor's downfall. Employees must have respect for their supervisors. Understanding roles and how everyone works within the team or department is all part of having a good chain of command. Those who operated inside the athletic department under McGee realized his style ultimately resulted in his downfall.

I often wonder where South Carolina's finances would be without the YES program. Hyman and Jeff Tallant (chief financial officer) were the best in the world with numbers. Lucky for Hyman, about the time he launched the YES Program, the Southeastern Conference bailed him out with its new television contract and larger paydays for conference schools. Granted, South Carolina needed facilities and as I have said, Hyman did a great job with this. However, I think the seat tax is not nearly as effective and productive as the increased royalties from the conference office.

An interesting sidebar: When Hyman took over as athletic director at South Carolina, he asked for an internal audit of the department. University auditors were assigned to the project. The result was a one million dollar deficit, which was very interesting when you look at the fact that McGee's administration had produced black number budgets annually.

When the report was released, many within the department were surprised—especially those within the business office. However, things seem to make sense when the next months went by. The head of the audit, Tallant, was hired by Hyman as chief financial officer for the athletic department.

Dr. Rod's
Treatment Plan

THE NATIONAL ATHLETIC
TRAINERS' ASSOCIATION

HISTORY SHOWS THAT COMPETITION was a very common thing among people in the past. Going all the way back to Greek civilizations, humans were always competing to find who is the strongest, fastest, or simply the best. There the "paidotribes" or physical education teachers and trainers of activity used poultices and applications to facilitate exercise. It is thought that these were the early ancestors of athletic trainers and the profession of athletic training. As sport become more recognized, the importance of people to take care of the injured rose, leading to today's alignment with athletic training.

As time went on and sports became more and more developed, organized, and popular, the need for medical assistance with injuries increased.

Normally a general doctor would take care of any injury or illness whether from athletic participation or not. It was not until the late nineteenth century that athletic training became more of a common thing with the development of interscholastic and intercollegiate sports.

Early on, athletic trainers were of questionable histories, having no real education and very limited if any experience. They mostly did as their name said, trained athletes, more or less like a coach or a teacher. It was not until years later that the athletic trainer's role changed to working with mostly the active athlete. But that soon also changed. Athletic trainers soon started working not only with athletes but in clinics, schools, hospitals, and even in the military.

In the 1930s, several college athletic trainers got together to try and start a national organization for athletic trainers. Between the late thirties and early forties, the group called the National Athletic Trainers' Association struggled to be recognized as an organization. It dissolved as a result of World War II, but in 1947 athletic trainers gathered together to create more regional groups which, today, are the districts of the National Athletic Trainers' Association. In 1950, the National Athletic Trainers' Association was officially formed and about two hundred athletic trainers joined. Their first annual meeting was in Kansas City, Missouri at the Muhlebach Hotel. By 1974, the NATA had over forty-five thousand athletic trainers members and now that number is well over thirty thousand.

Headquartered in Dallas, Texas, the National Athletic Trainers' Association has had a big role in recognizing the need for a set of professional standards and appropriate professional recognition. The National Athletic Trainers' Association also has helped to unify certified athletic trainers across the country by setting a standard for professionalism, education, certification, research and practice settings. Over the years, the membership organization has splintered off the functions of educational domains and competencies and an additional division for credentialing. Today, the Commission on Accreditation of Athletic Training Education (CAATE) is the agency responsible for the accreditation of three hundred and fifty- plus professional (entry-level) athletic training educational programs. The American Academy of Family Physicians (AAFP), the American Academy of Pediatrics (AAP), the American Orthopedic Society for Sports Medicine (AOSSM) and the NATA cooperate to sponsor the CAATE and collaborate to develop the Standards for Entry-Level Athletic Training Educational Programs. It is CAATE's mission to provide comprehensive accreditation services to institutions that offer athletic training degree programs. Further, they verify that all CAATE-accredited programs meet the acceptable educational standards for professional (entry-level) athletic training education.

To become a BOC-certified athletic trainer, you must earn a degree from a college or university with an accredited athletic training program, then— depending on your state regulation—take and pass the exam administered by the Omaha-based Board of Certification (BOC). The educational requirement of a professional degree was implemented in 1997, and phased out the traditional apprenticeship route to certification. While the change was difficult, the end result has been good for the profession.

Since it was formed, the NATA has been a driving force behind the recognition of the athletic training profession. From holding national conferences to the creation of National Athletic Training Month held in March strides have been made in further the profession.

In 1990, the American Medical Association decided to include athletic trainers as fellow allied health professionals. With this approval from the American Medical Association, athletic trainers were recognized as competent healthcare providers that can aide in the prevention, recognition, and rehabilitation of athletic injuries.

ACKNOWLEDGEMENTS

AS I EMBARKED ON WRITING this book, people told me you never realize all the people who help make it happen. This was certainly true, and I begin by thanking Rick Horrow, executive publisher and his vice president, Karla Swatek, for accepting my ideas for this project. Karla has served as a source of confidence in the tough times, and provided much needed guidance throughout this project.

I have never been confused as a good writer. Probably all my high school and college English teachers will attest to that. I have enjoyed the opportunity to express some of my principles and use stories from my career to exemplify them. The use of readers has been a big help. While they have been many of my peers, I truly appreciate their help.

I want to make sure I say thank you to a lot of people. This is my opportunity to tell them just what they mean to me. Like the turtle sitting on top of the fence post, "he did not get there by himself!"

Staff members can be a source of strength and reinforcement. Phil Hedrick was the first full-time football assistant athletic trainer I had at South Carolina. Our affiliation dates to his undergraduate days at Appalachian State. Good staff members are hard to find, but I found two in Phil Hedrick and Bill Martin as we worked closely caring for the football team at South Carolina.

Other staff athletic trainers over the years at various schools: Mark Rogers, Dennis Williams, Stephanie Rosehart, Brainard Cooper, Sue Biles, Nikki Harman, Tara Chase, Kerry Gordon, Erin Thomas, Kris Mack, Malissa Martin, Cindy Thomas, Craig Deneger, and Jamie Moul. Some were on the educational front, others worked directly with me in student-athlete healthcare. The fact remains: Good personnel are your biggest asset, and bad personnel are your biggest liability. Good employees are hard to find, and even tougher to keep. Bad employees are a liability and you can never get rid of them! I always tried to hire people who were smarter than me, and that usually was not difficult.

I have believed for years that students keep us young. Students ask questions that keep the faculty challenged. Students pose the challenges that require the faculty and clinical staff to stay on top of the literature, best practices, and stay current. With that said, I reflect on the many athletic training students from Lenoir-Rhyne to Appalachian State and most recently at South Carolina. In addition to those in the undergraduate program are those in the graduate programs, many of whom served with me and our staff as graduate assistant athletic trainers. The South Carolina athletics department was affiliated with the university's medical school and, thus, our athletic training room served as a clinical site for medical students, residents, and sports medicine fellows over the years. To all the students I have been fortunate to work with, thank you.

An athletic trainer's best friend is the team physician. You will read much about these relationships in this book. Athletic trainers and physicians work closely together in sports medicine. Effective teams have great rapport with these professionals. Communication is a hallmark of this relationship. There cannot be agendas. Again, successful outcomes reflect these hallmarks. There also must be a mutual respect and understanding of what each does relative to the healthcare of student-athletes. Let's get started with some of the key relationships I had with staff members and team physicians in meeting our goal for healthcare of student-athletes.

My physician friends have been many. From my undergraduate Appalachian State days I learned from Drs. Evan Ashby, Buck Derrick, Lowell Furman, Bill Herring and Marc Kadyk. My first true team physician I had the opportunity to work with the forever memorable Dr. Benny Goodman.

I continued with the existing Appalachian State physicians when I took over in Boone, and Dr. Pat Geiger had come to join Dr. Ashby's staff. In 1990, my indoctrination into NCAA Division I sports medicine was supervised by Dr. Bob Peele. Bob was so well-connected in the medical and social community. He knew everyone. His partners at Midlands Orthopedics in Columbia appreciated sports medicine, especially Robbie DaSilva and Jim O'Leary, who assisted Dr. Peele and served student-athletes for many years.

Primary care sports medicine was taught to me and I will always appreciate what these physician all-stars do for patient care, from Mark Leski to Tom Armsey to Tom Terrell to Jason Stacey. These guys were the key to success, and did a phenomenal job with patient care and education of their sports medicine fellows.

High school days were wonderful for me. I was a student athletic trainer and Allan Glenn was a student manager for Coach Len Maness' basketball team at Fayetteville's Terry Sanford Senior High School. Allan had a good friend who lived right around the corner from him, Sam McCrary. The three of us grew into a tight group through high school. Our friendship and ability to keep in touch was challenged due to geography. Following our 1975 graduation from high school, Sam embarked on his college career at Mercer University, Allan was off to Pembroke State (NC), and I headed west for Appalachian State University. About a year later, Sam decided to move closer to home and enrolled at Pembroke State University, where Allan also was studying. The two were student athletic trainers. Sam actually began to work with Allan as a student athletic trainer at Pembroke State. I always thought it was so odd that Sam had pursued a career in athletic training. He certainly had a love of sports. However, he never expressed any of the desires for such a career during our high school days. Sam eventually transferred to the University of Nevada-Las Vegas and completed his athletic training education requirements in that program. By this time, I was working at Lenoir-Rhyne, and I recall him stopping in Hickory during one of his treks across the country. That was 1983. It was my last conversation with Sam until 1991.

King Dixon, who was the athletics director at South Carolina and his wife, Augusta, informed me that one of her friend's daughters was married to an assistant athletic trainer for the New York Mets. It turns out that was my old friend, Sam. King told me Sam had married Beth Gar from Laurens, S.C., and she was working at a Columbia sporting goods store. Shortly thereafter, Sam and I connected again and kept in touch when he returned to his home in Lexington, S.C. during the offseason. Sam eventually left Major League Baseball and opened a gymnasium in Lexington, only a few miles from my house.

Following my departure from South Carolina, I dropped by Sam's gym to see how he was doing. A few months later, I began working out with Sam. He connected me with Clifton Parker, and now we work out together with Sam each Monday and Friday at 6 a.m. Clifton is a great partner, and someone I certainly respect these days. Today, Sam keeps me in check. It kills me that we were apart for so long.

I want to reference "man's best friend," and that would be good old Buc and Ginger. These were two great dogs, Buc, a Springer Spaniel, and Ginger, a Labrador-Golden Retriever mix. They gave us so much for so many years until they both died during the summer and fall of 2011. Buc was a royalty dog, and must have been part cat, as he survived some nine lives. They both gave much more love than they garnered from this family.

Another group who we have always been fond of is Greg and Erin Harmon's parents; Mike and Jean Thomas and Steve and Debbie Harmon. Following the 2001 Outback Bowl game, Susan and I had planned to take our four kids out to dinner to celebrate in our southern tradition. We joined a group of South Carolina Low Country friends led by Mike and Jean Thomas and Steve and Debbie Harmon and their children, Erin and Greg. Greg was one of my student athletic trainers and today is my best friend. We had one heck of a time that night, January 2, 2001, a big day for any college football fan, and especially the Gamecocks. My clan of six joined this esteemed group at Tampa's Ruth's Chris Steak House.

I turned my crowd loose—appetizers, salad, entree, dessert. Susan and I enjoyed cocktails with our friends. We embraced a good bottle of wine. Two and a half hours later, it came time to face the organ grinder—but there was no bill. The bill had been taken care of by our Low Country hosts. These folks are great, and it is not about the $600 bill they consumed. To this day, we continue to have so many fond memories around these families.

I regret not having kept up with my high school friends. Shelly Norris, Lynne Tomlinson, Tony Byrd, Steve Byrd, Joe Beck (brother of professional golfer Chip Beck), Mike Warren . . . many of these people I have not seen since our graduation. Due to my work in college athletics, I never attended high school reunions. I have never been much for going back to my former colleges, either Lenoir-Rhyne or Appalachian State. Maybe now that I am in the consulting business I will do a better job of connecting with friends from my past. I have truly enjoyed my recent time and reconnection with Sam McCrary and Allan Glenn. Facebook is a great mechanism to keep in touch with old friends and classmates.

The older I get, the more I enjoy time with family and friends. We love grilling out and occasionally are joined by former neighbors Roger and Carla Hutchins, and their daughters, Hannah and Hailey, as well as Rob and Kelly Carruthers, and their sons, Holden and Cooper. We enjoy having dinner with all our kids every Saturday or Sunday evening, especially when they are all in town. Family time is precious to Susan and me, especially as we mature and watch our kids grow.

When I left the University of South Carolina, I thanked God for the friends Susan had with the tennis leagues in Lexington, South Carolina. There were certainly the familiar town gown politics with tennis leagues, but I must say that her teammates heard little of this. The fall of 2007 saw much free time for me, and I tried to come out to see Susan and her 3.0 tennis league teammates play. The quality of the food spread coordinated by Tissie Mathews was much more important than the play on the court.

Friends really are so important. Peggy Moseley, Virginia Crooks, Francis Young, Patty Richard, Ann Bethea, Suzanne Flowers, Maria Ponder, Cindy Outz, Suzanne Wilkins—all have played with Susan at one time or another. You get to know this fine group of women and their significant others. Social events are special with this group as everyone is included. These women were much more sincere in their friendship than anything I had ever been exposed to.

Finally, to my friends and peers who have reviewed these pages of manuscripts. It has been a journey to get notes from DayTimers to the pages of this book. Thanks to Phil Hedrick, Kent Atkins, Robb

Williams, Patti Pleasants-Boone, Bill McBrayer, Ralph Patterson, Sam Booth, and last but not least, Susan. Thanks so much for all your insight and perspective.

BIBLIOGRAPHY

Albright, J. P., Powell, J. W., Smith, W., Martindale, A., Crowley, E., Monroe, J., et al. (1994). Medial collateral ligament knee sprains in college football. Effectiveness of preventive braces. Am J Sports Med, 22(1), 12-18.

Baker, B. E., VanHanswyk, E., Bogosian, S. t., Werner, F. W., & Murphy, D. (1987). A biomechanical study of the static stabilizing effect of knee braces on medial stability. Am J Sports Med, 15(6), 566-570.

Barth, J. T., Freeman, J. R., & Winters, J. E. (2000). Management of Sports-related concussions. Dental Clinics of North American, 44(1), 67-83.

Beard, D. J., Kyberd, P. J., Fergusson, C. M., & Dodd, C. A. (1993). Proprioception after rupture of the anterior cruciate ligament. An objective indication of the need for surgery? J Bone Joint Surg Br, 75(2), 311-315.

Beynnon, B. D., Johnson, R. J., Fleming, B. C., Peura, G. D., Renstrom, P. A., Nichols, C. E., et al. (1997). The effect of functional knee bracing on the anterior cruciate ligament in the weightbearing and nonweightbearing knee. Am J Sports Med, 25(3), 353-359.

Beynnon, B. D., Pope, M. H., Wertheimer, C. M., Johnson, R. J., Fleming, B. C., Nichols, C. E., et al. (1992). The effect of functional knee-braces on strain on the anterior cruciate ligament in vivo. J Bone Joint Surg Am, 74(9), 1298-1312.

CATS. (2011). College Athletic Trainers Society

ESPN. (2010). Montgomery sues for defamation.

Fleck, S. J. (1999). Periodized strength training: A critical review. Journal of Strength and Conditioning Research, 13, 82-89.

Freeman, M. A., Dean, M. R., & Hanham, I. W. (1965). The etiology and prevention of functional instability of the foot. J Bone Joint Surg Br, 47(4), 678-685.

Glazier, M. (2009). Report to the President - University of Central Florida. Unpublished manuscript.

Grace, T. G., Skipper, B. J., Newberry, J. C., Nelson, M. A., Sweetser, E. R., & Rothman, M. L. (1988). Prophylactic knee braces and injury to the lower extremity. J Bone Joint Surg Am, 70(3), 422-427.

Hansen, B. L., Ward, J. C., & Diehl, R. C. (1985). The preventive use of the Anderson knee stabler in football. The Physician and Sportsmedicine, 13(9), 75-81.

IRS. (2011). COBRA Health Insurance Continuation Premium Subsidy. Retrieved October 6, 2011, 2011

Lassiter, T. E., Jr., Malone, T. R., & Garrett, W. E., Jr. (1989). Injury to the lateral ligaments of the ankle. Orthop Clin North Am, 20(4), 629-640.

Liu, S., & Mirzayan, R. (1995). Current review--functional knee bracing. Clinical Orthopaedic Research, 317, 273-281.

NATA. (2011). Recommendations and Guidelines for Appropriate Medical Coverage of Intercollegiate Athletics. Retrieved September 3, 2011

NCAA. (2005). Sports Medicine Handbook (Eighteenth Edition ed.).

NCAA. (2010a). 2010-11 NCAA Division I Manual.

NCAA. (2010b). Sports Medicine Handbook (Eighteenth Edition ed.).

Quillian, W. W., Simms, R. T., & S., C. J. (1987). Knee-bracing in preventing injuries in high school football. International Pediatrics, 2, 255-256.

Rovere, G. D., & Bowen, G. S. (1986). The effectiveness of knee bracing for the prevention of sport injuries. Sports Medicine, 3(5), 309-311.

Safran, M. R., Benedetti, R. S., Bartolozzi, A. R., 3rd, & Mandelbaum, B. R. (1999). Lateral ankle sprains: a comprehensive review: part 1:

etiology, pathoanatomy, histopathogenesis, and diagnosis. Med Sci Sports Exerc, 31(7 Suppl), S429-437.

Safran, M. R., Zachazewski, J. E., Benedetti, R. S., Bartolozzi, A. R., 3rd, & Mandelbaum, R. (1999). Lateral ankle sprains: a comprehensive review part 2: treatment and rehabilitation with an emphasis on the athlete. Med Sci Sports Exerc, 31(7 Suppl), S438-447.

Schriner, J. L. (1985). The effectiveness of knee bracing in preventing knee injuries in high school athletes. Medicine and Science in Exercise and Sports, 17, 254.

Sitler, M., Ryan, J., Hopkinson, W., Wheeler, J., Santomier, J., Kolb, R., et al. (1990). The efficacy of a prophylactic knee brace to reduce knee injuries in football. A prospective, randomized study at West Point. Am J Sports Med, 18(3), 310-315.

Smith, R. W., & Reischl, S. F. (1986). Treatment of ankle sprains in young athletes. Am J Sports Med, 14(6), 465-471.

Statistics, U. S. B. o. L. (1990). Consumer Price Index. For Calendar Year 1990.

Statistics, U. S. B. o. L. (1991). Consumer Price Index.

Statistics, U. S. B. o. L. (1992). Consumer Price Index.

Statistics, U. S. B. o. L. (1993). Consumer Price Index.

Statistics, U. S. B. o. L. (1994). Consumer Price Index.

Taft, T. N., Hunter, S., & Funderburk, C. H. (1985). Preventative lateral knee bracing in football, Annual Proceedings of the American Orthopaedic Society for Sports Medicine. Nashville, TN.

Taylor, D. C., & Bassett, F. H., 3rd. (1993). Syndesmosis Ankle Sprains. The Physician and Sportsmedicine, 21(12), 39-46.

Teitz, C. C., Hermanson, B. A., Kronmal, R. A., & Diehr, P. H. (1987). Evaluation of the Use of Braces to Prevent Injury to the Knee in Collegiate Football Players. Journal of Bone and Joint Surgery, 69(1), 2-9.

Tropp, H. (2002). Commentary: Functional Ankle Instability Revisited. J Athl Train, 37(4), 512-515.

USC Athletic Department Financial Statements and Schedules, J., 1989 - May 31, 1990. (1990). Athletic Department Financial Statements and Schedules.

USC Athletic Department Financial Statements and Schedules, J., 1990 - May 31, 1991. (1991). Athletic Department Financial Statements and Schedules.

USC Athletic Department Financial Statements and Schedules, J., 1991 - May 31, 1992. (1992). Athletic Department Financial Statements and Schedules.

USC Athletic Department Financial Statements and Schedules, J., 1992 - May 31, 1993. (1993). Athletic Department Financial Statements and Schedules.

USC Athletic Department Financial Statements and Schedules, J., 1994 - May 31, 1994. (1994). Athletic Department Financial Statements and Schedules.

Verbrugge, J. D. (1996). The effects of semirigid Air-Stirrup bracing vs. adhesive ankle taping on motor performance. J Orthop Sports Phys Ther, 23(5), 320-325.

Walters, R. (2000). Research tackles prophylactic knee bracing. Biomechanics, 7(12), 34-47.

Wikipedia. (2002). Devard Darling, http://en.wikipedia.org/wiki/Devard_ Darling.

Wikipedia. (2011). Operation Lost Trust. Retrieved October 27, 2011

Winters, J. E., Sr. (2001). Commentary: Role of Properly Fitted Mouthguards in Prevention of Sport-Related Concussion. J Athl Train, 36(3), 339-341.

Wisniewski, J. F., Guskiewicz, K., Trope, M., & Sigurdsson, a. (2004). Incidence of cerebral concussions associated with type of mouthguard used in college football. Dental Traumatology, 20(3), 143-149.

CHRONOLOGY

- June 1975 - graduation from Terry Sanford Senior High School
- August 1979 - graduation from Appalachian State University (Bachelor of Science)
- August 1980 - graduation from Appalachian State University (Master of Arts)
- August 1980 - hired as Instructor and Athletic Trainer at Lenoir-Rhyne College, Hickory, North Carolina
- July 1983 - married Barbara McCauley Walters
- June 1984 - began work on Doctor of Arts at Middle Tennessee State University, Murfreesboro, Tennessee
- July 1985 - hired as Head Athletic Trainer at Appalachian State University
- December 7, 1986 - birth of David Rodwell Walters III
- May 14, 1988 - graduation from Middle Tennessee State University (Doctor of Arts)
- June 20, 1989 - birth of Ryan Michael Walters
- March 1990 - hired as Head Athletic Trainer at the University of South Carolina
- May 1991 - elected District Secretary to Mid-Atlantic Athletic Trainers' Association

- June 14, 1991 - Walters Inc. - Consultant in Sports Medicine registered as corporation
- September 1992 - University of South Carolina accepts invitation to join the Southeastern Conference
- June 1997 - installed on National Athletic Trainers' Association Board of Directors
- September 1997 - formal separation from Barbara Walters (divorced February 1999)
- November 1998 - promoted to Assistant Athletic Director for Sports Medicine
- December 1999 - married to Susan Marie Ferguson
- March 2000 - named Director of Testing for University of South Carolina student-athletes
- June 2003 - awarded NATA's Most Distinguished Athletic Trainer award
- June 2005 - inducted into NATA's Hall of Fame
- March 2006 - moved to full-time administrative position as Assistant Athletic Director for Sports Medicine at University of South Carolina
- February 2007 - resignation from University of South Carolina
- June 15, 2007 - full-time work with Walters Inc.

ABOUT THE AUTHOR

ROD WALTERS WAS BORN June 29, 1957 to David and Christine Walters. The oldest of three children, Walters was raised in Fayetteville, North Carolina. He attended public schools within the Fayetteville City School system graduating from Terry Sanford Senior High School in 1975. He attended Appalachian State University and received two degrees there; the Bachelor of Arts in Physical Education in 1979 and Master of Arts in 1980.

In 2007, Walters left the University of South Carolina to delve full-time into his consulting work, and has provided outstanding consultations and is a much sought after public speaker through Walters Inc.—Consultants in Sports Medicine. His services have been engaged by colleges and universities seeking evaluation of healthcare programs, corporations needing insight into Athletic Training and Sports Medicine; and thousands of attendees of his Athletic Training and Education Opportunity seminars.

An innovative professional, Walters has enjoyed a storied career as a collegiate athletic trainer. Most recently, Walters has provided outstanding consultations and is a much-sought after public speaker through Walters Inc.—Consultants in Sports Medicine. Basing his expanded role on his mantra, "the best way to sell, is to make sure the client is educated about the concept."

A member of the National Athletic Trainers' Association, he served on NATA's Board of Directors from 1997 - 2003. He received the NATA's Most Distinguished Athletic Trainer Award in 2003 and was inducted into the NATA's Hall of Fame in 2005. He was recognized as a Distinguished Alumni at Middle Tennessee State University in 2011. He is a member of the American Orthopaedic Society for Sports Medicine.

Walters worked in the field of athletic training for twenty-eight years. He received his undergraduate and master's degrees at Appalachian State University and his doctoral degree from Middle Tennessee State University. Walters is a graduate of the Athletic Training curriculum at Appalachian, and has been an advocate for good relationships between the clinical practice of Athletic Training and what is taught in the curriculums and classrooms.

Walters was head athletic trainer at Lenoir-Rhyne (NC) College for five years before joining the staff at Appalachian and moved to the University of South Carolina in 1990, a member of the nation's top athletic league in the Southeastern Conference. Walters served South Carolina for seventeen years.

Walters is married to Susan Ferguson of Columbia, S.C., and they have four children and a grandchild.

In *Tape, I-C-E, and Sound Advice: Life Lessons from a Hall-of-Fame Athletic Trainer*, Walters takes readers from the locker room to the sidelines, to athletic training room exam tables, and on the road with teams, chronicling many long road trips and shifts-worth of his experiences over his professional career.

RICK HORROW'S SPORTS PROFESSOR SERIES

Curated by "The Sports Professor" Rick Horrow, host of Bloomberg TV "Sportfolio," Morgan James' **Sports Professor Series** is the first-ever collection devoted to the dollars-and-cents side of sports.

Golf Wisdom of the Legends: Fairways of Life
Matt Adams

Golf Channel commentator Adams celebrates the wisdom, passion, and purpose found in the words of golf's great champions.
228 pages • ISBN: 978-1600378652
Paperback 5 x 8 in. • $19.95 US • ebook $9.99

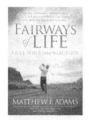

Return of the Gold:
The Journey of Jerry Colangelo and the Redeem Team
Dan Bickley

Sportsman Jerry Colangelo sets out to change the stained image of USA Basketball; includes the perspectives of all-time greats like Michael Jordan, Bill Russell, Julius Erving, and Jerry West.
216 pages • ISBN: 978-1600376375
Paperback: 6 x 9 in. • $25.95 US • ebook $9.99

Insightful Player:
Football Players Lead a Bold Movement of Hope
Chrissy Carew

Inspiring stories from active and former National Football League players that also provoke positive action.
240 pages • ISBN: 978-1614480549
Paperback 6.69 x 9.61 • $19.95 US • ebook $9.99

When the Game Is on the Line: From the Man Who Brought the Heat to Miami and the Browns Back to Cleveland
Rick Horrow

Horrow reveals the stories behind the biggest sports deals of the past 20 years, over 100 of which he has brokered.
244 pages • ISBN: 978-1600378997
Paperback 6 x 9 in. • $17.95 US • ebook $9.99

Beyond the Box Score:
An Insider's Guide to the $750 Billion Business of Sports
Rick Horrow and Karla Swatek

An in-depth look at the drivers in sports impacting the fan experience. Foreword by former NFL Commissioner Paul Tagliabue.
200 pages • ISBN: 978-1600376436
Paperback: 6 x 9 in. • $16.95 US • ebook $9.99